Russell and After

The politics of adult learning (1969–97)

In memory of Henry Arthur Jones, 1917–2002

Russell and After
The politics of adult learning (1969–97)

Peter Clyne

With additional editing by John Payne

promoting adult learning

Published by the National Institute of Adult Continuing Education (NIACE)
(England and Wales)
21 De Montfort Street, Leicester LE1 7GE
Company registration no: 2603322
Charity registration no: 1002775

First published 2006
© NIACE 2006

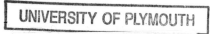
NIACE has a broad remit to promote lifelong learning opportunities for adults. NIACE works
to develop increased participation in education and training, particularly for those who do not
have easy access because of barriers of class, gender, age, race, language and culture, learning
difficulties and disabilities, or insufficient financial resources.

For a full catalogue of NIACE's publications, please visit

www.niace.org.uk/publications

Cataloguing in Publications Data
A CIP record for this title is available from the British Library

ISBN 10: 1 86201 138 9
ISBN 13: 978 1 86201 138 0

Cover design by Design2Print
Designed and typeset by J&L Composition, Filey, North Yorkshire YO14 9PF
Printed and bound in Great Britain by Cambridge University Press

Contents

Acknowledgements and dedication

Thanks are due to a number of people who have informed, assisted and encouraged me as I have undertaken this labour of love. The Russell Committee was appointed by the Secretary of State in 1969. Its report, *Adult Education: A Plan for Development* was finished in late 1972, and published in early 1973. I was fortunate to be appointed Research Assistant to the Committee, hence the starting date for this book.

For some considerable time I have looked forward to writing about the reasons why decisions affecting adult learning were taken. Others have documented the changes, listed the dates, noted the sums of money involved and identified the principal organisations affected. I wished to explore behind the scenes. Who was involved? Why did change occur at a particular time? From where did the pressure for change come? What was learned as a consequence of change? Throughout more than 40 years in adult learning – whether as a lecturer, college manager, inspector, local authority officer or consultant – I have been guided by a comment from a teacher who said: 'I am interested to know what you have done but I am more interested to know why you did it.' As the years rolled by, I expanded the teacher's comment to become a question to myself: Why am I doing what I am doing in the way that I am doing it?

This book seeks to ask and answer many of the 'why' questions related to adult learning since 1972. In the middle of the 1960s, as an adult college vice-principal, I had the good fortune to attend a training course on the management of adult learning led by the then principal of the City Literary Institute in London. The course leader was Henry Arthur Jones, known to all involved in adult learning as Arthur Jones, or Arthur. When I began work on this book, I realised that he was the person, above all others, to whom I should speak and from whom I should seek guidance. I wrote to him with a view to arranging a meeting. His recollections, judgements, lucidity and wisdom had always been informative and, on many occasions, inspiring. Arthur replied to my letter. He was unwell at the time but, nonetheless, he made the effort to respond to my letter in encouraging tones. Due to his illness, he said that I should interview others on my list first and I should see him later. He died before I could meet him, but I have his letter as a treasured possession. My first meeting with Arthur was at the beginning of the training course. In the years following I met him frequently and worked with him and for him. We travelled together to other countries to experience adult learning practice. Unceasingly, I learned from him. This book is dedicated to the memory of an outstanding adult educator who loved his fellow men and women.

Some of the people who have helped me with information and advice and copies of letters and other documentation have asked to remain anonymous. I have respected their wishes for confidentiality. Others are mentioned in the text. I am indebted to people with whom I have worked who have kindly supplied me with documentation and advice relating to teaching adults and adult learning in a wide range of organisational arrangements and establishments. In particular colleagues at the National Archives (then called the Public Records Office), NIACE, Ruskin College, the Open University, the Institute of Education at London University, and the Institute of Continuing Education (then Extra-Mural Department) at the University of Cambridge. In terms of number of students and number of courses, the largest providers of adult learning opportunities since 1972 have been the Local Education Authorities (LEAs). However, LEA staff are less likely than their counterparts in universities and the Workers' Educational Association to write extensively about the provision. Most of my career was spent in local authorities. In an attempt to fill the many gaps left by the lack of comprehensive reports on LEA provision, I have corresponded with and interviewed a number of colleagues with LEA experience and supplemented this information with my own collection of notes and diaries covering the past 35 years.

Peter Clyne
London, 2005

Foreword

The politics of adult learning

Having set out the background and context of adult learning during the twentieth century, this book documents the politics of adult learning from 1969 when Shirley Williams, the then Secretary of State for Education and Science, appointed the Committee of Inquiry into non-vocational adult education in England and Wales (Russell Committee). By considering the debates and arguments, placing the various reports and recommendations in their political and economic contexts and reflecting on the particular and personal contributions and influence of leading policy-makers and activists of the times, the book describes why and how certain decisions were or were not taken.

This is an insider's job. Peter Clyne was seconded by the Inner London Education Authority to work as Research Assistant to the Russell Committee. For the following 30 years, his work was related to many of the initiatives, policy programmes and reports concerning the development of adult learning in England and Wales referred to in this book. Use has been made of publicly available documents and information gained from interviews, correspondence and meetings. In addition, by drawing on the author's diaries and notes, the publication becomes a personal statement. The commentary covers the period to 1997. The book thus covers nearly all of the twentieth century, but leaves readers to draw their own conclusions about the relevance to contemporary readers of these twentieth-century debates about the purpose and organisation of adult learning.

References to the Russell Report indicate paragraphs in the published report (DES, 1973). There is a comprehensive list of acronyms to assist the reader and a full bibliography.

The first eight chapters were written by Peter Clyne. He was prevented by illness from completing the task he had set himself. John Payne was invited to complete the book by adding a short introduction and a ninth, concluding, chapter and by copy-editing the eight existing chapters and preparing the text for the publisher. We both take responsibility for the Afterword. We have a shared commitment to a particular approach to adult learning as a right for all citizens. We believe that adult learning can make a difference to the life experience and life chances of those who have benefited least from initial education and who often experience numerous other difficulties in their lives. We are convinced that turning this commitment into a reality remains a task for policy-makers and adult educators of the twenty-first century, just as it was for those throughout 1969–97, the period documented in this book.

Peter Clyne
Battersea, London

John Payne
Frome, Somerset

2006

Introduction

Policy is both text and action, words and deeds, it is what is enacted as well as what is intended. Policies are always incomplete insofar as they relate to or map on to the 'wild profusion' of local practice.

(Ball, 1994, p. 10)

Introduction: social and economic change and adult learning

This book encompasses the years 1969–97. It shows how many of the issues that have preoccupied adult educators in England and Wales over this period were anticipated by the work of the Russell Committee, and the ways in which the Russell Report illuminated policy and practice during the next quarter of a century. The book does not attempt to reach any conclusions about what has happened since 1997, or the extent to which developments in adult learning policy and practice in that more recent period have either fulfilled or abandoned the promise of Russell, although we recognise in the Afterword that this will be a question many readers will ask themselves.

The opening chapter lays the groundwork for the book, tracing the policy developments that influenced adult education from the groundbreaking work of the Adult Education Committee of the Ministry of Reconstruction, which was responsible for the 1919 Report (Ministry of Reconstruction, 1919/1980). It demonstrates how the years leading up to the establishment of the Russell Committee in 1969 were years of great ferment and optimism in educational circles. During the period of the Committee's deliberation (Chapter 2) optimism became rather more muted. While the Russell Report, appearing in 1973, attempted to reproduce something of the vision of 1919, it also attempted to be 'realistic' about what might be achieved in practical terms. It took account of the fact that within the Department of Education and Science (DES) itself, there had been a significant lack of support for, or commitment to, the work of the committee. It also took account of the change from the Labour Government of 1969 to the Conservative Government of 1973, and the likelihood that support from the government of the time was unlikely to be enthusiastic. The result was that despite the wisdom and energy of its work, the final report was a restrained call for modest improvement rather than a clarion call for radical action. Chapter

3 demonstrates that the Russell Report was one of a number of attempts internationally in the 1970s to bring adult education rather more centre stage as an
element in social policy. After outlining the contents of the Alexander and
Murphy reports in Scotland and Ireland, the chapter concentrates on the work
of UNESCO, emphasising how few of the ideas available internationally were in
fact taken up within England and Wales.

Chapter 4 marks a shift away from the world of politicians and civil servants,
and a closer emphasis on the professional adult education world. It gives a
complete and succinct account of the recommendations made by the Russell
Report. Chapter 5 examines the response of the 1970–4 Conservative
Government to Russell. It goes on to show how the potential goodwill of the
1974–9 Labour Government foundered on the economic deterioration
following the increase in international oil prices in 1973, and the resultant
enforcement by the International Monetary Fund (IMF) of reductions in public
expenditure in 1976.

Chapter 6 shows how the hoped-for developmental growth of adult education
did not happen, tracing this back to the precise terms of reference of the
committee. Instead, 'development' was seen in terms of specific projects
addressing particular issues identified within the professional field, such as
guidance or work with disadvantaged groups. Organisationally, this involved
the setting up of the Advisory Council for Adult and Continuing Education
(ACACE), and then the Unit for the Development of Adult Continuing
Education (UDACE) and REPLAN, and eventually a greater role for NIACE as
the 'national organisation for adult learning'. But as Chapter 7 records, the
necessary resources to implement across England and Wales the ideas and innovatory practice coming out of these various units was seldom available to LEAs
or other providers of adult learning. At the same time, the existence of such
initiatives, and the individuals who drove them, created by 1997 a powerful
sense that the time was ripe to move forward to a brave new world of lifelong
learning. As Chapter 8 shows, the issues by 1997 were rather different from those
at the time of the Russell Report in 1973. New challenges were presented by the
growth of new curriculum areas such as basic skills (including English for
Speakers of Other Languages for migrant workers and refugees) and by the challenge of an economy in which skills obsolescence and redundancy were now
major issues. Where Russell had looked forward to economic change and the
demands it might make on adult learners in the future, by 1997 the challenge of
economic change was a daily experience for many people. The future had
arrived.

Throughout the book, care has been taken to emphasise the social, economic
and political contexts in which particular adult learning policies and practice
emerge. The temptation has been resisted to suggest that particular policies (as
opposed to the values that underpin those policies) are in some sense 'right'. As

Harold Wiltshire wrote of the 1919 Report (Ministry of Reconstruction, 1919/1980, p. 7): 'We live in a different world materially, economically, politically, socially and culturally. And we ourselves have changed; we no longer possess, and we even find it difficult to sympathise with, that confidence in the future which inspires this *Report*.' The 1970s was a period of economic and social conflict and marked the high point of trade union membership and influence in the UK. In retrospect, it also marked the beginnings of its long decline. Edward Heath called the February 1974 election on the theme of 'Who governs Britain?' and lost. From then on, there was a clear commitment within the Conservative Party and the business community to bring an end to the power and influence of the trade union movement. With the election of the 1979 Conservative Government, led by Margaret Thatcher, specific policies were put in place to bring this about, and the remoulding of the UK economy accelerated.

The period also marked the early stages of what has come to be known as globalisation, with inefficient and old-fashioned British industries increasingly facing competition from other countries with more efficient production methods and/or lower costs. Old industries such as steel, shipbuilding and coal mining went into near-terminal decline as public subsidies were withdrawn. Spending on public services was cut wherever possible, bearing in mind both the reduced tax inflow and increased social security outflow produced by mass unemployment, which peaked at over three million in the early 1980s. In this context, adult education found a peripheral role in dealing with some of the most pressing problems of adult retraining, but was not central to the government's economic restructuring programme. In addition, as we have recorded in this book, policy-making was complicated by the presence of two government departments – the DES and ED – with overlapping interests in the field of adult learning. It was not until the 1990s, as the country gradually recovered from the shock therapy administered to it by successive governments, that issues of skill requirements in the 'new' economy, the relationship between skills and their educational underpinning, and the role of government policy in securing a supply of skilled labour, began to rise towards the surface of government policy-making. Even at the end of our chosen period, issues of the link between adult learning and quality of life, or the links between adult learning and other policy fields such as health or the arts remained firmly off the public agenda.

If the 1990s appeared relatively peaceful in the UK, certainly compared with the confrontations of the two previous decades, forces were stirring which were to lead on to the unstable, often frightening world of the twenty-first century. Nationalism, partly at least in response to the increasing sense of a globalised, homogenised world, became again a significant political force. The Soviet Union broke up into its constituent parts, and countries such as Czechoslovakia and Yugoslavia that had been part of the European map since before World War II also fell apart. In the latter country, ethnic tensions were complicated by religious rivalries. Religious fundamentalism (in places as far apart as Kosovo and Chechnya) became a force that threatened at various times to spread its particular brand of destabilisation far beyond national boundaries. Intervention by foreign countries or international agencies was usually either ineffective or gave rise to further problems. As the world became a more violent and dangerous place, increasing numbers of people found it impossible to live in their own country. This flow of refugees was augmented and often complicated (since it was often difficult to distinguish between the two) by economic migrants who saw the wealth of countries such as the European Union (EU) countries and the USA on television and in films and wanted to share in it. One of the major products of the period was the growth of inequality between the rich and the poor, not only between countries but also within countries. These inequalities occurred between an elite and the masses in the poor countries, and between a rich elite, a comfortable majority and a poor minority in the advanced industrial countries. Many commentators now see inequality as the greatest challenge of the new century.

So what precisely are the challenges for adult learning in the twenty-first century and what, if anything, can we learn from the Russell Report, the debates and projects that it spawned, and subsequent developments, not all of which could have been foreseen by the committee members? This book chapter seeks answers to four broad questions. Here are the first three:

1. What, if anything, have we learned from the successes and failures of the past?
2. What can we learn from experience elsewhere for adoption or adaptation here in the UK?
3. Why do we still consider adult learning as a by-product of education or employment policies rather than as a core strand of social policy?

The fourth question follows on directly from the first three questions. To what extent can 'adult learning' still be considered a unified field of professional endeavour? Is there anything that links the work of staff in grassroots adult community learning (ACL) with staff teaching mature adults in further and higher education, or in long-standing providers of adult learning such as the Workers' Educational Association (WEA) or the residential colleges, or with members of voluntary community organisations securing their own learning on their own terms? So the fourth question is:

4. What are the values that underpin the concept of adult education as vocation and to what extent has this been replaced by a more straightforward approach to it as 'just a job'.

I
Setting the scene

The first ingredient of political stability is an informed citizen. The first ingredient of economic progress is a skilled worker. And the first ingredient of social justice is an enlightened society. Education is, thus, the key to global peace and well-being.

(Kofi Annan, Secretary-General of the United Nations, in an address to the American Council on Education, February 1997)

What are we talking about? The language of adult learning

For many years, debating how we describe what we are considering has been an amusing, interesting, but largely pointless and unrewarding experience. The use of similar or identical terminology has often sought to convey different intentions and meanings. It has been equally problematic for readers and listeners to assume that different words implied different meanings. Following the publication of the Ministry of Reconstruction's 1919 Report (Ministry of Reconstruction, 1919/1980), much debate centred on the terminology employed and alternative interpretations on phrases and individual words. The Adult Education Committee, established as a sub-committee of the Reconstruction Committee in July 1917, was charged with considering 'the provision for, and possibilities of Adult Education (other than technical or vocational)'. Readers should be aware that language changes. Quotations from publications and documents should be read in the context of the time, place and language of their points of origin. In this book, as far as is practicable and respectful to the language of quoted people and publications, the term 'adult learning' will be used, indicating the belief that the subject constitutes a 'seamless robe' covering the entire spectrum of types and levels of structured learning undertaken by adults. The debate about language and terms is largely a diversion. Nevertheless, in the years leading up to the appointment of the Russell Committee and throughout the years covered by this book, the debate continued.

Contributors to this debate included academics, programme providers, national and local politicians and Her Majesty's Inspectorate (HMI). In the UK, the processes of teaching and learning, associated with structured programmes for adults, have been generally designated as 'adult education'. Some have argued against the loose and unthinking use of the undefined term 'adult' – what age, what learning contexts? Similarly, it has been suggested that 'education' implies a formal and bureaucratic delivery of a package to recruited recipients, whereas the emphasis should be on a negotiated learning experience, with the teacher and the taught operating as a partnership. In his research, Joseph Trenaman (1967) found that 45 per cent of the UK population held negative attitudes towards the word 'education'. The negativity was expressed as suspicion, indifference, fear and hostility. At the time, Trenaman was working in the further education department of the BBC. His studies led him and others to be committed to concentrating on the process of learning rather than the descriptors. He sought to avoid using the word 'education' wherever and whenever possible. Nonetheless, despite the widespread acceptance of the validity and importance of his findings, conclusions and recommendations, 'education' continued to be employed as a title and descriptor of an intellectual process experienced by adults.

A number of the most original, relevant and effective adult learning initiatives have not been described or recognised as 'adult education'. The experiences and processes had sufficient meaning for the learners without requiring any title or designation, which might well have been inaccurate and could have given rise to feelings of alienation. Participants often will have been unaware that what they were doing was being described by others as 'adult education'. The reality throughout the second half of the twentieth century was that many people who pursued their learning in the context of apprenticeships, work-based or job-related training, or post-qualification or post-graduate study would not have considered that they had participated in adult education at all. Men and women who have pursued their learning within the framework of skill and knowledge acquisition by means of community-based or interest group related learning would not necessarily have recognised their activity as adult education or adult learning. Much attention paid to the report of the Russell Committee, and to reports that preceded and followed it, dwelt on the terminology employed. This often marginalised or, at least, gave inadequate attention to the substance of arguments, conclusions and recommendations in the published documents. There is no virtue nor value in regretting the fact that the terms of reference of the Russell Committee specified 'non-vocational' adult education, which subsequently became synonymous, in some of the literature, as being courses not related to work; nor surmising over the use of the term 'adult and continuing' in the designation of the Advisory Council for Adult and Continuing Education (ACACE).

Reflecting on the value attached to adult learning, Allen Parrott (2002) concluded that

> over the past 30 years, the nature of this debate has completely changed. Concepts like 'liberal education' have been consigned to the historical

dustbin, while the radical quest for social justice through education apparently died . . . It is obvious that the utilitarians and instrumentalists have 'won'. . . the traditional notion of value as a moral and ethical concept has been taken over by the two different meanings of 'value' concerned with money and mathematics.

The argument will go on. Some would argue that Parrott's conclusion was unduly general and pessimistic. It may be that 'the utilitarians and instrumentalists' won the battle but the war has not yet ended. In an internal paper produced for Ruskin College in 1991, Stephen Yeo, Principal of the College, insisted that: 'Like all the best adult education of the past two hundred years in Britain we are part of a movement rather that the providers of a simple service.' The extent to which the many different and, at times, competing providers, could ever have been said to be elements of one single movement continues to be debated. In any case, it is not clear what kind of 'movement' is intended. Some historians of adult learning have reflected that, at the end of the nineteenth century and during the first quarter of the twentieth century, the movement, of which adult learning organisations and other social action bodies formed parts, was the early Labour Movement in the UK. As Roger Fieldhouse (1996) has pointed out, the adult education 'movement' was divided between a rather more formal wing represented by the WEA, and a more radical wing represented by the Plebs League and the National Council of Labour Colleges. Others have judged that providers of adult learning, almost through a process of osmosis, changed and developed in response to expressed and latent needs of the people and, in that respect, can be said to have formed an informal but, nonetheless, evident movement for progress. In a WEA publication, Raymond Williams (1983a), a much-respected adult educator of the post-World War II period, firmly expressed his belief, in his teaching and writing, that adult learning was both an essential component of the engine driving social change and also a cause and motivator of social change.

In his University of Nottingham inaugural lecture (25 November 1966), Professor Harold Wiltshire (1976) suggested that, 'adult education is not competitive and it is not selective and it is, therefore, almost the only sector of our educational system that can throw a bridge (though a frail one) across the rather frightening gap in our society between the educationally well-endowed and the educationally ill-endowed'. He argued that it *could* throw a bridge not that it *has* thrown a bridge. The gaps between aspiration and achievement, theory and practice, are wide. Even if it is accepted that adult learning could form a bridge, the picture he painted remained one of a divided society with those with the greatest need for learning opportunities, suited to their aspirations and potential competence levels, on one side of the divide, and those with material well-being and easy access to learning, on the other. The most likely providers of learning opportunities for adults, capable of bridging the gap identified by Harold Wiltshire, would not have been widely considered to have been traditional providers of learning opportunities for adults. Voluntary organisations devoted to particular interests (for example, music, pigeon fancying and philately) or concerned with social matters (for example, child development, disability and illness, pre-school learning and care) were more likely to bridge the gap than the then traditional programmes offered by universities and LEAs. The concept of 'bridging the gap' was a move away from the radical reformist agenda and a return to the earlier concept of a ladder or hierarchy of learning. This was not the view of the Russell Committee believing, as it did, that no type of learning nor subject area was intrinsically of greater importance than any other.

In 1979, an internal report of the HMI Working Group on Recurrent/ Continuing Education paid attention to the descriptors in use and their different meanings and contexts. Hindsight causes us to question the narrowness of the group's vision. Nonetheless, at the time, the report usefully identified many issues, current in the debates before and after the publication of the Russell Report. The group's working definition was that recurrent or continuing education, seen as interchangeable words, comprised 'opportunities for men and women to continue to develop their knowledge, skills, judgement and creativity throughout adult life by taking part, from time to time in learning situations which have been set up for the purpose as part of the total public and private provision of education and training'. This definition assumed a passive or reactive role on the part of the prospective and actual learner; namely, that the learner can take up the opportunity if it is provided by some person or organisation. There was little room in the definition, or adopted approach, for learner-led or negotiated learning; little scope for acknowledgement of incidental or individual learning.

Within the context of the Organisation for Economic Cooperation and Development (OECD), European education ministers had discussed the term 'recurrent education', introduced by the Swedish minister, in 1969. At this meeting, the French minister expressed a preference for the term *éducation permanente*. Yet both Swedish and French ministers agreed that, in the two very different political, social and educational contexts in which they operated, post-primary education planning should include learning for adults. In 1975, a further meeting of European ministers agreed to adopt the term 'recurrent education' as a guide to the future development of education planning and service provision. However, there was no agreement as to how the adoption of 'recurrent education' would be expressed in policy developed nor, more importantly, in the design of national education systems. The term was accepted but little regard was paid to whether the term would have the same meaning in the different countries. Even within an expanded EU, including both the UK and Sweden, national education systems remained the responsibility of national governments. The Russell Report was to both adopt a definition of adult education very close to that of recurrent or permanent education ('opportunities for men and women to continue to develop their knowledge, skills, judgement and creativity throughout adult life', paragraph 8) and to assert that '"permanent education" is a long-term concept and we have not time to wait for it' (paragraph 51).

It had already been unquestionably established that simply adding a modest adult learning development to an ever-expanding child and youth education structure would not deliver the required much-needed progress for adult learning. However, while accepting the evidence and conclusion, some countries, including the UK, would not countenance replacing the existing front-loaded system to indicate acceptance of the fundamental changes suggested by the French, Swedish and a number of other ministers. To give serious attention to introducing structural change to the overall educational system was not thought to be politically acceptable. That such required change would be likely to benefit all age groups was not held to be sufficient justification for action. The UK was one of a number of countries expressing the view that the education of adults should be bolted on to the existing initial education system to the extent that available resources allowed. Although the economic circumstances had already begun to deteriorate in the 1970s, after the years of expansion in the 1950s and 1960s, the absence of political and social vision and confidence was regrettable. The overall absence of priority for adult learning was dispiriting for those in 'the field'. The front-loaded model for education remained.

Adult education opportunities were expanding in the 1960s and continued to expand, although at a slower rate, in the 1970s. The 1979 HMI internal report recorded a widening of the range and nature of provision of learning opportunities for adults in the late 1960s and 1970s. A Conservative government had been elected in 1970 with a clear commitment to supporting work-related and instrumental learning. Learning for an economic purpose was to be given priority in terms of public funding. The Manpower Services Commission (MSC), the government's employment-related quango, had been launched in 1973 soon after the publication of the Russell Report. It was a reminder that the vocational/non-vocational divide would continue despite the view of the Russell Committee that education and training for adults should be seen to form a coherent whole, differentiated only by the motives, aspirations and intentions of the learners. While much of the detail within the report of the HMI Working Group touched on matters which arose after the Russell Report was published, it is appropriate to refer to the report, as a whole, in this scene-setting first chapter. It clearly indicates aspects of the debate within and outside the Russell Committee. The HMI saw an accepted relationship between education for adults and 'economic, social and labour market policies'. They noted a greater understanding, by providers, of the needs of adults for 'education and training at intervals over a lifetime' and a greater willingness to respond accordingly. Third, they confirmed a greater willingness to recognise 'that learning takes place within the context of formal and informal education and training'. Then, as now, it was noted that most post-initial vocational education and training was provided for people with higher level skills and qualifications. At the time, HMI noted that the then recently launched Training Opportunities Programme (TOPs) was designed as post-initial education and training for people with lower educational attainment. Although offered in educational and non-educational premises, the programme was initiated and financed in accordance with government labour market and employment policies.

In the context of a deepening economic crisis following the 1973 oil crisis and the devaluation crisis of 1976, the 1979 report was an explicit indication that adult learning, as far as the government was concerned, was not dependent on the policies or actions of the Department of Education and Science (DES). It was also an indication that certain types of learning opportunities for adults might be best delivered in premises other than those designated as primarily educational. It also reflected the view expressed by the Prime Minister James Callaghan at Ruskin College in 1976 that 'education' should in future be more closely tied to 'work'. In its discussion document, *Towards an Adult Training Strategy* (MSC, 1983), the MSC was concerned to offer improved learning opportunities for adults, seen to be markedly different from the offers to young people. The MSC noted that much of the 'shop floor' level work it was funding was narrowly focused on what were judged to be work-related essential skills and, in some instances, even job-specific skills. Such an approach was effective in neither the short nor the long term. By contrast, programmes designed and launched to improve training at management and supervisor levels, were increasingly containing a broader more balanced approach towards meeting personal as well as work-related learning needs. The MSC was promoting adult learning programmes with a vocational or work-related focus, incorporated within a broader view of the total learning needs of individuals. It was geared to respond to the identified needs of an adult community, within a framework structured to provide a more skilled workforce.

Later, throughout the 1970s and 1980s, there was increasing understanding by the traditional and more generally recognised adult learning providers that much post-initial work-related and work-based education and training was offered by bodies not previously thought of as mainstream providers of adult learning programmes. The spectrum of learning providers extended from narrowly focused sole-purpose employment-related private training providers, through the multifaceted provision of LEAs, to targeted university opportunities of higher education for mature adults, and to both general and narrow-interest voluntary organisations. It was a time when many providers had to realise that, however important and widely respected their own provision may have been, there were other bodies offering services and learning opportunities. These were sometimes in a more relevant, accessible and appropriately structured form. Often the learning opportunities were not described as education for adults.

In 1979, HMI were of the view that adjustments to the existing structures and systems would be sufficient to accommodate the sense of recurrent and continuing education. This view was influential in governmental and parliamentary circles. Contemporary evidence from OECD studies and reports and the accumulated experience and knowledge of providers indicated that simply adding modest resources for adult learning to the ever-expanding front-loaded model of education would never bring about equality between generations nor provide what adults needed. Instead, it would further benefit younger people and ignore or marginalise older people. HMI suggested a shift in emphasis in terms of resource allocation and a commitment to ensuring that 'education is much more closely related to other social and economic policies'. In making this comment, the Inspectorate was supporting a conclusion reached by the Russell Committee some years earlier, but also reflecting the new tone stemming from Callaghan's Ruskin College speech in 1976.

In developing this theme in their report, HMI asserted that 'it is necessary for the policy makers to try to discover where they think the community is going and to recognise that there is an education-work-leisure life-cycle in which paid work, unpaid work, and leisure feature and are all of great importance to each individual'. A broader definition of 'work' was suggested, recognising that large-scale unemployment was leading to earlier retirement, a shorter working week, job sharing and reduced overtime. It was assumed that this trend would eventually lead to 'more demand for adult education'. At the same time, it was noted that reduced unemployment was likely to lead to greater demand for on-the-job and work-related education and training, thereby achieving the necessary adjustment to maximise personal and economic benefits to be derived from technological changes and demands. HMI judged that education and training services had different functions and responsibilities through the structure of government but that they should be seen as 'complementary aspects of a single process of recurrent and continuing education'. Throughout the period under discussion, the words 'recurrent' and 'continuing' were often used together or separately without explanation, giving additional emphasis to the point that the argument about terminology often pushed aside consideration of the fundamental education/training issues.

Language sometimes gets in the way of understanding or, as Eric Hobsbawm famously said: 'We seemed to be using the same vocabulary but we did not appear to be speaking the same language.' In a paper, presented to the 1983 Standing Conference on University Teaching and Research in the Education of Adults (SCUTREA) conference, Alan Rogers (1983) gave expression to a widely shared frustration: 'Let me get definitions out of the way – I shall from now on use "post-initial education" for the whole field of the education of adults;

"continuing education" will be for vocational and closed group courses; "adult education" will be used for the traditional socially purposive and open education.' He continued by saying, about these terms, ' I don't like them at all, but we must have some shorthand or we'll never finish'. Although the language used and the shorthand headings varied from context to context and person to person, it was generally understood that the balance of types and purposes of adult learning across the wide range was changing during the 1980s. Vocational and job-specific training was assuming an ever-greater importance and prominence as a focus of public policy and funding schemes. Pressure for this change was coming from government, political organisations, industries and employers' bodies and from individuals seeking better work prospects. This was an illustration of the push towards instrumentalism and linking educational policy more closely with economic and industrial policy. Some educational organisations and institutions supported the instrumental approach to learning provision. The fruitless argument raged: is it 'education' or 'training'?

As we turn to a detailed consideration of the detailed policy initiatives over the 60 years leading up to the Russell Report, it is clear that we must look behind the words used to determine exactly what their authors intended by those words. We must also consider the aims and purposes which the subjects of adult learning – the students – brought to their studies. What did they think they needed to learn, and why? What were their preferred ways of participating in learning?

Adult Education Committee of the Ministry of Reconstruction: the 1919 Report

The Adult Education Committee (AEC) which produced the 1919 Report was bound, by its terms of reference, to focus attention on what was described at the time as 'non-vocational adult' education. Fifty years later, the Russell Committee was required to be similarly focused. In respect of the terms of reference of both committees, practitioners and enthusiasts in the field, who had hoped to see terms of reference embracing the full range of education for adults, were disappointed. However, their disappointment was somewhat appeased when the reports of the committees were seen to have covered a wider spectrum of adult learning.

The AEC was established by the Ministry of Reconstruction at the end of World War I 'to consider the provision for, and the possibilities of, adult education (other than technical or vocational) in Great Britain, and to make recommendations'. The committee was established *against* the wishes of the Board of Education which considered that adult education was a matter for the Board's attention and responsibility and not for the Ministry of Reconstruction. In the different situation 50 years later, the Russell Committee was supported and serviced by the Department of Education and Science and required

> . . . to assess the need for and review the provision of non-vocational adult education in England and Wales; to consider the appropriateness of existing educational, administrative and financial policies; and to make recommendations with a view to obtaining the most effective and economical deployment of available resources to enable adult education to make its proper contribution to the national system of education conceived of as a process continuing through life.

Although there were similarities between the terms of reference for the AEC and the Russell Committee, there were two important differences between the contexts within which the committees worked. First, the brief of the AEC extended across Great Britain. The Russell Committee's brief was limited to England and Wales. Second, the AEC reported, through the Ministry, to the Prime Minister. The Russell Committee, having been established by the Secretary of State for Education and Science, reported back to the Secretary of State. That the 1919 Report was submitted directly to the Prime Minister, through the Ministry, emphasised the intention to locate policy development for adult learning as a central plank of the work of the government as a whole. A combination of political, industrial and economic difficulties, plus the absence of a high level governmental commitment to adult learning as a priority matter, meant that a number of the recommendations of the 1919 Report were not implemented. Despite that disappointment, acceptance of the 1919 Report was the first indication of recognition by a UK government that adult learning embraced more than was covered by 'education' alone.

The 1919 Report has been arguably the most frequently quoted publication in the English language about adult learning in the UK. On the dust cover of its 1980 reprint of the report (Ministry of Reconstruction, 1919/1980), the University of Nottingham stated that it 'makes readily available to a modern audience the most famous document in the history of English adult education'. The inspirational language, optimistic tone and comprehensive attention to its brief, made the report a milestone in the literature and an example for subsequent committees dealing with adult learning. It was produced for 'a land fit for heroes' in the new Great Britain expected to rise from the degradation of the slaughter of the innocents during World War I. Therefore, it was inevitable that the report would point out a way to an expected enlightened and optimistic future when meeting the anticipated large-scale demand for learning opportunities would lead to communal and social contentment. The report called for an expanded and publicly recognised and funded role for universities with more and better paid staff. The establishment of extra-mural departments was recommended. The first was in Nottingham in 1920. This recommendation, and the recommendation for an increased role for the WEA and other voluntary organisations, led to the definition of 'Responsible Bodies' in the 1924 Adult Education Regulations (England and Wales).

In his letter to the Prime Minister, David Lloyd George, presenting the 1919 Final Report, the Chairman of the AEC, Arthur L. Smith, Master of Balliol College, Oxford, insisted that

> . . . the necessary conclusion is that adult education must not be regarded as a luxury for a few exceptional persons here and there, nor as a thing which concerns only a short span of early manhood [sic], but that adult education is a permanent necessity, an inseparable aspect of citizenship, and should therefore be both universal and lifelong . . . That the opportunity for adult education should be spread uniformly and systematically over the whole community, as a primary obligation on that community in its own interest and as a chief part of its duty to its individual members.

Without defining the terms used, the letter then argues that adult education should find 'its proper place in the national educational system'.

Allowing for the variation in language over the years, the aspiration and vision expressed by the 1919 Committee and its Chairman are echoed in many reports thereafter. While the mass of new adult students, envisaged by the committee, did not arrive in the predicted numbers in university and LEA classes, or in the branches of the WEA, the vision of the committee and the positive nature of its conclusions and recommendations enthused many. The difference between hope and aspiration, on the one hand, and the actual outcome, on the other, can largely be explained by the fact that the report was considered by the government and other potential funders and providers at a time of economic constraint, when essential attention was given to many more down to earth 'bread and butter' issues including housing, health, employment and school education. Similarly unfortunate was the fact that the Russell Report was followed by the oil crisis and economic downturn in the 1970s. The 1919 Report was trapped in the aftermath of World War I. Nonetheless, the report repays further reading and study, more than 80 years after its initial publication, for the attention it gives to issues relating to the personal and social consequences of exclusion and deprivation which continue to be agenda items at the beginning of the twenty-first century.

The 1919 Report (paragraph 330) clearly sets out the purpose and political importance of adult learning, as seen by the committee:

> The adult education movement is inextricably interwoven with the whole of the organised life of the community. Whilst, on the one hand, it

originates in a desire amongst individuals for adequate opportunities for self-expression and the cultivation of their personal powers and interests, it is, on the other hand, rooted in the social aspirations of the democratic movements of the country. In other words, it rests upon the twin principles of personal development and social service. It aims at satisfying the needs of the individual and at the attainment of new standards of citizenship and a better social order. In some cases the personal motive predominates. In perhaps the greater majority of cases the dynamic character of adult education is due to its social motive.

The 1919 Report was explicitly a political, as well as an educational, report, starkly asserting the social purpose of adult learning as a process designed to strengthen civil society, enhance social justice and create informed citizens. Adult education was thought to be good for a purpose; more than good in itself. It should be seen to be instrumental in intent. Yet the report failed to give adequate acknowledgement to the vocational benefits of much adult learning, whether or not courses and programmes were promoted with vocational intentions and aims.

This viewpoint from the committee will have been politically correct at the time, but in conflict with the socio-philosophical value attached to the liberal tradition, clearly expressed in the language, tone and philosophy of the next paragraph of the report, paragraph 331: 'We do not think that it is possible or desirable to eliminate from adult education the discussion of controversial questions, indeed one of the greatest values of adult education is that highly controversial subjects can be freely discussed in an atmosphere of mutual confidence and tolerance.' Harrison (1961) captures the same sense. He insisted that adult learning should be seen as an activity designed and used for a social purpose. Therefore, it should be acknowledged that the learning intention, on the part of the adult, would relate to social, political, cultural and/or religious aspects of life. It is important to bear in mind that much of the hoped for expanded and strengthened provision of adult education, post the 1919 Report, was expected to comprise work and employment training. Prior to World War I and during the war itself, LEAs and the WEA gave attention to vocational education to benefit the individuals concerned and the wider national interest. This was seen as part of the 'social motive' mentioned many times in the report. It was the time of the so-called 'great liberal tradition', with a number of universities seeking to become active and involved in their local communities.

In re-reading this and other paragraphs from the 1919 Report, it is crucial not to let the language get in the way of an understanding of the meaning and intention. In so many ways, 1919 is unlike the early years of the twenty-first century. Use of language is only one of the ways. When considering changes and developments in adult learning over a period of many years, attention must be given to the sense and intention of the vocabulary and the social, political and cultural contexts of the times. In the opening paragraphs of its report, the Russell Committee pays respects, and acknowledges its debt, to the 1919 Report. In particular, they quote in paragraph 10 the view of the 1919 Report:

> We do not wish to underrate the value of increased technical efficiency or the desirability of increasing productivity; but we believe that a short-sighted insistence upon these things will defeat its object. We wish to emphasise the necessity for a great development of non-technical studies, partly because we think that it would assist the growth of a truer conception of technical education, but more especially because it seems to us vital to provide the fullest opportunities for personal development and for the realisation of a truer conception of citizenship. Too great an emphasis has been laid on material considerations and too little regard paid to other aspects of life.

This clear and determined commitment, expressed in the 1919 Report overall, to an inclusive adult education movement, designed to deliver learning opportunities with personal, communal and social purposes proved to be inspirational. The passion for purposeful learning was shared widely. Extension and tutorial programmes, delivered by nineteenth-century universities to working-class industrial communities, had been a form of Victorian philanthropy (Simon, 1990). It accorded with the norms of the times. Later, at the end of the nineteenth century and up to and including the period of World War I, universities and the newly created WEA were committed to the belief that the expansion of learning opportunities for adults should be an important element of the rapidly changing political and social movements of the day. This was the focus of endeavour of Albert Mansbridge, R.H. Tawney and G.D.H. Cole, as leading individuals in the WEA and extra-mural adult learning in the first half of the twentieth century, and it continued to influence and inspire generations of activists and participants. This was the time when providers of learning opportunities thought themselves to be offering an introduction to high culture, university degree study and general higher education to members of the working class. Nonetheless, the social purpose, all-inclusive rhetoric of the 1919 Report was not translated into policy and action. A strong sense of the 1919 Report was to laud the great and liberal tradition and protect the connection between liberal education for adults and the universities.

The 1919 Report led directly to the creation of extra-mural departments in most universities in the 1920s and 1930s. However, acceptance of the report, in principle, and of its recommendations, failed to give due recognition to the contemporary and potential contribution of LEAs to adult learning, which were understated in the report. Bill Devereux (1982) observed that, of the more than

250 pages in the 1919 Report devoted to 'A Survey of Adult Education', merely six dealt with provision of adult learning programmes by LEAs. In these six pages, there was an emphasis on London. The London County Council (LCC), predecessor of the Inner London Education Authority (ILEA), had taken action in 1913 to establish a network of evening institutes (literary, general, men's and women's), in sufficient number and of sufficient strength to create the pattern which was to last, subject to necessary updating, until 1990, when ILEA was abolished and the service dismantled. Throughout the period 1913–90, London took a national lead in the provision of adult education. It provided a greater number of learning opportunities than the national average. At the time of abolition, this was generally agreed to be about one quarter of the total for England. A framework of support services for professional staff and adult learners was created. Perhaps most important of all, constant attention was paid to the very important relationship between adult learning and changing social and economic circumstances.

From the 1919 Report to the Education Act 1944

Each generation of adult educators and trainers has embarked on its work in the knowledge that the extent and nature of programmed learning opportunities have always been conditioned by funding limitation and political policy priorities. Adult educators have never been able to do all that they would have wished to do; nor has there ever been agreement about what it is that they wish to achieve, beyond general rhetorical statements about the virtue of ensuring that learning opportunities for all should be available. Committees of enquiry do not work in a vacuum nor are they insulated from what went before. The Russell Committee acknowledged its debt to the 1919 Report and paid attention to the Education Act 1944. In addition, it noted other milestones along the adult education road. Many important legislative decisions, government circulars and reports were mentioned in the Russell Report. In the remainder of this chapter, brief consideration is given to the major domestic national influences on the shape of adult learning in the period before the Russell Committee started its work.

Two meetings, held in London in 1918, chaired by Albert Mansbridge, the then General Secretary of the WEA, led to the inaugural meeting of the World Association of Adult Education in March 1919. Despite its name, the new organisation never established either a broad membership or credibility as a worldwide body. It set itself the challenge of aiding 'the establishment, or development, in all parts of the world, of movements and institutions for promoting adult education, and to promote cooperation between them'. The World Association published papers, organised conferences and offered advice and information through its office in London. Later, in January 1921, Mansbridge chaired another meeting in London which gave rise to the British Institute of

Adult Education, a branch of the World Association, and a forerunner of NIACE. Within four years, the institute became a separate and independent representative body for adult learning in Great Britain. The institute grew rapidly in size, range of work and extent of influence.

The President of the Board of Education created an Adult Education Committee in 1921. In many ways this was a forerunner of ACACE, being a group of appointed individuals charged with the responsibility of offering advice to the board. Initially, the committee, in common with the board itself, moved away from the emphasis in the 1919 Report on the university links to adult learning and argued for a stronger coordinating and leadership role for LEAs. Later, during the 1920s and early 1930s, the committee paid more attention to the value of partnerships at the local level, between LEAs, universities and the voluntary sector, particularly but not exclusively the WEA. The potential value of this partnership arrangement was reflected in Section 42.4 of the Education Act 1944 which dealt with the procedure to be followed by LEAs in producing their schemes of further education. Unfortunately, this was one element of the Act that was not implemented fully. Partnership at the local level depended on willingness on the part of the LEAs rather than the fulfilling of the legislative requirement. The Adult Education Committee produced many reports to the government on policy ideas. Of special note is the influence of the committee on the terms of the Board of Education (Adult Education) Regulations 1924. The Regulations formed a break with the past. As noted in the Ashby Report (Ministry of Education, 1954), prior to the publication of the Regulations of 1924, the board had consistently expressed the view that most, if not all, further education below the level of university tutorial classes, should be the responsibility of LEAs. The Regulations set the ground rules for a major change in policy and practice by permitting universities, the Districts of the WEA and other appropriate approved bodies to apply for recognition as 'Responsible Bodies', entitled to receive grants for the established three-year tutorial classes and for classes and courses below that academic level.

Throughout the period covered by this book, even if there were not always obvious shared policies and perspectives as between the various committees, councils and task groups, there was a network of individuals who frequently sat together. In his commentary on the reception of the 1919 Report, Bernard Jennings (Ministry of Reconstruction, 1919/1980) wrote:

> It is difficult to distinguish between the influence of the report and the continued influence of the leaders of that movement, some of whom had in effect written the Report. The incestuous tendencies of the principal adult education organisations created a network through which such men (sic) as Mansbridge, Temple, Greenwood, Tawney, Alfred Zimmern, Haldane, A L Smith and the latter's successor at Balliol, A D Lindsay, exer-

cised considerable influence. The WEA central executive, the Central Joint Advisory Committee for Tutorial Classes, the committees of the British Institute and the World Association for Adult Education, and the Adult Education Committee of the Board of Education, had interlocking memberships. Temple, for example, was the first chairman of the AEC [Association of Education Committees] as well as being President of the WEA. Mansbridge was a member of all the above committees, except the WEA central executive, and also served on the Royal Commission on Oxford and Cambridge. This influential group had the ear of successive Presidents of the Board of Education, one of whom, Lord Eustace Percy, served as a committee member of the BIAE [British Institute of Adult Education] before taking up his office.

What Jennings recorded in respect of the early to middle 1920s applied equally to the years from the establishment of the Departmental Committee on the Youth Service in England and Wales (Albemarle Committee) in 1958 to the creation of ACACE in 1977.

The report of the Consultative Committee of the Board of Education on the Education of the Adolescent (The Hadow Report) (Board of Education, 1926) was published in 1926. Membership of the Hadow Committee included Albert Mansbridge and R.H. Tawney, both of whom had been members of the committee that produced the 1919 Report. The committee was not charged with the brief to report on post-school learning. Nevertheless, it commented that 'it is desirable that teachers in Modern Schools and Senior Classes should endeavour to secure the continued education of their pupils after school age by drawing attention to such facilities for further instruction, whether cultural or vocational, as are available in the area'. Raising the minimum school leaving age from 14 to 15 years took place in 1947 after incorporation of the recommendation in the Education Act 1944. The Hadow Committee had recommended that the change should take place in 1932. The general encouragement to extended education for all, as adopted by the Hadow Committee, gave a measure of national recognition and approval to the 'village college' initiatives of Henry Morris in Cambridgeshire. His concept of an all-age educational institution, staffed, programmed and managed in a manner consistent with his rather romantic view of rural life was expressed in a major statement submitted to the LEA in 1924. During his time as Chief Education Officer in Cambridgeshire, five village colleges were established. They became the acknowledged precursors of the community schools and community colleges created in the 1960s and thereafter. This approach to local all-age provision was greatly influenced and encouraged by the Sports Council's view that sports and leisure facilities could and should be developed for general community use on school sites and the Albemarle Report's recommendation (in 1960) that school-based youth wings and youth centres should be available for adult and community use outside the time when they are occupied for youth work activities.

Jonathan Rose (2002) quotes from the memoirs of J. R. Clynes: 'I began to conceive that these words that I loved were more than pretty playthings: they were mighty levers whereby the power of the whole world could be more evenly and fairly distributed for the benefit of my kind.' Clynes was the son of a farm labourer who, after working in the textile mills in Oldham, became an MP in 1906 and was a minister and deputy leader of the Labour Party in the 1920s. The early years of the twentieth century and, in particular the four years of World War I, witnessed dramatic changes in social and community behaviour and attitudes. Large numbers of women began to breach the barricades which had protected male control of many institutions and areas of education and employment. Women were employed to do 'men's work' during the war. As a result of the carnage during World War I (1914–18), many children were brought up by their mothers in single-parent homes. Women had become more assertive, more demanding and more challenging to the government and to the 'establishment' of the day. They challenged the assumptions about the position of women. Returning servicemen and people who had lived through the war at home were determined that the social and political changes, on top of the impact of two generations of compulsory mass education for children, should lead to a refusal to accept that the future would automatically repeat the past. The written word had become an invaluable facilitator of education, information, debate and argument. It formed a central thread of working-class culture, crucial to the concept of mutual education evident in community and work organisations, including trade unions, churches, libraries, WEA and university extension programmes. Throughout the 1920s and 1930s, 'mutuality' was a word applicable to the lifestyles and values of a large section of the population. To some degree, it was rediscovered in the community development and priority area work of the 1960s, which both informed the Russell Committee and strengthened the recommendations of the Russell Report. This was before radio and television had a dramatic effect on the ways in which the public gained access to information and learning.

The National Council of Social Service, later the National Council of Voluntary Organisations, was founded in 1919. During the interwar years, the organisation encouraged, supported and initiated action to develop a spread of village halls and community centres across the country. The increase in the number and quality of village halls and community centres led to a growth in the practice and appreciation of arts and crafts, including music, drama, performing and creative arts. Enhanced interest in folk music and dance, and traditional urban and rural crafts was evident. None of this heightened activity was given general recognition as being part of the mainstream of adult learning. Even after the passing of the Physical Training and Recreation Act (1937), designed to respond to government concern about the physical condition and general health and welfare of the nation, it took time before there was an acceptance that the Act could have far-reaching implications for adult learning.

Memorandum 172, issued by the government in 1938, dealt with the implementation of the Physical Training and Recreation Act. It gave power to local authorities, not necessarily LEAs, 'to establish or support community centres and recreational institutes and urged the general extension of opportunities for physical training and recreation for older and younger students'. Prior to the Act, the LCC had insisted that people wishing to participate in physical training and recreation classes should attend one or more courses in other subjects. After the Act, the Council changed its policy and permitted students to enrol for such courses only. The LCC, in common with very few other LEAs, took full advantage of the opportunities presented by the Act and sought funding from central government departments and the housing committees of the LCC and inner London boroughs to build premises and pay for staff and equipment. Devereux (1982) describes in detail the benefit of the Act on the development of adult education institutes in London resulting from the ability of the LCC to work jointly with borough councils and other services in a creative way.

The programmes of building and upgrading village halls and community centres meant that the specific intention of the government to see an improvement of the physical training, health and welfare of the nation was coupled with a growth in facilities available for wider programmes of adult learning, often promoted by the WEA and other voluntary sector bodies, rather than by the LEAs or universities. Years later, the Russell Report argued that adult education should be accepted as being an education-oriented social service, often operating alongside and in conjunction with other social services; public, private and voluntary.

The Education Act 1944

Adult educators in the late 1960s came to hope that the Russell Report would be the much needed and much delayed historical milestone in adult learning, following many years characterised by uncoordinated and modest initiatives. Konrad Elsdon (2001) makes the point that the appointment of the Russell Committee 'seemed to represent a finally successful outcome of the pressures over a long period from a host of outside forces as well as from the inspectorate'. The pressures were evident over a period extending back to the middle to late 1940s when it became obvious that the 1944 Act would not deliver the necessary legal framework for the much needed learning opportunities for adults in the post-war period. This was a particular disappointment to all concerned with adult learning, given that a large proportion of the 1945 incoming Labour Government and Cabinet, including the Prime Minister, Clement Attlee, had been involved in adult learning as students, teachers and organisers. Some had been WEA students and activists. Others had participated, as students and teachers, in groups and classes promoted by universities, trade unions and LEAs. Rose (2002) records that many of these politicians freely acknowledged that they owed much to the skills and knowledge gained in this way. Despite this, adult learning lacked a strong and determined advocate in the Cabinet backed by a publicly acknowledged overwhelming case for radical change. Ellen Wilkinson, as Minister of Education, did not command the same powers of persuasion in government as Aneurin Bevan displayed when leading the creation of the National Health Service in 1947–8. Nor did she show the same unyielding conviction. H.D. (Billy) Hughes MP, later to be Principal of Ruskin College, a distinguished national officer of the WEA for many years, and a leading member of both the Russell Committee and ACACE, was, for a time, Ellen Wilkinson's Personal Parliamentary Secretary. Nonetheless, he was unable to move adult learning up the political agenda.

The Education Act 1944 did not mention either 'adult education' or 'continuing education'. It included the term, 'further education' as the third stage of a 'statutory system of public education' – primary, secondary and further. Details related to delivering the three stages of public education were set out in Part II of the Act. The general duty placed on LEAs was confirmed in Part II.7 of the Act, 'securing that efficient education throughout those stages shall be available to meet the needs of the population of their area'. LEAs were required to ensure that they made 'adequate' provision for all three stages. In respect of the primary and secondary stages, 'adequate' could be measured in terms of the number of children between 5 and 15 in any given area, for whom efficient full-time education was to be compulsory. No similarly precise, quantifiable measure of adequacy was outlined in the Act, or related circular or regulation, with regard to further education. Further education was dealt with in seven sections of the Act. Four of the seven sections referred to the never implemented proposals for 'county colleges' and for compulsory part-time education for young people up to 18 years of age who had left school before that age. One section described the preparation of 'schemes of further education' to set limits to the powers available to LEAs in seeking to 'secure the provision of facilities for further education'. This was subsequently elaborated in Circular 133 (Ministry of Education, 1947a) and in Pamphlet No. 8 'Further Education' (Ministry of Education, 1947b). One section outlined interim arrangements for the period prior to the date of implementation of the Act, leaving only one section, Section 41, directly addressing the provision of further education for adults.

The Act gave attention to adult learning, largely within the context of LEA duties, but it did nothing to ensure that learning for adults was likely to gain the central position of importance that the time and the circumstances required. Section 41 of the Act confirmed the duty to be laid on LEAs 'to secure the provision for their area of adequate facilities for further education'. It also sought to ensure that LEAs, in seeking to fulfil this duty, would 'have regard to any facilities for further education provided for their area by universities, educational associations and other bodies, and [to] consult any such bodies as aforesaid and the local educational authorities for adjacent areas'. The nature of any possible sanctions against a defaulting LEA was not explained in either the Act or in related regulations or circulars. Frustration regarding these matters remained for many years. Section 41 called for:

(a) full-time and part-time education for persons over compulsory school age; and

(b) leisure-time occupation in such organised training and recreative activities as are suited to their requirements, for any persons over compulsory school age who are able and willing to profit by the facilities provided for that purpose.

The wording of the Act, with regard to adult learning, was most unhelpful. Adult learning tended to be marginalised, in thinking and planning, in view of the loose and weak reference to 'leisure-time occupation'. Subsequent to the passing of the Act, and in recognition of the necessity to improve and increase the provision of vocational, craft and industrial education and training, LEAs were required to prepare Schemes of Further Education provision for their areas, to include adult learning (Ministry of Education, 1947a). The two parts, (a) and (b) of Section 41, were to be treated very differently. The first part was to be interpreted as narrowly meaning vocational education largely for young people embarking on their working life. The second part was designed to cover adult learning to enrich leisure time in the context of defining and contributing to the needs of a civilised society. The intended but unreal division between vocational and non-vocational, and the greater priority, in terms of policies, programmes and resources, given to work-related courses and education for employment for young people, became clearer. This division, damaging though it was recognised as being, had lasted from 1918 and had become more rigid with every passing year. It was to be a concern of the Russell Committee, ACACE and many other bodies during the years following the 1944 Act.

Despite the shortcomings of the 1944 Act and its imprecise and totally inadequate treatment of adult learning, the Russell Committee was absolutely clear as to what it sought to achieve in describing a comprehensive service of adult learning:

The specification of needs that has emerged from our study is of crucial importance for the health of our society and the quality of life of individual citizens. We are not concerned with the mere garnishing of leisure hours but with the full personal development of men and women in environments that are often inimical to creativity and independence of mind. And we are concerned with *all* the people, not simply with those whose prior acquaintance with education has led them to demand more. We take our cue from the Education Act 1944 which speaks of 'the education of the people' and 'the provision of a varied and comprehensive service in every area'. The comprehensive service of adult education that we are advocating and of which details are set out in Part III [of the Russell Report] is an inescapable component of that provision (paragraph 59).

From the Education Act 1944 to the Russell Report

The 25 years preceding the appointment of the Russell Committee in 1969 was a time of much legislative and policy activity which had an important bearing on adult learning. In this scene-setting chapter, preliminary consideration is given to the most important features of policy and activity which, together, prepared the ground for the Russell Committee's conclusions and recommendations. More detailed attention to principal policies and changes will be found in later chapters. The period also saw many building and development programmes, making it possible for providers of learning to argue that, with extra resources and a firm legal basis for adult learning, significant increased growth would be assured.

When members of the Russell Committee met for the first time, they were able to reflect on a period of 25 years since the 1944 Act characterised by much thinking and heart-searching about education. Many committees had been established by governments and other interested bodies. Reports had been published. Legislation had passed through Parliament. While much of this activity was initially considered to be marginal to the provision of learning opportunities for adults, it soon became apparent that adult learning policy-makers and programme planners needed to be aware of what was happening. Without any committee having explicit responsibility for advising the government and others on how best to respond to the learning needs and desires of all adults, policy decisions were being taken which, by default, had an impact on adult learning. A brief description of a number of important background influences on the work of the Russell Committee is set out in this section of the chapter.

Part II of the Russell Report was headed 'Review of Existing Provision'. In introducing a summary of major documents of the years from 1944 to 1971, the committee stated that 'the sequence of official publications suggest a declining concern with adult education' (paragraph 78). The Labour governments from 1945 to 1951 paid particular attention to ensuring that school education was well established after World War II. In this regard, they were deemed to have been very successful. However, the same cannot be said in respect of adult learning. Governments defaulted. The experience of successful basic education programmes in the armed forces during the war, the need to train and retrain large numbers of returning men at the end of the war, the fact that many women had been recruited to work in industry, the service sector and the professions during the war and needed their experience certificated to enable them to continue after the war, all pointed to a priority need for a national impetus for adult learning. It had been expected by adult learning workers that this would have been recognised by the government. The omission of adult learning from the list of socially and economically significant service improvements implemented between 1945 and 1951 was a considerable disappointment.

The damaging and unjustified split between vocational and non-vocational adult learning contributed greatly to the air of insecurity which overlay adult learning in the years preceding 1969, when the Russell Committee was appointed. However, the 1944 Act acknowledged the importance and potential contribution of voluntary organisations to adult learning, acting in partnership with LEAs, universities and other bodies. The Russell Committee underlined the importance of cooperation and partnership in local provision, to be initiated and supported by the LEA:

> Every local education authority should aim to provide a broadly-based and varied programme of adult education which is sensitive to local needs and quick to respond to them, assisting university extra-mural departments, the WEA and other voluntary agencies where appropriate but acting directly over much of the field ... A full provision of adult education should also include 'community workshops' to which adults can resort in their own time and not simply to attend formal classes. (paragraph 185)

The 1944 Act had pointed in the direction of Community Colleges as establishments in which the education of children and adults could take place. The Ministry of Education pamphlet, *Further Education* (Ministry of Education, 1947b), gave guidance to LEAs. This exercise neither released resources nor was it uniformly significant in policy and programme planning terms throughout the country. The requirement placed on LEAs, to follow the issued guidance, was allowed to wither away by the then Ministry of Education. It had no major lasting impact on the quality, quantity or variety of adult learning opportunities.

The 1944 Act led to fundamental changes in the structure of secondary education in England and Wales. It also gave rise to a major school building programme in order that the schools could accommodate the extra pupil numbers consequent upon raising of the minimum school leaving age to 15, effective in 1947, and the universal availability of secondary education. As the new buildings became available in the late 1940s and 1950s, so they were increasingly used to house classes of adult students in out-of-school hours. This pattern was repeated in 1972, when the minimum school-leaving age was further raised to 16 years. Additional Raising of the School Leaving Age (RoSLA) buildings appeared on many school sites to house the extra pupils, some temporary but some permanent.

During the 1950s and 1960s, many local authorities obtained funding from central government for building, adapting or modernising village halls and community centres. This funding was in accordance with the terms of the Physical Training and Recreation Act 1937 and administered through leisure and recreation departments rather than education. In addition, much local community-based adult learning was launched as one element of the work of social and community development officers and workers employed by New Town Corporations and ad hoc bodies established to oversee the building of major residential estates on the outskirts of large cities.

In 1952, Responsible Bodies were threatened by the Ministry of Education with a budget freeze for the year 1952–3 and a 10 per cent reduction in 1953–4. Following considerable protest from 'the field' and intervention by the then Prime Minister, Winston Churchill, the proposed 10 per cent cut was lifted but the budget freeze remained. The Minister of Education, Florence Horsbrugh, appointed a committee, chaired by Eric Ashby 'to review the present system by which the extra-mural departments of universities, the WEA and the other Responsible Bodies provide local facilities for adult education, with special reference to the conditions under which the facilities are organised, and are aided by grant from public funds'. Although the Ashby Report (Ministry of Education, 1954) made no dramatic or fundamental recommendations for organisational change, it did recommend that grants to Responsible Bodies should be based on the quality of organisation, teaching and learning, an assessment of the learning needs of the area covered by the individual responsible body and the provision being made by other adult learning bodies. This was to bring HMI closer to the work of the Responsible Bodies.

Much adult learning was taking place outside recognised and overtly educational structures and organisations. In 1958, the government established the Albemarle Committee to review the Youth Service in England and Wales. Richard Hoggart was a leading member of the committee and a significant contributor to the committee's report. He was to be very influential in the following twenty-five years or more in the development of many aspects of adult learning. He contributed to international adult learning through his work at UNESCO, and was chairman of ACACE from 1977 to 1983. It was Hoggart who defined and described the 'sociological background against which it [the Albemarle Report] set the youth service' (Maclure, 1965). That part of the Albemarle Report (Ministry of Education, 1960) headed 'The World of Young People' graphically and comprehensively described the background to the lives of many young people between 14 and 20 years of age, the age bracket delineated for the youth service. Yet teenagers inhabit the same world as people younger and older than themselves. Hoggart's words were of direct and important relevance to adult educators, at the time he was writing and for the decades to follow. They bear repetition at length:

> The society which adolescents now enter is in some respects unusually fluid. Old industries change their nature as new processes are adopted; new industries appear and help to shift the location of industry itself. New towns arise, and new estates on the outskirts of old towns deplete the established housing areas and alter their social composition. A series of Education Acts, notably that of 1944, are causing some movement across class and occupational boundaries and should in time cause more. So British society is beginning to acquire greater mobility and openness. The effects of these changes are not always marked at present; some groups seem to live much as they have lived for many years. Yet as the changes develop, so old habits, old sanctions, old freedoms and responsibilities will be called into question and new relationships demanded . . .
>
> We mention below some of the generalisations commonly made about adolescents today. We believe that most of them are untrue and distorting. But they have hardened into some of the most striking clichés of the last decade [the 1950s]. It is frequently said, then, that young people today belong to 'a generation of teenage delinquents'; that they have rejected family life and are 'featherbedded' by the Welfare State; that they are increasingly materialistic; 'couldn't care less'; and have no moral values. Probably the most accurate reply to such assertions is also the most obvious: that today's adolescents are much like those of other generations. Yet we would add this: that when we compare what is often said about adolescents with the overwhelming unanimity of regard expressed in the evidence of those with long and intimate experience, especially in 'difficult' areas, we are left predominantly with a sense of respect and admiration for most young people's good sense, goodwill, vitality and resilience.

The sense of these paragraphs remained as valid at the end of the century as in 1960. Language will have changed with the passage of time but the essential truth remains; that the world does not stand still for any generation at any time. It is the task of those involved in adult learning organisations and services to recognise this fact. In the light of this essential understanding, high quality provision should be made in a manner, at times and in locations appropriate to those wishing to participate.

Among the Albemarle Committee's recommendations, accepted by the government, was the need for a national building programme. This was of great consequential benefit to future adult learners in many parts of the country. The number of free standing youth centres, sometimes designated as youth and community centres, and of youth wings on school sites, increased dramatically during the 1960s. By the time the Russell Committee started its work in 1969, many adult students were pursuing their studies in these new premises which, because of their prime purpose as youth service facilities, were generally located in residential areas of towns and cities. This often made them more easily accessible than major establishments, such as schools and further education colleges, traditionally used for adult learning. Funding from the LEA Further Education Building Programme was used to transform or extend some youth wings to become youth and adult wings. In some places, they became parts of designated community schools and community colleges. Determining where the line should be drawn between youth and adult, in terms of times of access, age limits, staffing and other resources was left to the responsible LEA. Many LEAs applied for extra resources to increase the amount of accessible accommodation and to increase the numbers of organisational, professional and administrative staff within the framework of an integrated youth and adult community service. These building developments, and their related staffing and other resources, helped to create a modest base for neighbourhood-located provision of learning opportunities for adults. The courses and other learning activities were often managed in conjunction with the programmed teaching and learning taking place in nearby schools, libraries, leisure centres or other suitable premises. Although the facilities were established and managed by LEAs, they were often made available for use by extra-mural departments, WEA and other voluntary organisations. The neighbourhood or area centre concept, recommended by the Russell Committee and underpinning the basic aim of the Educational Centres Association (ECA), was closely related to the post-Albemarle developments.

The Robbins Report (Committee on Higher Education, 1963) recommended that arrangements should be made to develop higher education opportunities for mature adults. Immediately, questions were raised as to whether the report was more about structure and form than about content and purpose. If the intention was to focus on the relationship between higher education, the national economy and employment, the target would be missed. Neither at the time of Robbins, nor subsequently, have the majority of people leaving higher education moved directly into paid employment related to their course of study or leaving qualification. While the situation has changed and improved somewhat in the forty years since the Robbins Report was published, for most young adults, the route from A Level examinations in school or college through higher education was not leading to work and employment so much as being the continuation of a narrow academic form of teaching and learning. Mature adults in higher education establishments, having successfully taken A Level examinations, or their equivalent, were on the same conveyor belt taking them through an elongated largely academic learning process, not necessarily an appropriate preparation for work. This is not to disparage academic learning. Rather it is to point out a fundamental weakness of post-school learning in the UK over many years. Politicians had argued erroneously for more higher education opportunities of the academic type for school leavers and adults when what the country needed was a better balance between higher level academic and vocational learning, and more opportunities for mature adults to move from paid or unpaid work into differently-designed flexible full-time and part-time forms of higher education. In 1963, Robbins argued for an increase in the number of higher education students with the removal of impediments faced by mature adults seeking opportunities. Universities were encouraged to admit 'non-standard' students.

Within three years, following trailing speeches by Anthony Crosland, Secretary of State for Education and Science, the White Paper *A Plan for Polytechnics and Other Colleges* (DES, 1966a) outlined the government's proposals to establish polytechnics as degree-awarding higher education establishments. The binary division was created. Unlike the new polytechnics, universities tended not to take seriously the government's wish to see more 'non-standard' mature students admitted. The new polytechnics and their related colleges became categorised, often totally unfairly, as second-class universities offering a range of vocational courses. The division was to last until the merger of polytechnics and universities into one university sector following the Further and Higher Education Act 1992. It still underlies public perception of the relative merits of different universities.

At the other end of the age spectrum, the Plowden Report *Children and Their Primary Schools* (Central Advisory Council for Education, 1967) gave an important impetus to family and parent education and strongly highlighted the relationship between individual education achievement and personal, social and communal poverty. This was as crucial a finding in respect of devising learner-friendly and easily accessible methods of meeting the learning needs of adults as it was in respect of the education of children. Using the survey evidence available to the committee, it was recommended that a number of Educational Priority Areas (EPAs) be designated in areas of multiple deprivation. The work of the staff teams in the EPAs in the late 1960s and early 1970s set out new and effective arrangements for offering learning in the community to many adults previously not in any way touched by local provision (Halsey, 1972). An important influence on the ultimate terms of the Plowden Report, with regard to early years learning and its links with parent learning, was the experience of the Pre-school Playgroups Association (PPA), now the Pre-school Learning Alliance (PLA). The PPA was created in the early 1960s following correspondence in the columns of *The Guardian* newspaper about the unsatisfied needs and wishes for education and work opportunities for young mothers and the value to young children of well-organised and well-led education and care in the early years. From largely middle-class beginnings, with an emphasis on care rather than learning for young children, the PPA rapidly became a national organisation of importance, acknowledged to be offering far-reaching learning opportunities for parents, principally mothers, and early learning for pre-school children.

In addition to the beneficial outcomes of the government's acceptance of the recommendations of the Albemarle Report, adult learning gained from increased governmental support for community-based arts and sports during the 1960s. The First Minister for the Arts, Jennie Lee, published a White Paper *A Policy for the Arts* (Lee, 1965). The White Paper was followed by encouragement and financial support by the DES and the Ministry of Housing and Local Government to local and regional arts facilities. New or improved premises were often erected in conjunction with existing or planned educational buildings. As a result, in the late 1960s and throughout the 1970s, there was a significant increase in the number of arts centres. Some were located in new buildings, some on shared sites with schools, and some in converted existing redundant buildings. Overall, the increase in facilities for arts appreciation, practice and performance invigorated adult learning programmes in many areas. Similarly, throughout this period, support offered to LEAs and other local authorities by the DES and the Ministry of Housing and Local Government led to an expansion in sports and recreation provision. Some of these new developments were on school and college sites and, from the outset, designed, equipped and managed with dual education/community use in mind. Many freestanding sports centres were built and floodlit, all-weather surfaces laid out for sports training and match play.

The government launched Home Office-funded Community Development Projects (CDPs) in 12 urban areas in 1969, one year after the start of the Urban Programme. As a dimension of the Urban Programme, coordinated by the Home Office, and also involving the Departments of Education and Science, the Environment (created in 1970), and Health and Social Security, the CDPs developed mechanisms and activities to alleviate social need. With regard to the education elements of the CDPs, they were designed to be community-based and community-led initiatives committed to learner participation in course design, curriculum and teaching and learning techniques. Many local initiatives to meet social and educational needs were funded in this way, especially projects and programmes for ethnic minority groups and other excluded groups, for whom the existing programmes and organisational arrangements were inappropriate or unacceptable for one reason or another. CDPs learned much from the experience of EPAs and vice versa.

Both approaches were based on the proposition that learning in the community should be seen to be more than individuals gaining from community-based learning, however valuable that gain might be. Ideally, the community should be seen to benefit from the process of learning undertaken by individuals and the learning outcomes that ensue. The approach adopted by the CDPs was consistent with the views being expressed by Raymond Williams and others at the time. In *Towards 2000* (1983b) Williams discussed the objective of looking for an 'educated and participatory democracy' and a 'learning democracy'. People should be individually involved in the operation of democratic institutions and in decision-making in ways absent in a representative democracy. In the language of the second half of the twentieth century, Williams was reconsidering a basic premise of the 1919 Report, that 'the adult education movement is inextricably interwoven with the while of organised life of the community . . . it rests upon the twin principles of personal development and social service . . . the dynamic character of adult education is due to its social motive'. That Williams felt obliged to address the issue indicates the lack of progress in the intervening years towards embedding adult learning in personal, social and national progress.

John Robinson (1982) described the 1960s as 'the expanding sixties'. The BBC had carried educational programmes on the radio for some time. In October 1962, the government made it possible, through new regulations, for television to carry adult education. This development was warmly welcomed by a range of adult learning bodies which had exerted pressure on the government, the BBC and the Independent Television Authority (ITA) for this move. Between 1963 and 1970, both the BBC and the ITA, through its individual commercial television companies, prepared and broadcast a varied and challenging number of education series. These related to science, modern languages, politics, economics, industrial affairs, the arts, history, health, family life, mathematics and other subjects. By the end of the 1960s, the BBC was well placed to prepare and launch the most far-reaching and significant series, 'On the Move', a television series for adults with poor literacy skills. This grew out of discussions in 1972 among further education officers at the BBC (Hargreaves, 1980). The internal discussions were encouraged by the consideration being given by the Russell Committee to the learning needs of excluded groups, especially people with basic learning needs, by the work of the present author as Research Assistant to the committee, by the publication of *The Disadvantaged Adult* (Clyne, 1972) and, finally, by the launch of the Right to Read campaign in the Autumn of 1973.

The BBC television series *Teaching Adults* was a crucially important indicator that the world of adult learning was changing, strengthening and becoming more concerned with delivering a good quality service. The series was first broadcast between April and June 1968 and repeated between October and December 1969. Many people considered that adult learning was too disjointed and incoherent for a general series to be capable of meeting the variety of training needs of people teaching in dissimilar situations. There was little evidence of people teaching adults in different contexts ever meeting to share experience, ideas and problems and to seek common ways of improving their teaching skills and professional satisfaction in the job. *Teaching on Equal Terms*, edited by Jennifer Rogers (1969), was published by the BBC to accompany the series. Worksheets were produced. Organisations and services concerned with teaching adults established viewing and study groups. The television series was important as the first national initiative harnessing television to the tutor training process in conjunction with the written word and group activity and led, at the local level, by tutor trainers. The series was about teaching adults, not about adult education. Had the 1960s not been a decade of change, growth and creativity, it is unlikely that *Teaching Adults* would have made such an impact. It undoubtedly helped to prepare thousands of tutors and organisers to receive and respond to the Russell Report in a more considered and confident manner than would otherwise have been the case.

Two other, interrelated, elements of the background to the work of the Russell Committee were the National Extension College (NEC) and the Open University (OU). In 1963, the NEC was established with the primary objective of improving and increasing access opportunities to higher education. It aimed to achieve this objective by working in close partnership with broadcasting authorities, by linking correspondence learning with residential schools and by producing materials which would be widely marketed and not solely restricted to its own registered students. Michael Young was the influential driving force behind the creation of the NEC. It was also his vision and use of the term 'Open University' which inspired the thinking about directly offering higher education opportunities through correspondence and distance learning, broadcasts and support materials and residential schools. The determination of Jennie Lee, as Minister for the Arts in the 1964 Labour Government, ensured that the OU, as an independent degree-giving higher education institution, open to all regardless of prior qualifications, came into being in 1969. Her clearly focused force carried the day against any opposition.

The government issued Further Education Regulations in 1969. Regulation 25 specified the 24 extra-mural departments of the universities, the 17 districts of the WEA and the Welsh National Council of the Young Men's Christian Association (Welsh YMCA) as being Responsible Bodies entitled to receive grants from the DES 'towards the cost of providing tuition in any course of liberal adult education in a programme approved . . . by the Secretary of State'. At the time, the DES also made grants to a number of voluntary organisations, other than the WEA, and towards national administrative costs of the WEA and its Service Centre for Social Studies.

2
The Russell Committee and its report

*Our vision is of a comprehensive and flexible service of adult education, broad
enough to meet the whole range of educational needs of the adult in our society.
It must therefore be integrated with all other sectors of the educational system
but at the same time firmly rooted in the active life of local communities;
and it must be readily accessible to all who need it, whatever their means or
circumstances. Only in such terms can we conceive of education 'as a process
continuing throughout life'.*

(Introduction, paragraph 3, Russell Report, DES, 1973)

Expectations at the time

In the 1964 general election, a Labour government was elected for the first time
since 1951. The re-election of this government in 1966, with an increased and
comfortable working majority, gave many individuals and organisations,
including HMI, the confidence to expect that a much needed and much
demanded committee of inquiry into adult learning might be appointed.
Throughout the years since 1944, pressure had been building for a fresh look at
adult learning. The previous chapter identified some of the many changes in
education and related public services that had an important bearing on adult
learning opportunities demanded and needed in England and Wales. In the UK
as elsewhere, the 1960s was a period of challenge and change in public policy
and services. Arguments raged around the morality of the Vietnam War, the
rapid and strong emergence of 'women's liberation' and 'black consciousness' as
the driving force behind moves towards greater equality and equity, and the
nature of society itself. The part organised adult learning could and should play
in social and community development and action was a constant topic of debate.

The 1960s was pre-eminently the decade of the birth of a number of significant social and voluntary movements. Adult learning, in many contexts, became
associated with the same issues being tackled by Shelter, the Child Poverty
Action Group (CPAG), Gingerbread (now the National Council for One Parent
Families) and other social action organisations. Jeremy Sandford's seminal television drama about homelessness and poverty, *Cathy Come Home*, was broadcast in 1967. In addition to striking the consciences of the nation, it caused

countless adult educators to think outside their cosy environments and become more creative and responsive. Arguments between advocates of 'participatory' and 'representative' democracy, in all the many settings of work, education and political affairs, created tension and, at times, violent dispute. David Caute (1988) opened his comprehensive documentary book, *Sixty-Eight: The Year of the Barricades* with the sentence: 'The year 1968 was the most turbulent year since the end of World War II.' The end of the dynamic 1960s was undoubtedly a good time for a committee to be appointed.

In the years before the appointment of the Russell Committee, correspondence between HMI often highlighted concerns and frustrations related to the state of adult learning. A letter of November 1962 from one HMI to another, a copy of which is in the hands of the present author, graphically expresses doubts and fears of the time. The letter comments on 'the hostility between the academic manqué and the practical man, of the holders of various vested interests all against a background of insecurity of status and personal predilections and frustrations'. It continues with remarks about the need to change the image of adult education, not helped by so many part-time tutors who 'are themselves imbued with this rather apologetic attitude to adult education as compared with their "main" work in schools'. It is suggested that the negative attitude and lack of vision is 'tied up with a British (including HMI) distrust of idealistic thought shown in eagerness to cover it by some blur-word or cliché like "education for leisure" or "for democracy", so as to be free to concentrate on "realities" like the tea-break or trapezoidal tables'. The letter argues that, despite 'marked resistance', HMI should assert, without apology or diffidence, that adult educators must be 'doers of something to the community, not purposeless reflectors, facilitators, oilers of a machine regardless of its direction'. It is suggested that society is culturally and ideologically divided every bit as much as being socially and economically divided. This may have given rise to an unthinking laziness which 'has raised itself to a self-conscious pride in living with an unwritten "constitution", a feeling that to be liberal one must be aimless and muddled'. There is, it is added, 'a curious suspicion that abstract ideas are somehow "posh"', together with a dislike of accepting any hierarchy of values. The views and attitudes displayed in this letter of 1962 were indicative of one strongly entrenched perspective evident in a wide-ranging debate about values and purposes of learning raging during the decade.

The debate continued throughout the 1960s, between people expressing an unswerving belief in a fixed hierarchy of learning and those convinced that adult learning should be seen as an essential part of a movement towards equity and equality between peoples and between areas of learning. All agreed that the lack of DES strategic thinking and planning left adult learning in a vulnerable state despite the ferment, liveliness and optimism of the times. It was not until the appointment of the Russell Committee in 1969 that a body was in a position to think deeply and widely and to reflect on all aspects of adult learning. Its terms of reference might have been narrow but the collection of evidence and the work of the committee were wide-ranging and, more than 30 years later, the report retains its relevance.

In February 1969, the committee was appointed with the following brief:

> To assess the need for and to review the provision of non-vocational adult education in England and Wales; to consider the appropriateness of existing educational, administrative and financial policies; and to make recommendations with a view to obtaining the most effective and economical deployment of available resources to enable adult education to make its proper contribution to the national system of education conceived of as a process continuing throughout life.

In view of the considerable disappointment that the terms of reference had restricted the Ministry of Reconstruction Adult Education Committee to 'non-vocational adult education' for its 1919 Report, it was not surprising that it was thought by many that the brief given to the Russell Committee was also too narrow and limiting. Given the optimism and boosted confidence evident in public services and society at large in the 1960s, the phrase 'the most effective and economical deployment of available resources to enable adult education to make its proper contribution' was taken by many people to imply that the limited and restricted budgetary allocations would continue, regardless of the strength of the final report. There was a suspicion that the government might already have decided what a 'proper contribution' might be. On the other hand, enthusiasts and activists were encouraged by the assertion that 'the national system of education [should be] conceived of as a process continuing throughout life'.

Throughout the period covered by this book, the attitudes and expectations of adult learning practitioners swung from optimism and enthusiasm to deep pessimism and feelings of helplessness. At times, it was thought that governments and individual ministers were listening and understanding. At other times, it seemed that 'messages' from the field were not even being listened to, let alone understood and considered. In general, adult learning counted for little in the overall scheme of governmental policy and planning. One senior civil servant, personally concerned with different aspects of adult learning during the last 30 years of the twentieth century graphically explained this situation to the present author, by saying that 'no serious civil servant with ambition would wish to be seen with adult education from the time the Russell Committee reported to the Secretary of State at the end of 1972 to the election of the Labour Government in 1997'. There was minimal support for the work of the committee or interest in its brief on the part of most senior staff in the DES at the time. There was an evident dismissal of the importance of the committee and its efforts. In a private conversation with the present author, one retired senior person, who worked in the DES in the early 1970s, reported the view that an influential civil servant spoke, disparagingly, of the committee as comprising two types – 'hard headed businessmen' and 'woolly minded professionals'.

Membership
The committee was chaired by Sir Lionel Russell, the then Chief Education Officer of Birmingham. It initially comprised 14 members. Due to ill health, two of the members withdrew from the work of the committee well before it was completed. The report was submitted to Margaret Thatcher, Secretary of State for Education and Science, in December 1972 and was published as *Adult Education: A Plan for Development* (DES, 1973). It should be noted here that the period of Labour governments which lasted from 1964–79 was interrupted by the Conservative Government of 1970–4.

Membership of the committee included a number of people with little or no experience or knowledge of any aspect of non-vocational adult education. It was noticeable that the committee membership did not include a student, an adviser/inspector from an LEA, or a person from the voluntary sector, other than from the WEA. The bulk of the work, including policy thinking, was undertaken by a minority of the members, supplemented by regular contributions from HMI. Much depended on the determination, commitment and perspectives of the leading adult education practitioners on the committee – Brian Groombridge, H.D. (Billy) Hughes, Henry Arthur Jones and Elizabeth Monkhouse, and on the HMI assessors working with the committee.

A potentially important member of the committee was R.D. Salter Davies, who had recently retired as Chief Inspector of Other Further Education [further education other than college work] in the Inspectorate. He was able to inject an historical perspective into the deliberations of the committee and contribute from more than 30 years as an HMI. Salter Davies was likely to have been a major influence on the DES and the Minister of State leading to the appointment and membership of the committee. The fact that he had retired before the committee began its work, thus gaining for himself a measure of independence, should have enabled him to establish a close and supportive working relationship with the chairman of the committee. His considerable knowledge of the working of the department could have been at the disposal of the members of the committee. There is no evidence, however, of such desirable closeness. His insights, contacts and understanding of systems and possibilities within government and outside, had they been appropriately employed, could undoubtedly have moved the committee's work forward more speedily. That this did not happen was a matter of regret. On his retirement, the post that Salter Davies had held was abolished, in itself an indication of the low priority given to adult learning in the DES and Inspectorate. Following his departure from HMI, it was considered by many of his inspector colleagues that adult learning had no discernable advocacy by HMI in the highest levels of the DES. To a great degree, Salter Davies appeared reluctant to apply his accumulated understanding and wisdom to the benefit of the committee's work unless asked, and he appears to have been rarely asked. This may have had the effect of making aspects of the report less creative and developmental than they could have been.

One member of the committee has been dismissive of the committee, its work and the report, in suggesting to the present author that the report was a deeply conservative document and 'not at all important'. This was not a widely shared judgement, either in 1973, when the report was published, or subsequently. The committee member suggested that it changed little. There were countless missed opportunities, including not capitalising on the enthusiasm raised in the Literacy Campaign, which coincided in time with the life of the committee, and not building sufficiently on the important community-based initiatives around the country (EPAs, Community Development Projects, outreach and community education workers).

A more widely held criticism was that there was an absence of cohesion, shared purpose and understanding in the committee. It was suggested that the poor support from the Department, and weak leadership of the committee by the chairman, inevitably led to the production of a report which some judged to have little fresh thinking and no clear discernible structure. The committee was not well supported by the DES with staff time or with sufficient financial resources to enable it to commission necessary work. One member of the committee has recently told the present author that the Department appeared to be 'oblivious to the impossibility of doing justice to the work of the committee without proper staffing and departmental support'. For only part of the committee's life, a research assistant (the present author) was employed with the primary, but not exclusive, brief to review and report on 'the nature and extent of the provision of adult education for disadvantaged groups'. Nonetheless, even among the most disappointed committee members or committee watchers, positive outcomes from the report and its recommendations were identified.

The Russell Committee was obliged to adjust to the different political climate with the change from Labour to Conservative in 1970, just as ten tears later ACACE needed to adjust the approach to its work to take account of the change from a Labour to Conservative government following the general election in 1979. On both occasions, the difference in attitude, policies and priorities between the two governing political parties was considerable. The Russell Committee and, later, ACACE were obliged to pay regard to the contrasting types of relationship between committees and government ministers and between committees and departmental civil servants, who were required to work

to fundamentally changed briefs, reflecting very different governmental policies
and priorities.

Operational arrangements

The committee sought to carry out its work in seven different ways:

i)   *Committee and sub-committee meetings.* The committee held 51
     meetings during the period between March 1969 and the submission
     of its report to the Secretary of State in December 1972. Sub-
     committees were established to consider different aspects of the
     work. The minutes and notes of the meetings indicate that the
     committee spent much time trying to achieve a measure of under-
     standing and agreement about their brief to consider 'the provision
     of non-vocational adult education'. Even in the final year of the
     committee's life, there was an obvious and damaging division of
     thinking and focus between the core group of experienced and
     knowledgeable adult educators and the non-educationists, including
     the committee members from industry. The meetings did not always
     move the committee forward. Undoubtedly, the lack of focus and
     direction in the meetings was a major contributor to the delay in
     finalising the work and producing the report.

ii) *Submissions of evidence.* Evidence was invited from anyone and
     everyone who wished to submit written material. Evidence was
     received from 236 organisations, establishments and groups. Written
     evidence was also received from 50 individuals. It is of interest to
     note that 17 major national organisations responded to the
     committee but, some years later, did not submit evidence to
     ACACE when it invited responses to *Towards Continuing Education*
     (ACACE, 1979c). Among these were the Arts Council of Great
     Britain, Committee of Vice-Chancellors and Principals, Community
     Relations Commission, Crafts Council, Independent Broadcasting
     Authority, the Residential Colleges Committee and the TUC. On
     the other hand, in 1979, Help the Aged, Institute of Careers Officers,
     Royal Society of Arts and the Sports Council responded to ACACE
     whereas they had not provided evidence to the Russell Committee.
     Oral evidence was received from 57 organisations, groups and
     individuals.

iii) *Formal visits.* Members of the committee, in small groups, undertook
     39 visits. Of these, 12 were to LEAs, 11 to universities and nine to
     districts of the WEA in England and Wales. These 39 visits were
     largely to meet policy-makers, and senior administrative and organ-

ising staff. In addition, they visited teaching and learning establishments in 13 LEA areas. On a visit to Edinburgh, committee members met representatives of Local Authorities, WEA Districts, universities and the Scottish Committee on Adult Education. There was no indication in the Russell Report of any exchange of evidence, information or advice between the two committees. Visits were also made to four continental European countries. Yet the report does not explain why the Federal Republic of Germany, Finland, Sweden and Yugoslavia were chosen and what was learned from the visits.

iv) *Informal visits.* Individual members of the committee made other visits to establishments and reported on them to the committee. These visits were largely undertaken by committee members acting in their professional roles and capacities other than as members of the committee. Some members of the committee sought individual opportunities to maintain regular contact with one or more aspects of adult learning provision. These contacts supplemented the formal contacts established on behalf of the committee. A number of members attended conferences, courses and meetings convened by a variety of organisations and establishments as a way of furthering the work of the committee.

v) *Papers produced by committee members and assessors.* The committee was very reliant on individual members of the committee drafting papers for consideration at committee meetings and leading discussion. The committee's assessors also prepared and submitted papers.

vi) *Research Assistant material.* Material produced by the committee's Research Assistant was used to inform discussions at regular programmed meetings of the committee and to provide draft text for sections of the committee's report. *The Disadvantaged Adult* (Clyne, 1972) was based largely on the work undertaken by the present author for the committee.

vii) *Questionnaire responses.* Data was collected by means of questionnaires distributed to LEAs, university extra-mural departments and WEA Districts. In May 1970, a questionnaire was sent to the Chief Education Officers of all 163 LEAs in England and Wales requesting data about many aspects of learning provision for adults in LEA areas to supplement the incomplete statistics collected by the DES. Data, collected by the Department, gave a partial picture of the provision of non-vocational education and was of limited value. It was indicative of the marginality of adult learning and the lack of agreed descriptions, definitions or understanding of the range of learning covered by the committee's brief, that the letter accompanying the questionnaire sought information relating 'to education not specifically designed to meet vocational requirements provided or grant-aided' by LEAs. In other words, adult education was still defined in negative rather than positive terms.

A second questionnaire concerning student fees was sent out in March 1971 to LEAs and Responsible Bodies. The Russell Committee noted that the Department regularly collected comprehensive statistics regarding the organisation, programming and teaching of non-vocational adult education by Responsible Bodies. However, such data had not been collected from LEAs and no statistics had been collected regarding fees paid by students or by organisations, employers or others on behalf of students pursuing non-vocational adult education.

Production of the report

When the committee was established in February 1969, four assessors to the committee were appointed. Of the four, three were HMI and one was an Assistant Secretary within the DES. One other HMI was appointed to be the Secretary to the committee. The support staff to the committee underwent a number of changes between September 1970 and September 1971. This, inevitably, caused a measure of disruption to the level of staffing support. Christopher Rowland HMI had been initially appointed as secretary to the committee. By virtue of his knowledge, experience and responsibilities, he was in touch with much contemporary adult learning provision. After being promoted to be a staff inspector, he moved, in September 1970, from being the secretary to being one of the assessors. He was succeeded, as secretary, by a departmental civil servant who did not have, nor could have been expected to have, similar knowledge and experience. This change gave rise to an enhanced contribution by the adult education members of the committee and by the HMI assessors. The HMI assessors were able to make an educational contribution to the work of the committee through background briefing and the production of position papers. One of the HMI assessors, Jim Simpson, was closely connected with international adult learning. He contributed information and policy ideas, emerging from UNESCO, OECD and the Council of Europe, to the committee's discussion, although there is no evidence in the report that the committee paid regard to his considerable international knowledge and experience. It is noteworthy that the committee neither formally sought evidence from any of the international organisations nor did the committee's report contain any significant information, conclusions or recommendations derived from international adult learning.

The present author has had the opportunity to draw on information from his own diaries and papers and from other papers relating to the work of the committee. He has spoken to and corresponded with some individual members of the committee and assessors to the committee. He has, additionally, communicated with a number of the people concerned with the operational arrangements for the committee's work and the production of the report. Partly as a consequence of the staffing difficulties mentioned above, and partly in recognition of his particularly comprehensive skills and knowledge, Henry Arthur Jones drafted much of the report. In addition to being a member of the committee, he had recently moved from his position as Principal of the City Literary Institute in London to be Professor of Adult Education in the University of Leicester. He also supervised the work of the committee's research assistant. It is to him that credit must be paid for the fine language of the report and for successfully tackling the difficult task of placing together the many pieces of the jigsaw to form a coherent picture of adult learning, within the limitations of the committee's terms of reference.

The report and its recommendations

Much has been said about the restricted terms of reference of the Russell Committee. However, little regard has been paid to the committee's efforts to ensure that the Russell Report reflected a view that adult learning cannot easily and usefully be divided, in the language of the time, between vocational and non-vocational adult education. Another contemporary phrase was used to assert that the different types of adult learning provision form 'a seamless robe'.

In the general statement (paragraph 2.1), preceding the list of recommendations at the beginning of the report, the committee emphasised three propositions underlying the report:

1. 'In our changing and evolving society the explicit and latent demands for all kinds of adult education have increased and will continue to increase.'
2. The existence of 'an enormous reservoir of human and material resources' which could be released 'for the benefit of individuals and the good of society' through 'a relatively modest investment in adult education.'
3. 'The successful development of adult education depends in very large measure on a consistent lead and direction being given by the Secretary of State.'

With hindsight, the three propositions can be seen to have been pious aspirations rather than achievable ambitions. The first proposition referred to 'demands for all kinds of adult education'. While 'explicit demand' implied 'demand', 'latent demand' signified 'need'. The social processes by which need might be translated into actual demand for learning were not elucidated. Neither the political nor the economic nor the educational policy contexts, nationally, during the 1970s, were sufficiently positive to enable the aspirations expressed in the second and third propositions to be realised. This meant, in turn, that the humanist commitment of the committee expressed in the General Statement was not fulfilled either:

> The value of adult education is not solely to be measured by direct increases in earning power or productive capacity or by any other materialistic yardstick, but by the quality of life it inspires in the individual and generates for the community at large. It is an agent changing and improving our society: but for each individual the means of change may differ and each must develop in his own way, at his own level and through his own talents. No academic subject or social or creative activity is superior to another provided that those engaged in it develop a greater awareness of their own capacities and a more certain knowledge of the totality of their responsibilities as human beings. (Paragraph 6, General Statement)

In so many ways, this paragraph was the summation of the timeless, liberal view of adult learning. The sense of the words would have been readily understood and wholeheartedly supported by Albert Mansbridge at the time of the foundation of the WEA in 1903, or by R.H. Tawney throughout his presidency of the WEA from 1928 to 1956. The paragraph expressed, in appropriate language of the day, the same general sentiments expressed by the Adult Education Committee in its 1919 Report. The sentiments would also have been held to be eminently reasonable by ACACE, appointed in 1977. However, this commitment to an all-inclusive view of adult learning was not shared by the government of the day or by any government thereafter, during the period covered by this book. Despite the limitations of the narrow non-vocational brief, the committee saw fit to confidently assert the value of learning in all its many forms. It is regrettable that the committee's far-sighted and generous view of learning, free from any taint of elitism and recognising the value of learning to the individual as well as to the wider community and economy, was not accepted as the foundation principle on which future decisions, plans, programmes and funding systems were to be based. Divisions have plagued adult learning. Sometimes they have been deliberately determined by legislation or regulation, while sometimes they have been the consequence of actions and decisions neither primarily nor directly concerned with adult learning. Although all-embracing descriptive terms, including recurrent, continuing and lifelong, have been employed in the language, their use has not been able to disguise a hierarchy of types of provision. The purpose designated by government or the provider of study or training has remained of primary importance, with the aims, objectives and purposes of individual learners generally ranked in secondary place.

It was not within the power of the committee to broaden its terms of reference to embrace the full range of adult learning. Nonetheless, the committee, while recognising that it was obliged to give attention to 'the provision of non-vocational adult education', pointed out that the Education Act 1944 made no reference to non-vocational adult education. Indeed, adult education, per se, was not mentioned in the Act. The Act referred to further education, taken to be post-school education embracing work and employment-related vocational education and training, and personal, social, cultural and non-vocational education. The report confirmed the committee's vision 'of a comprehensive and flexible service of adult education, broad enough to meet the whole range of educational needs of the adult in our society' (paragraph 3). The committee acknowledged and endorsed the opinion expressed in much of the submitted evidence that it is the motives of the learner which determine the use to which learning might be put. It is for the learner to decide whether learning is undertaken for vocational reasons, to assist in a job search or the better performance of a job. The learner might consider that what is described as vocational by the education and training provider is worth pursuing for the love of learning. 'We therefore see no virtue in attempting a sharp line of division' (paragraph 4). However, the committee did accept that the wording of its terms of reference, specifying 'non-vocational adult education', obliged it to exclude detailed attention to what it described as 'the major areas of higher, technical and art education'. An indication of the committee's broad vision of adult learning is the fact that much of the evidence submitted to the committee came from organisations primarily concerned with what was designated as vocational education and work-related education and training. These included individual trade unions, TUC, Confederation of British Industry (CBI), Central Training Council and four Industrial Training Boards. The widespread interest in the work of the committee, the desire on the part of many organisations and individuals to take advantage of the opportunity to contribute to the debate about the future of adult learning, and the general determination to look more broadly at adult learning than the terms of reference required, were all factors conditioning the approach of the committee to its work.

The report merits re-reading, not only for its style, language and tone but for the committee's eminently reasonable and positive approach to many of the issues of the day, some of which continue to be matters of concern 30 years later. Elsdon (2001, p. 51) made the point, about both the Russell Report and a Ministry of Education review of LEA evening institutes in 1956, that 'the text did not provide enthusiasts with quotations to beat about the heads of unyielding governments, but was full of much needed practicable suggestions which could be picked up without waiting for changes of heart on high'. His frustration, shared by many others, shone through in his further comment that, 'it is not impossible that the cause of Adult Education might have prospered a little better if more of its vocal proponents had been as concerned with the practicalities of the field and of politics as they were with philosophy'. These quotations from Elsdon allude to a tension that ran through discussions among adult educators during the second half of the twentieth century. Should tactics employed in debates, campaigning activities and writings concentrate on possible short-term gains for adult learning or should they be dedicated to mapping the long-term plan, based on a commitment to adult learning as a movement for change and social improvement? To accept modest improvement to an existing system might be thought to endorse the view that the system could and should be continuing. For those who had been long convinced that they could foresee a better society emerging, to which a fundamentally changed provision of adult learning would contribute, it was difficult to accept that changes on the margins would be worthwhile achieving. They would offer immediate obvious benefit to some adult learners but not to others. They might even reinforce inequalities in society.

The recommendations of the committee were not radical. They did not define a new view of education throughout life. Recommendations were not related to a single coherent philosophy of learning or teaching, nor were they set within an organisational framework encompassing the entire range of publicly funded personal and social services. They were practical recommendations, not worded in a form likely to alienate, disturb or surprise anyone giving them serious attention. In drafting the main sections and recommendations of the report, Henry Arthur Jones was at pains to ensure that idealistic statements in the text of the report about what was desirable, were balanced with carefully considered, reasonable and realistic proposals for modest gains, capable of early achievement. Jones had also supervised the work of the present author in the preparation of *The Disadvantaged Adult* (Clyne, 1972) and written the Foreword to the report.

With the passage of time, given the many legislative, administrative and organisational changes introduced by governments, it is inevitable that some of the recommendations now appear to be concerned with matters of ancient history. However, it is of interest and value in aiding understanding of the past to explore the action or inaction following each of the main recommendations. Discussion about the politics of adult learning during the latter part of the last century, as set out in this book, will be linked to the recommendations of the Russell Report and the issues they raise wherever possible. In the General Statement that preceded the recommendations, the committee highlighted what it identified as its ten most important recommendations, given the state of adult learning in 1972:

   i)   The first recommendation concerned a structure for adult learning
         provision. A Development Council for Adult Education for England

and Wales should be established (paragraph 160.4). Regional Advisory Councils in England and the Welsh Joint Education Committee should create adult education sub-committees where they did not already exist (paragraph 165). Local Development Councils should be formed in each LEA area (paragraphs 173–5). The committee made recommendations as to the purposes, functions, membership and relationship to the Department of the proposed national Development Council (paragraphs 161–4). This recommendation, as far as the national Development Council was concerned, fell on the deaf ears of the Secretary of State and the government more generally. Some four years later, in 1977, the Advisory Council for Adult and Continuing Education was appointed. The word 'Development' had too many frightening financial connotations for both the Conservative Government at the time, and for the successor Labour Government.

ii) The second recommendation urged the continuation of a partnership between statutory and voluntary bodies in the provision of learning opportunities for adults with increasing support for the voluntary sector from both the DES and LEAs (paragraphs 224–5). The committee was impressed by the size of the contribution of voluntary organisations, large and small, to adult learning. It noted that 'few of them may provide classes directly and independently in the way major providers do' (the LEAs, universities and the WEA were identified as major providers). It was not until a few years later, when ACACE undertook a study of the role and contribution of local voluntary organisations in adult learning, that the full extent of the national contribution of voluntary organisations became widely appreciated. In drawing attention to the importance of partnership, the committee understated what had been happening in cities, towns and villages up and down the country for many years. Indeed, the 1919 Report records the valuable contribution of community and social action and development to overall adult learning. Study groups, lecture series, displays, performances, concerts and exhibitions formed the visible public tip of a massive iceberg of community learning which also included study programmes, one-off lectures, study tours, training courses and qualification examinations for members and supporters. The lack of basic reference data, coupled with the inability of the committee to commission much original research due to paucity of support funding, meant that the committee was largely unaware of the range, nature and extent of adult learning outside formal educational establishments, other than that mentioned in evidence, written and oral, submitted to the committee. The committee recognised the existence and importance of this learning activity, but did not have detailed information about the scope and variety of such learning.

At the annual conference of the Standing Conference on University Teaching and Research in the Education of Adults (SCUTREA) in 1971, Edward Hutchinson, Director of NIAE, said:

> '(T)he emphasis on class enrolment as the main criterion of involvement in adult education leaves out of account any kind of learning situation in a general community context, such as the work now being pioneered in association with the Liverpool EPA [Educational Priority Area] project to say nothing of the associative activities of voluntary bodies – TGs [Townswomen's Guilds], WIs [Women's Institutes] etc. etc. Even within class enrolment limits, there is the additional problem on the LEA side of deciding what range of work in 'Major Establishments' (Colleges of Further Education at various levels and Colleges of Art) is 'adult' education because it does not lead to any certificate of competence.'

iii) The third recommendation should, more suitably, have been the first and overarching recommendation. The committee urged the Secretary of State to take appropriate action to stimulate the development of adult learning (paragraphs 155–60). In accordance with the terms of the Education Act 1944, she should give guidance to LEAs with regard to their responsibility to secure provision. The guidance should include a definition of the 'varied and comprehensive service' mentioned in the Act and she should require LEAs to ensure that all sections of their local communities are able to participate. The committee argued that many of the recommendations set out in its report would assist the Secretary of State in taking the necessary action. Sadly, this recommendation was neither implemented by Margaret Thatcher, nor by any of her successors. Despite the many changes in the political and legislative arrangements for adult learning in the years following the Russell Report, the lack of a firm legal basis for adult learning, and a statutory definition of 'adequacy', continued to be a frustration and a running sore in the relationships between governments, providers of programmes of learning and student bodies.

iv) In the fourth recommendation, the committee called for a planned increase in the number of full-time staff employed in adult learning with appropriate career and salary structures (paragraphs 356–78). This recommendation particularly applied to LEAs. It stressed the importance of ensuring that suitable training opportunities would be available for full-time and part-time staff (paragraphs 403–17). The committee recommended grants from the department to meet the costs of subject organising tutors and resident tutors in the universities (paragraph 389) and organising tutors and development officers in the WEA (paragraph 391). Most teaching was undertaken by part-time teachers who often brought to their work expertise and knowledge gained in other paid employment or unpaid pursuit of an area of interest. The committee recognised that there were insufficient full-time organisers, curriculum managers and subject teachers to maintain a strong core of personnel who could be entrusted with the responsibility of improving the quality of teaching, and keeping teaching practice up to date. Training for full-time staff expanded in the years following the publication of the report, led by a number of university departments and LEAs. This was due, in part, to the Russell Committee's observations on the quantity, quality and training of adult learning teachers. Of greater importance was the coincidence in time between the production of the Russell Report and the discussions and action following the James Report (DES, 1972b). The government accepted the recommendations of the James Committee to improve and increase initial training and in-service training of school-teachers. At the same time, the government accepted that a larger number of full-time staff in further education should receive both initial training and opportunities for in-service training. In so far as many further education lecturers were teachers of adults, the increase in staff training programmes was welcomed. On the other hand, there was general disappointment that there was no reference to adult education staff or to part-time further education teachers, many of whom taught adults. The James Report was followed by two reports produced by the Haycocks Sub-Committee of the Advisory Committee for the Supply and Training of Teachers (ACSTT). The first Haycocks Report (ACSTT, 1975) related to the training of full-time teachers in further education. The training needs of the multitude of part-time teachers of adults remained largely unmet, despite the recommendations of the Second Haycocks Report on the training of part-time teachers in Further and Adult Education (ACSTT, 1978a). A separate report targeted the training needs of full-time staff in non-vocational adult learning (ACSTT, 1978b). It was not until a comparatively small number of LEAs agreed to offer payment to part-time staff for attending training sessions that the numbers in training grew significantly in those areas (see also Chapter 7). Elsewhere, growth in numbers of trained part-time staff was modest.

v)   Much of the evidence submitted to the committee identified the need for a recognisable route for adults seeking access to qualifications (paragraphs 286–99). In their fifth recommendation, the committee stated that 'adult education programmes should provide opportunities for adults to complete secondary, further and higher education and offer access to qualifications at all levels'. This recommendation led to a rapid growth in the variety and number of Fresh Horizons, Second Chance, Access and New Opportunities courses in the 1970s. HMI strongly supported and encouraged this growth. Examining Boards were urged to continue and increase their work on designing more flexible and suitable examination courses for mature adults (paragraph 289). The work of the NEC and the OU was important in this regard.

In 1978, recognising the importance and justice of extending access opportunities to higher education and the professions to grossly under-represented sections of the population, the DES made funds available to enable seven LEAs, including ILEA, to programme tailor-made access courses for members of ethnic minority groups. The number of purpose-designed access courses rose dramatically. Enrolment on the courses subsequently broadened from minority ethnic groups to any sections of the population that, hitherto, had not had such opportunities. However, less than one month after the Russell Report was submitted to the Secretary of State, John Henry, County Education Officer for Surrey and a leading member of the Society of Education Officers, in addition to having been a member of the Russell Committee, appeared to undermine one important aspect of the report's conclusions and recommendations when he was quoted in the journal *Education* (5 January 1973): 'I would have thought that we were getting close to the time when one certainly started to slow down the rate of development in the field of higher education, both in terms of economic use of the output of qualified manpower and even in terms of education for education's sake.' A major thrust of the Russell Report's conclusions and recommendations was that, as adult learning provision changed and increased, the needs of people with the greatest unmet learning needs should be given some priority. To call for a slow down in 'the rate of development in the field of higher education' was to argue, in effect, that the exclusion of many mature adults from higher education should continue.

vi)   In response to the findings of the committee's Research Assistant concerning learning opportunities for disadvantaged adults, the sixth recommendation urged that more attention and targeted provision should be available for 'disadvantaged adults' (paragraphs 277–85). This term, widely used in the report and in the debates thereafter, was considered to be, simultaneously, helpful and supportive by some in terms of practical outcomes for learners, and unhelpful and condemnatory by others who would have preferred a discourse of rights and entitlement. The committee was clear in its comments that the then situation was unacceptable and should not be permitted to continue. Many of the people with the greatest and most urgent learning needs found themselves ignored or found the existing programmes inaccessible or unsuitable.

vii) The committee's seventh recommendation called for an increase in the amount of accommodation available for adult learning (paragraphs 315–31). Some needed to be purpose built or specially adapted (paragraph 332). However, in addition, the committee considered that more premises, suitable for adult learning, were required in conjunction with schools (paragraph 334) and further education colleges (paragraph 332). The committee importantly urged the provision of learning opportunities for adults in premises 'most suitable to the public' – youth and community centres, libraries, village halls, etc. (paragraphs 327, 338–9). In common with the committee producing the 1919 Report, the Russell Committee recognised that much adult learning was inspired and encouraged by participation in day to day social life, often in very informal settings. This was a firm acknowledgement by the committee that much adult learning should be community-based, as was the case in inner London and some few other places following the Physical Training and Recreation Act 1937 and government acceptance of the recommendations of the Albemarle Committee.

In terms of both the physical environment and teaching and learning practices, it was recognised as being invaluable to 'start where the students are'. Many potential adult students did not find existing university departments, further education colleges or schools conveniently placed, welcoming or suitably furnished and equipped. With regard to accommodation for industrial training and other employment-related learning, the Association of Teachers in Technical Institutions (ATTI) later commented that the committee had greatly understated the need for purpose-designed and -built working premises to facilitate an expansion in provision for adults. Despite the firm recommendation regarding accommodation, at the DES and LEA levels, adult learning continued to be treated as one element of further education, and little purpose-built accommodation was provided for general adult education. The annual Further

Education Building Programme, funded by the DES and formulated by LEAs, was overwhelmingly concentrated on vocational and academic teaching and learning for young people of 16 to 19 years of age. With the changing age profile of the student population outside schools, showing a rapidly increasing proportion of students who were mature adults, this was most unhelpful.

viii) The eighth recommendation related to universities (paragraphs 211–23). The committee was of the view that funding to universities should continue to come from both the University Grants Committee (UGC) and directly from the DES (paragraph 213). The committee considered that funding from the UGC should be in respect of work in specified areas – liberal studies, balancing studies to complement earlier specialisation in education, role education, industrial education (liberal and academic courses related to human relationships in work), project work (group research or enquiry techniques), training of adult educators and pump-priming for development work (paragraph 213). The committee made the point that universities would be expected to agree their particular contribution to one or more of the specified areas of work with partner organisations locally, ideally through the deliberations of the Local Development Council. As Development Councils and Advisory Councils were not established in every part of the country, partnership and cooperation in programme planning often depended on local goodwill rather than structures.

ix) Matters of concern to the WEA (paragraphs 226–41) were dealt with in the ninth recommendation. In its evidence to the committee, the WEA had indicated that recent developments in the work of the association could be expanded with backing from the DES. The committee recommended that the WEA should be funded by LEAs and the DES and that additional resources be allocated by the DES for 'certain priority fields'. The report endorsed and recommended the four priorities identified by the WEA in its evidence to the committee. Experimental and informal education work in conjunction with other organisations 'for the socially and culturally deprived living in urban areas' was the first priority, acknowledged in the report to the effect that 'New avenues for activity have begun to appear in courses run in cooperation with OXFAM, SHELTER and similar socially oriented organisations' (paragraph 232.3). Working in factories and other workplaces in consultation with trade unions was the second priority. Third, political and social education for people engaged in local government (councillors and staff) and social and political organisations was identified. Liberal and academic study below university level, to be programmed in conjunction with similar activity often arranged by LEAs, became the fourth priority.

x)   The committee, in its tenth main recommendation, called for an expansion of residential adult education. It called for more opportunities for short (paragraph 203) and longer-term (paragraphs 247–55) residential study and an improvement in the facilities used. With respect to the short-term residential colleges, the committee urged LEAs to 'continue to develop or support colleges so as to serve to the full the general needs of their areas and regions, as well as to serve a national catchment for some special courses' (paragraph 203). The committee argued for more short-term colleges, especially in the north of England. Unfortunately, largely due to the financial problems facing central and local government as a consequence of the economic crisis following the Middle East oil crisis of 1973, some short-term colleges were closed during the 1970s. Others had their course programmes and staffing reduced by the LEAs concerned. The committee also identified a need for an additional long-term residential college in the north of England (paragraph 255). Northern College for Residential Adult Education was established in 1978 with support from the LEAs of the region and trade unions. A leading advocate of the value of long-term residential adult education was Billy Hughes. As a member of the Russell Committee and Principal of Ruskin College, he warned the Residential Colleges Committee in March 1971 that the value for money assessments introduced by the government could lead to possible worsening of the staff–student ratios and a change in the relationship between the colleges and universities as a consequence of the projected increase in the numbers of young people qualifying for and being admitted to places at universities. The long-term colleges were relieved to find that the report had recommended continuation of the direct grant from the DES. Assistance by grant from the DES towards the improvement and extension of college accommodation in the late 1960s had proved crucial. Colleges were pleased to note that the report recommend continuation of this assistance.

It will have been noted that, in a number of cases, appropriate action did not follow the ten 'most important recommendations' as set out in the General Statement preceding the specific detailed recommendations at the beginning of the report. Nonetheless, as will be described in Chapter 5, sufficient positive developments and changes took place in the years immediately following the publication of the report to justify the conclusion that the Russell Report marked a fundamental and long-lasting breakthrough for adult learning. The years that followed were years of uncertainty for many, but perhaps for the first time since 1919, adult learning was acknowledged as a topic of importance meriting consideration at the highest levels of government. Pressure from providers and learners was exerted on decision-makers at local and national levels to a degree not seen before. There was a noticeable improvement in the quality of teaching and learning while creative and imaginative examples of good practice became more widely known.

3

The Russell Report and the wider world of adult learning

In the long term, however, there will be no solution to the problem of a better life except in a society imbued through and through with the principle of lifelong education and in an education closely bound up with the advances and achievements of society.

(In Search of Lifelong Education, UNESCO, 1972)

(T)he access of adults to education, in the context of lifelong education, is a fundamental aspect of the right to education and facilitates the exercise of the right to participate in political, cultural, artistic and scientific life.

(From the recommendation on the development of adult education adopted by the nineteenth session of the General Conference of UNESCO in 1976)

Towards the end of the 1960s, demands for greater national and international recognition of the importance of adult learning were increasing in both number and strength. The OECD and UNESCO sought to pull together ideas and information, then to create worldwide movements for change and progress in the wake of the positive reception given to their reports. In Ireland and Scotland, national committees of enquiry were appointed to give detailed attention to the state of learning and to make recommendations. This activity took place as the Russell Committee was deliberating. In this chapter, brief consideration is given to a number of reports and events that dealt with topics also featured in the Russell Report. The Russell Committee made some reference to adult education outside England and Wales. Adult learning, in its various forms, was a matter of concern and importance in many countries and with many governments. Whether or not the Russell Committee chose to take note of what was being discussed and decided elsewhere, the fact that the wider debates were taking place influenced the attitudes and priorities of providers and funders of adult learning in the UK, during the period when the Russell Committee was deliberating and thereafter.

Adult Education in Ireland (The Murphy Report)

Adult Education in Ireland (committee appointed by the Prime Minister, 1973) was published in the same year as the Russell Report on adult education in England and Wales. The Irish Committee, chaired by Con Murphy, was appointed in May 1969 by Brian Lenihan, Minister of Education. It was given wide terms of reference: 'To report on the needs of the Community in the matter of Adult Education, and to indicate the type of organisation to be set up in order to serve those needs.' Adult education was defined by the committee as being concerned with facilities for people no longer in the full-time school system to enable them to 'learn whatever they need to learn at any period of their lives'. No distinction was made between formal and informal education or between vocational and non-vocational education. The difference between the terms of reference of the Murphy and Russell Committees could not have been starker. Murphy was to consider the full range of adult learning, whereas Russell was asked to pay regard to 'the provision of non-vocational adult education'.

An interesting distinction was drawn between education and learning by the Murphy Committee. To a greater degree than was the case with the Russell Committee, the Murphy Committee paid attention to the language, organisation and curriculum of learning. Paragraph 1.2.2 of the Murphy Report asserted that 'education does include learning, but learning is also part and parcel of every human experience whether this experience be conscious or not'. The same paragraph continued by stating that, for an activity to be correctly described as adult education, it must have five features:

1. It must be 'purposefully educative' in so far as the motivation of the learner must include the wish to alter knowledge, skills or attitudes.
2. The activity must be 'systematic' with the likelihood of 'achieving progress towards the learning objectives'.
3. The learner's activity should be 'sustained for more than a single session'.
4. The activity should be guided by a person other than the learner 'in contrast to self-directed learning', and
5. The activity should be 'continuously evaluated or assessed and reinforced'.

Later in the report, the Murphy Committee moved away from its initial narrow definition of education, the fourth feature of which might have excluded correspondence and distance learning, education through the media and the OU.

The Murphy Report referred to adult education as a flexible movement capable of enabling all adults to participate in learning for its own sake, for personal and occupational benefit and for the benefit of the community and society at large. Community and social development was a central feature of the

Murphy Report which envisaged a strong, dynamic and progressive adult education movement as being a crucial instrument for this purpose. Training and the support of community activists and leaders were seen to be principal aims of a revived adult education programme.

The Murphy and Russell Reports were published in the year Ireland and the UK joined the then European Economic Community (now the EU). The significance of this wider context in which Ireland and Irish adult education would now be placed was not lost on the authors of the Murphy Report. In Ireland, it was considered to be of great importance by the Murphy Committee that adult education should 'reflect Irish values, beliefs, culture, as at present and in relation to future social change', seek to understand European culture and values while, at the same time, protect 'our Christian culture and our principles' in a Europe seen as being primarily concerned with economic and humanistic objectives. By entering the fields of educational and political philosophies and principles, the Murphy Committee showed itself to be more focused than the Russell Committee on the wider influence and importance of adult learning. In this regard, the caution of the Russell Committee reflected a realistic assessment of the uncertain political climate at the time. The Russell Committee was concerned to ensure that consideration of its report should pay regard to the range, nature and volume of learning opportunities, and the necessary funding arrangements. To venture into a consideration of broader issues was to risk being branded as too political. The Murphy Report was a strongly focused blueprint for adult learning in Ireland. Taking as its starting point a view of Ireland as a country within an expanding European organisation and expressing a world view, it argued that adult learning providers 'have an obligation to promote an awareness in adults of' a number of issues including 'the nature and extent of Ireland's involvement in international agencies; their responsibilities and duties to promote world justice and peace' and 'the need for commitment to and concern for the needs of the Third World' (paragraph 3.2.25).

Regarding adult education as a movement for change and improvement, the Murphy Report, in common with the Russell Report, stressed the importance of partnership and cooperation among voluntary and statutory agencies. Voluntary and community organisations, employers' and employees' associations, library and museum services and sports and arts organisations were identified as having particular contributions to make to an overall adult education movement. It is ironical that *Museums in Education* (DES, 1971) is quoted in the Murphy Report but not in the Russell Report: 'To conserve is the museum's first priority: to educate and entertain is a close second.' The Russell Committee did not draw on the work of a number of government-promoted studies being conducted in related fields of social, leisure and educational services in the UK at the same time. This was consistent with the obvious, and understandable, intention of the Russell Committee to produce a report capable of achieving widespread support and early implementation without the risk of complicated delaying debates and possible argument between interested parties. Russell refers to the desirability of establishing partnership arrangements between adult learning agencies and the library service in the light of the terms of the Public Libraries and Museums Act 1964. However, the report did not describe the benefits to be gained from the creation of formal joint 'sub-committees' (paragraph 353). Although there was not the wholehearted, nationwide creation of Local Development Councils for Adult Education, that the Russell Committee had hoped for, they were established in some LEA areas, variously called 'Development Councils' or 'Advisory Councils'. Often, the membership included representation from local public services, other than education, including social services, libraries and museums, planning and health. With particular reference to the learning needs of disadvantaged individuals, groups and communities, the present author, in *The Disadvantaged Adult* (Clyne, 1972), emphasised the importance of joint planning and provision across a number of public services and voluntary organisations, many of which would not be primarily and specifically committed to education, however defined.

Despite the already proved success in the UK of the NEC, with its strong correspondence element, the Murphy Report quoted the view of Professor E.G. Wedell (1970) in a Council of Europe publication, that 'education by correspondence is a sector of the educational provision which evokes among education experts very varying responses'. Neither Wedell nor the Murphy Committee discussed the alleged positives and negatives of the 'varying responses'. The Russell Committee offered no comment in its report on the observation made by Wedell in the Council of Europe document. The Council of Europe strongly believed that adult learning, by this means, was of great value to people in particular personal, domestic or employment situations and should be embraced wholeheartedly. The NEC and the OU, in addition to the correspondence courses promoted by trade unions, churches, professional organisations and private companies, had all proved the existence of great demand and unmet need, and the effectiveness of distance education both from the learner's point of view, and also as an efficient use of scarce resources for the provider. Such success might be contrasted with the grudging comment in the Russell Report: 'Correspondence education has also so far made only a restricted contribution to adult education' (paragraph 132).

Murphy's only reference to the Russell Report is found in the section on a desirable local statutory structure for Ireland. Having considered the Russell Committee's view regarding the appropriateness of the LEA structure as the basis for delivering the bulk of publicly financed adult learning, the Murphy report outlined its proposed structure for education, as a whole, and suggested the LEA model as suitable for application in Ireland. Although the ground covered by the Murphy and Russell Committees had many similarities, there is no evidence of the two committees sharing information at any stage. The Murphy Committee undertook visits to England, Wales, Scotland, the Netherlands and Denmark, but these trips were more to identify national good practice than to begin to develop a European model of adult education that might match the political, social and economic aims of the EU.

As with the later Alexander Report (1975) in Scotland, the Murphy Report urged the need to merge adult education, youth work and community development in one integrated service. The justification for this recommendation was that fragmentation of interrelated services and resources was thought likely to be wasteful. The Russell Report did not consider the advantages and disadvantages of deliberately creating an integrated LEA community education service. In the years following the publication of the Russell Report, a number of LEAs in England and Wales did achieve a measure of integration by merging adult education and youth work. Indeed, as Russell recognised (paragraph 89.3), some LEAs had functioned in this way prior to 1973. Other LEAs merged the administration and organisation of the two services, although they were delivered as separate programmes in the community. Having determined that an integrated service would prove to be the most effective organisational arrangement, the general conclusions and recommendations of the Murphy Report concentrated on adult learning rather than the broader vision of a youth, community and adult service.

In addition to making a general plea for greater acceptance by the government of the importance of adult education and of the need to allocate sufficient funds, the Murphy Report urged an increased involvement of the universities in adult learning and the establishment of residential centres. It also called for the development of radio- and television-related education, use of new technologies, information and counselling services for adults, correspondence courses and the possibility of a focused OU provision for Ireland. Increased support for and recognition of the importance of AONTAS (the national non-governmental organisation (NGO) for adult education) was called for, as was the establishment of links between Ireland and other countries through international multinational agencies, and cooperation between AONTAS and national NGOs in other countries. This paralleled the recommendation of the Russell Committee that NIAE in England and Wales should receive more financial support and should be encouraged to play a greater leadership role in national adult learning developments.

Lifelong Learning in Ireland (The Kenny Report)

In 1981, the Irish Minister of Education established 'an advisory body to prepare a national development plan for adult and continuing education'. In his Chairman's Foreword, Ivor Kenny placed the Kenny Report (Commission on

Adult Education, 1983) within a wider economic and political context conditioned by a rapidly changing world:

> We can adapt to this changing world by learning. When change is the most significant feature of the age, the first demand of those who live through it is for adaptation, for understanding, for grasping the significance of what is happening to them and around them. If our rate of learning exceeds our rate of change, we adapt. If it does not, we fail.

This perspective was of particular concern as the Irish nation and its economy worked to adjust to the challenges of the EU. The report commended the recommendation of the Committee of Ministers, made to the member states of the Council of Europe, on adult education policy (November 1981) that the mission and purpose of adult education should be to promote critical attitudes among people as consumers, users of the mass media, citizens and members of their communities.

The commission gave attention to policies and practices in other countries and in international organisations. In 1978, the Irish government accepted the International Labour Organisation's Convention 140 on paid educational leave, but the Convention had not been ratified and no policy had been implemented at the time the commission completed its report. The far-reaching Convention called for: the promotion of educational leave from work with pay for training; general, social and civic education; and trade union education. Whereas the Kenny Report specifically called for the Convention to be ratified and implemented, the Russell Report, ten years earlier, had not referred to the Convention in its recommendation on the matter but suggested that

> ... the CBI [Confederation of British Industry] and the TUC [Trades Union Congress], in consultation with appropriate government departments, should be invited to take action to ensure that we do not lag behind other European countries in affording adequate opportunities for educational leave. (Paragraph 48)

The Kenny Commission embraced the Convention in full and recommended accordingly. On the other hand, the Russell Committee acknowledged that the ILO had been studying educational leave since 1965 and quoted the conclusions of the UNESCO General Conference of 1965 inviting member states 'to grant workers leave, paid if possible, necessary for training in the framework of permanent education' (paragraph 271).

In 1980, ACACE conducted a survey of participation in adult learning in England and Wales. As the Russell Committee had noted, there was a dearth of comprehensive statistical data. ACACE sought to establish baseline data. The Kenny Commission adapted the ACACE survey questionnaire to suit Irish circumstances and compared the Irish findings with those published by ACACE:

> The ACACE Survey showed that in England and Wales 20 per cent of the adult population over 17 years of age had taken part in adult education during the previous three years, and that a further 27 per cent had undertaken some form of study at some stage prior to the last three years since leaving school or college. Thus in England and Wales, the non-participant part of the adult population appears to be 52 per cent as against 73 per cent in Ireland.

In common with findings in other countries, the commission concluded that, among non-participants, there was a disproportionately high number of older people, working-class people and residents in rural areas. These conclusions had especial resonance in Ireland, a country that had lost many younger people to emigration, and which had a higher percentage of people living in rural areas than was the case in England.

Adult Education: The Challenge of Change in Scotland (The Alexander Report)

The Scottish Committee on Adult Education, chaired by Sir Kenneth Alexander, was appointed by the Secretary of State for Scotland in May 1970. Its report (Scottish Education Department, 1975) was published in March 1975. The work of the Alexander Committee took four years, overlapping with the work timetables of the Russell and Murphy Committees. The terms of reference of the committee were even narrower than those set for the Russell Committee and far more constrained than the terms of reference of the Murphy Committee:

> To consider the aims appropriate to voluntary leisure courses for adults which are educational but not specifically vocational; to examine the extent to which these are being achieved at present; and with due regard to the need to use available resources most effectively, to make recommendations.

During a visit made by members of the Russell Committee to Edinburgh, a joint meeting was held with members of the Alexander Committee. Members of the Russell Committee also met representatives of Scottish education authorities, WEA districts and universities during the same visit. There is no evidence that the two committees of enquiry exchanged evidence other than through these meetings.

As was the case elsewhere in the UK, educational legislation for Scotland made no reference to 'adult education', nor had such a term ever been statutorily defined. Although the Alexander Report mentioned the perceived importance of regarding education as being lifelong, there was little consideration of the relationship between adult learning and other phases of education. The Alexander Committee made few references to primary, secondary or further education. It considered adult education, or 'voluntary leisure time courses', to be 'courses of instruction which have no specific vocational purpose and which are voluntarily attended by a student in the time when he (sic) is not engaged in his normal daily occupation'. For the purposes of this type of education, the committee defined an adult as being any person who has reached the statutory school leaving age (16 years). An examination of the available data related to adult learning in the year 1972–3 showed that 88 per cent of enrolled students in Scotland joined education authority provision. Extra-mural departments enrolled 9.5 per cent and the WEA enrolled 2 per cent. The remaining 0.5 per cent was enrolled by central institutions. Overall, some 4 per cent of the post-school population participated in 1972–3.

The organisation and structure of provision in England and Wales differed from the arrangements in Scotland. Statistics contained in appendices to the Russell Report related to the year 1968–9 and included students of 18 years of age and above, 'enrolled on courses of non-vocational adult education' provided by LEAs and Responsible Bodies only. The Russell Report's statistical tables indicated that, in 1968–9, 5.5 per cent of the total population above the age of eighteen was enrolled. LEAs enrolled 87.5 per cent of the total number of students. Responsible Bodies enrolled the remaining 12.5 per cent. The England and Wales national statistics were somewhat distorted by the overwhelming strength of ILEA provision in inner London. It was not surprising that the Russell Report noted that 'the proportions of students provided for by the Responsible Bodies is the lowest in the South East region [which included London] (7 per cent) but the highest in Wales (24 per cent)'. ILEA enrolled in excess of 20 per cent of the gross LEA total for England and Wales in each year from 1968–9 to 1989–90, when ILEA was disbanded. There was a dramatic reduction in the enrolled numbers across the 12 inner London boroughs and the City of London after 1990, which in turn lowered the overall average participation rate for England (Cushman, 1996).

The Alexander Report concluded that an increased volume and expanded range of learning programmes could be made available by maximising the potential economies of scale to be derived from merging the education authorities' youth and community and adult education services. It urged the provision of a more relevant and accessible programme to meet the needs of under-served and disadvantaged sections of the population. Recommendations included giving a high priority to areas of multiple deprivation and maximising the use of colleges of further education for adult learning. More staff and improved training for all staff were recommended. The creation of an effective information, advice and counselling service for adults was recommended, as was the establishment of a Scottish Council for Community Education.

The Alexander Report was published in 1975. In the same year the Local Government (Scotland) Act 1973 was implemented. Traditional local authorities were reorganised into a small number of regional authorities. Within the overall context of local government reorganisation, and in view of the difficulties facing the national economy, it was not surprising that little real progress was achieved towards implementation of many of the recommendations. Where integrated community education services were established by education authorities in Scotland, it was soon evident that adult learning was generally taking a back seat as youth and community work was pushing ahead. Among the various alternative structures to the existing arrangements in England and Wales considered by the Russell Committee was 'sole provision by the local education authority, somewhat after the practice in Scotland' (paragraph 149). Russell rejected the Scottish model, believing that the existing pattern with a multiplicity of providing bodies and funding sources was appropriate and should be retained. University extra-mural departments made little headway towards adopting a community development approach to taking university level learning into areas previously not reached. Education authorities, through new joint committees, failed to identify sufficient funds for the WEA and other voluntary agencies to expand community-based work. It became clear that adult learning in Scotland, as in England and Wales, was not able to gain the strong political backing at central or local levels called for in the reports.

United Nations Educational, Scientific and Cultural Organisation (UNESCO)

The first UNESCO International Conference on Adult Education was held in Elsinore in Denmark in 1949. It was attended mainly by delegates from Western Europe, thus not meriting being described as a 'world' conference. In 1960, Montreal was the location for the second UNESCO International Conference which was attended by representatives from 51 countries, as compared with only 29 countries at Elsinore. The Montreal conference considered the theme 'Adult Education in a Changing World'. The final report of the Montreal conference included a clear assertion that: 'Nothing less will suffice than that people everywhere should come to accept adult education as a normal, and that governments should treat it as a necessary, part of the educational provision of every country.' John Lowe (1975) argued that this was probably the first international statement that lifelong learning should be a principal element of educational policy for all governments. The editors of *International Perspectives on Lifelong Learning*

(Istance *et al.*, 2002) commented that 'it is no coincidence that the discourse on lifelong learning has flourished most at the international level, detached from the structures of power and decision making that dominate national systems'. While this must be accepted as a useful reminder of the danger of pursuing academic study out of touch with the 'real world', it should not be thought to be beyond policy-makers' and practitioners' abilities to rethink fundamentals.

Between the International Conference in 1949 and the Nairobi General Conference of 1976, UNESCO consistently gave absolute priority to 'the fight against illiteracy' while, at the same time, broadening its concerns to embrace wider aspects of basic learning needs (language and numeracy), learning to reduce exclusion and learning for occupational benefits. The International Conference in Montreal in 1960 confirmed the continuing priority to work towards the eradication of illiteracy while, simultaneously, paying regard to the identifiable and particular learning needs of women and families. The learning needs of women had been first identified as a priority area of concern for UNESCO in 1946. The assumption in most western European countries was that these matters were of more concern in developing countries than in the industrialised countries, which did not need to change their approach to adult learning policies, planning, priorities and programming. It was a number of years after the Montreal Conference before governments and providers in the UK gave priority attention to the unmet literacy needs of many adults and the expansion of special programmes for women and families.

By the late 1960s, most industrial countries had made a speedy recovery from losses and destruction caused by World War II and its aftermath. Social change had accompanied economic growth with consequential rise in the general standards of living. Newly independent countries were gradually establishing the economic bases on which community well-being could be built. The potential contribution of education to social and community development was generally accepted. However, the organisation of education systems and their curriculum contents remained substantially the same as they had been before World War II. The aims and purposes of education had not been sufficiently redefined to pay regard to the challenges of the new and different world.

Following the confidence and determination evident in Montreal in 1960, adult learning became more visible in policies and programmes in many countries. Nonetheless, as planning was taking place for UNESCO's Third International Conference on Adult Education, to be held in Tokyo in 1972, very few governments were placing adult learning securely within the framework of national education policies. Few countries were making adequate financial provision for adult learning and few countries were making focused efforts to reach those adults with the greatest need of learning opportunities. Finally, in respect of industrialised countries, few governments were even beginning to come to terms with the implications for adult learning, among a range of public services, of an ageing population. By this time, it was becoming essential that policy-makers and providers of adult learning programmes should strongly attack clichés and preconceptions like 'you can't teach an old dog new tricks'. Another challenge was the arrival of large numbers of immigrants from developing countries, often with languages, cultures and religions different to those of their new home. Prejudices and unjustified assumptions about age, ethnicity and the ability to learn had to be set aside.

The size and arrangements of the Tokyo conference and the publication of the Faure Report, *Learning to Be* (UNESCO, 1972), considered in detail in the next section, demonstrated clearly how much the international world of adult education had moved on in the 12 years since the Montreal conference. While continuing to give attention to illiteracy issues, the Tokyo conference also considered country reports submitted by some 97 delegations. These identified other urgent themes for discussion at the conference itself and for detailed follow up, including the learning needs of women in different economic, social and domestic circumstances; immigrant, migrant and refugee workers; family planning; and the special learning needs of young people after compulsory schooling. Education and training was becoming more and more costly. Despite having the best of intentions, some governments found themselves unable to fund an appropriate public education service for all young people let alone for mature adults. Colonial governments in Africa, Asia and elsewhere had tended to concentrate on the education of national elites rather than on the education of all young people. At the same time, much of the curriculum in schools and colleges was unsuitable for the changing circumstances of a post-colonial world. Governments, determined to reform the educational systems for children, often expressed regret that little could be done, within available budgets, to improve and increase opportunities for adults. The Tokyo conference concluded that, in making their best efforts to improve and increase adult learning opportunities, governments should not simply seek to add adult learning activities and programmes to the school system.

The dominant theme of the Tokyo conference was the need for learning opportunities for disadvantaged adults, described in the final report of the conference as 'the forgotten people'. In his commentary on the Conference, John Lowe (1975) made three general points that could have applied equally to the Russell Report and its recommendations. First, all forms of communications and educational technology should be employed. Second, there should be a move away from subject-centred learning to problem-solving learning and, third, non-formal learning should be given greater prominence. The conference confronted the dilemma facing all people committed to adult learning as a movement for change and social improvement offering a greater measure of equity to excluded and isolated people and poor sections of populations. Everyone accepted the fine words and the ringing rhetoric while acknowledging that, as long as learning opportunities for adults are offered in schools and colleges and modelled on school and college curricula, the extent to which local people will respond will depend on their experience of initial education. The more you have, the more you want and the more prepared you are to respond to adult learning programmes. This issue of exclusion and inclusion reinforced the need to give greater prominence to non-formal and informal learning and increased the general recognition and respect for learning in the community, outside the framework and structures of educational establishments. At the same time it also raised the consequent difficulty of what sort of action by national governments could encourage and support such informal learning. A very important outcome of the Tokyo conference was the creation of the International Council for Adult Education (ICAE) in 1973, supported by the patronage of UNESCO and followed speedily by the creation of regional bodies to cover the world. As an NGO, the ICAE was thereafter able to both support and develop systems, services and organisations on a national and regional basis. At the same time, and despite its weak financial basis, it acted as an advocate for adult learning worldwide.

Throughout the 1960s and most of the 1970s, the ways in which education contributed towards economic development in many countries became obvious and were widely acknowledged. Education and training for adults was increasingly designed and funded to prepare individuals for work in new industries, to introduce new skills to adult workers, obliged to leave declining basic industries, or to enable existing workers to acquire new skills to be able to continue their employment. Then, as now, there was a lively debate between those people whose faith in a better future rested on giving priority allocation of resources to young children and, on the other hand, people who were convinced that the better future depended on our priority attention to the learning needs of adults. Julius Nyerere, first President of Tanzania and a leading adult educator, is quoted in *Campaigning for Literacy* (UNESCO, 1984) as saying: 'First we must educate adults. Our children will not have an impact on our economic development for five, ten or even twenty years. The attitudes of adults ... on the other hand, have an impact now.' Twelve years previously, introducing the report *Learning to Be*, Edgar Faure (UNESCO, 1972) noted that: 'the rising generations cannot be properly trained in an illiterate environment'. This plea for a policy leading to structural and organisational change was to be made by others throughout the 1970s and beyond. It influenced, for example, the Literacy Crusades in Nicaragua in the early 1980s. It was realised that the learning needs of societies generally and individuals within societies could never be met through a front-loaded education system. Simply doing more of the same, or adding to the resources available in the children's school systems, would not have the desired effect of benefiting those adults who had not completed a satisfactory initial education.

One of the weaknesses of the Russell Report was that the committee appeared to have learned little from the work of multinational organisations and the ideas and practices of other countries. It was, therefore, somewhat ironical that paragraph 428.5 of the Russell Report should state: 'There is a need for an abstracting service covering the literature of adult education on a world basis, for practitioners in this country find difficulty in keeping abreast of the thinking and developments elsewhere.' The point was directed at the National Institute ('of Adult Education' to 1983 and 'of Adult Continuing Education' since 1983) and recognised to be an important one. NIAE increased and strengthened its contacts with other national and international NGOs in the years following the publication of the report in 1973. Many of the collaborative contacts were channelled through the newly formed ICAE and the European Bureau of Adult Education (now the European Association for the Education of Adults).

Learning To Be (The Faure Report)

In 1970, UNESCO established the International Commission on the Development of Education; chaired by Edgar Faure (former Prime Minister of France and Minister of Education in France in 1970). This important commission reported (UNESCO, 1972) just a few months before the report of the Russell Committee was presented to the Secretary of State. The Russell Committee appears not to have either learned from the work of the commission or submitted evidence to the commission. This was regrettable. They could have learned much from each other. Both bodies spent time considering a range of topics in common, including paid educational leave, barriers to access to learning, the needs of unemployed people, education counselling and advice services, the particular learning needs of women, and learning opportunities for disadvantaged men and women.

The UNESCO Commission paid considerable attention to the relationship between education and society, more generally. It sought an answer to a fundamental question: should education systems be expected to reflect the general patterns and structures of society at the time or should education act as an agent of social change? It also considered the possibility that it could do both at one and the same time. The commission was convinced that nations should support and encourage the interrelated concepts of 'lifelong education' and the 'learning society' in which all experiences should be used and recognised as opportunities to acquire knowledge and skills. The commission understood 'the learning society' to be the full integration of the organisation and processes of structured education into the social environment. Learning towns and cities initiatives drew from many of the ideas in the Faure Report as well as those in Donald Hirsch's (1992) report on 'learning cities', presented to the OECD Second Congress on Educating Cities, held in Gothenburg. Although this never became government policy in the UK, it had some impact at a local level. Within a few years a network of some 20 learning cities was created in Britain, each adopting a policy and operational style appropriate to its own local circumstances but sharing a commitment to building community cooperation and inter-agency partnership designed to enhance individual and communal learning. Initial enthusiasm for the idea lasted only as long as providers of statutory and local public services were prepared to adjust their policies, priorities and practices to match the emerging plans and proposals of local people and their activist leaders. Such adjustment of decision-making systems by 'the powers that be' had to be accompanied by the allocation of resources to maintain the momentum, so crucial to the success of learning cities. The concept of the learning country (in the case of Wales at the time of devolution and Slovenia soon after independence) was similarly rooted.

The Faure Report spoke of 'lifelong education' and 'the learning society'. In so doing, it moved beyond education to consider learning in a wider sense. Lifelong learning, or lifelong education, as stated in the report, was to be more than bolting together separate, although related, phases of educational provision – school, further and higher education. Lifelong education was seen to be 'a principle on which the overall organisation of a system and hence the elaboration of each of its parts, are based'. It was for everyone. Interestingly, the commission questioned the concentration of learning opportunities in educational establishments and institutions, believing that formally constituted educational bodies are often not as well placed as trade unions, community and other voluntary organisations to reach some sections of the population. All social and community organisations and institutions have the potential to be used for the purpose of learning. Only in this way is 'a self-aware learning society' built. In some respects, this aspect of the report's conclusions was similar to the learning dynamics of many community and social development initiatives in industrialised and developing countries, of equal validity in rural and urban settings. Such initiatives created a virtuous cycle in which individual learning would feed into social and community development, while social and community development would facilitate and structure individual learning.

In concentrating on the personal development of the learner at the centre of learning processes and delivery mechanisms, the Faure Report stressed the importance of tracking, strengthening and extending the learning pathway. With the benefit of hindsight, it can be seen that the Faure Commission was unduly optimistic in thinking that sufficient resources and the necessary political will would be evident in all countries to carry forward the thinking to enable new patterns of learning to be created in a short time. The commission's creative thinking was confounded by the ever-widening education and wealth gaps between individuals and groups within countries and between countries, which in turn reflected the long period of economic downturn and community decay as traditional industries declined in the industrialised countries following the

1973 oil crisis. In view of the rapid and radical changes in technology and the content of the curriculum for initial education, less well-educated parents were increasingly at a disadvantage in supporting and encouraging their children at school. Income distribution was becoming more unequal and would continue to be so. In many countries, domestic family structures were less secure and, hence, less supportive. A large and growing proportion of households were headed by lone parents, usually women, whose income levels, social status and future potential were all reducing. Unwillingness or inability of governments to introduce fundamental structural changes to the organisation, administration and delivery of education were to contribute to the widening divisions in society and communities, particularly evident in the later years of the century.

As a contribution to the debate in Sweden, following the reform of adult learning in 1969, the Swedish Confederation of Trade Unions insisted that 'a just distribution in the field of adult education does not mean equal shares for everyone but more for those that have received less' (in Rubenson, 2002). This view was current in the 1970s discussions regarding equality and equal opportunities in UK education, but Sweden was alone in attempting to reflect this goal systematically in its education policies. In the UK, many policies, ostensibly designed to give all adults opportunities to achieve, succeed and, thereby, benefit from education, were doomed to fail, given that some people required initial or additional support, which was often not available. The frustrated adult learner might well have asked: How can I be expected to compete in the race on equal terms when I am not even at the starting line? In giving attention to the theme of adult education and the disadvantaged (paragraphs 187–8 and 277–85), the Russell Committee stressed the importance of accepting that there could be no comprehensive adult learning service to meet the needs and aspirations of all, unless hurdles and blockages that discouraged or prevented access were removed.

Recurrent Education: A Strategy for Lifelong Learning (The Clarifying Report)

Soon after the publication of UNESCO's Faure Report, the OECD published the seminal report; *Recurrent Education: A Strategy for Lifelong Learning* (OECD/CERI, 1973). It was written by two well-respected OECD staff members, Denis Kallen and Jarl Bengtsson, who were supported by Ake Dalin, an independent consultant. The OECD report set many of the parameters for considering the development of adult learning in the 1970s and thereafter. The report was given the operational title of 'Clarifying Report' by its authors. This title set out the prime aim and purpose of the report, and thereafter it became known by this title. In setting the context for the debate following its publication, the preface of the report stressed three points as justification for adopting a notion of recurrent education 'as an alternative to the ever-lengthening period of continuing education for youth':

1. It insisted that the expansion of education opportunities for young people had brought about neither the required, nor the desired, social equality.
2. Given the rapid social and economic changes already evident in most parts of the world, some form of continuing or permanent education would be essential.
3. The clear and damaging separation of learning by experience from the formal education structures and curriculum was seen to require urgent attention.

This report was the first major statement concerning adult learning to assert, with supporting evidence and unchallengeable justification, that a new approach was necessary: 'The concept of recurrent education is based on a different approach – namely that education opportunities should be spread out over the individual's lifetime.' The report explained in a clear way how and why the front-loaded model, extending education opportunities for young people, could never achieve equal educational opportunities for all people throughout their lives, nor enable all individuals to gain greater control over the social and occupational aspects of their lives. One of the consequences of focusing attention overwhelm-ingly on the learning needs of young people, at a time when the needs of adults were pushed to the margins, was that the learning and knowledge gaps between younger and older adults was widening. The report argued that the introduction of a new structure for public education and training to introduce recurrent education would reduce this gap. The report also argued that, by continually loading the front-end of the educational model, a meritocracy would be rein-forced. This would, inevitably, lead to greater inequality as people with a more favourable educational start increasingly benefited from their advantage, leaving a poor 'underclass' further and further behind. It reflected widespread concern at the time that the expansion of education for young people had already increased divisions in society rather than leading to greater equality. Having argued for a structural change, the report's authors acknowledged the unlikelihood of politicians and governments generally adopting wholesale change and, thereby, reversing firmly entrenched policies and priorities. Therefore, the report's thesis became more evolutionary than revolutionary in advancing the case for enhancing learning opportunities for adults. It advocated the creation of a social framework embracing education as one of a number of activities having clear and valuable learning outcomes.

The Clarifying Report, in common with the Murphy Report, discussed the difference between 'education' and 'learning'. Education was defined in the

Clarifying Report as an organised and structured programme of learning 'confined to an intentionally created situation', while learning was described as 'an essential characteristic of the living organism'. Whether subsequent writers and education thinkers agreed or disagreed with the definitions used in the report, all will have found the style and language of the report helpful to the continuing debate. The report has served adult learning very well. Its influence is clear in the development of lifelong learning as an organising concept for the further development of adult learning in the 1990s. There is no evidence that the Russell Committee sought information or advice from the authors of the OECD report nor is there evidence of the reverse having taken place. Like the Russell Committee, the OECD addressed the issues of inequity and inequality. Russell was diffident in its comments on the social and occupational roles, and the potential contributions to society as a whole, of the education service. This may have been due to the changed political and economic climates between the time the committee was established in 1969 and the publication of the report in 1973. There was a determination, on the part of the Russell Committee, to produce an acceptable report, even at the risk of it not being as assertive and radical as many awaiting its publication would have wished. While neither report revolutionised educational structures, either in the UK or internationally, both reports directly influenced the increasing attention paid in public policy and professional discourse to those groups in society that had not yet benefited from increased expenditure on initial education.

Having considered the difference between 'education' and 'learning' and suggested that additional resources committed to the front-loaded model of education in society would not have a positive outcome for adults or society as a whole, the OECD report insisted that 'it would be absurd to reproduce else-where the shortcomings of the conventional system'. Instead, it suggested, policy-makers should be seeking creatively every opportunity to recognise, respect and increase the non-institutional learning of adults. Even offering people fee concessions or cost-free learning would achieve little for those with the greatest learning needs. They might be keen to learn, but on their own terms and in their chosen settings. They might well have barriers to overcome, other than finance. In their different ways, both the OECD report and the Russell Report called for an expansion of 'outreach' developmental activity, often of a non-educational nature. In the jargon of today, the OECD report called for 'joined-up thinking' leading to joined-up policy-making and planning including a visible and effective level of participation by those most likely to play their parts in the learning process as teachers and, above all, as learners. It argued that, unless this process was introduced, the potential of adult learning as a life-enhancing activity would be much reduced. The Clarifying Report asserted that: 'The relatively modest role of education in attaining social equality has made obvious the fact that educational policy is only one element – and not the most

important one – in achieving the wider social objectives that education pursues.'
The validity of this assertion was borne out in the years following publication of
the Russell Report, which had recommended a focus on learning opportunities
and initiatives to benefit adults with the greatest educational and social needs.
Experience of a variety of community-based learning activities in the 1970s and
thereafter confirmed that changes in educational policy or priorities, designed to
serve people with the greatest learning needs, would have no more than a
marginal impact unless accompanied by action to remove the same people from
financial, environmental and social poverty.

Russell in the context of international adult learning

Although members of the Russell Committee visited four countries – Federal
Republic of Germany, Finland, Sweden and Yugoslavia – there is no indication
in the report as to why these particular countries were chosen and how the
knowledge gained influenced the work of the committee or the contents of the
report. References to work in other countries are few and far between. No
contact appears to have been made with either UNESCO or OECD, both of
which were, as we have seen, deeply involved at the time in the production of
major reports of lasting significance. This is not a particular criticism of the
Russell Committee, since the absence of contacts with other countries or international organisations was typical of the times. Within the body of the Russell
Report (paragraph 46.1), reference is made to the then recent Swedish decision
that all adults should have an 'entitlement to the equivalent of the basic
minimum of education rising as that minimum is raised for the children'. Russell
suggested that this arrangement 'has much to commend it'. However, the subject
does not appear to have been discussed in any detail by the committee and no
related recommendation is included in the report. An entitlement to adult
education was never on the agenda in the mood of the 1970s and 1980s in
Britain. In a later policy discussion paper, NIACE (1990) recommended that the
government 'should consider the means for the provision of a free-of-charge entitlement for every adult to learning opportunities equivalent to at least 60 hours
of study per year on an accumulating basis, to be used for either education or
training'. Two years later, a commitment to implementing a form of entitlement
to adult learning was included in the Labour Party's manifesto for the 1992
general election. But it was only in the new century that a limited commitment
would be made for free adult learning for those with existing qualifications below
a given threshold. The wheels of policy grind slowly indeed.

While finding the notion of 'permanent education' attractive, the committee
asserted that it must be seen as 'a long-term concept and we do not have time to
wait for it' (paragraph 51). This odd turn of phrase indicates one of the principal
weaknesses of the Russell Report as a whole, which, in so many respects, was an

eminently reasonable, encouraging, confident and forward-looking statement, much welcomed by 'the field' and influential in the development of so many aspects of adult learning in England and Wales for the remainder of the century. In so far as the terms of reference of the committee sought recommendations 'to enable adult education to make its proper contribution to the national system of education conceived of as a process continuing through life', it would have been helpful had the committee explored the concepts of 'permanent education' and 'lifelong education' which were being discussed widely in international organisations and in other countries. Had that been done, it is likely that the committee would have made reasoned recommendations for a programme of structural change and funding over time. It is regrettable that the committee did not take the opportunity, during its three years of deliberations, to give careful consideration to permanent education or lifelong learning on the grounds that 'we do not have time to wait for it'.

In the immediate period after the publication of the Russell, OECD and UNESCO reports, one of the most pointed contributions to international events was given on 27 June 1973 in Paris. Sir Toby Weaver, the then recently departed Deputy Secretary at the DES, addressed an OECD conference on 'Future Structures of Post-Secondary Education'. He referred to the Russell Report virtually as an aside, despite the fact that it had only recently been published. He made a number of reactionary and defensive comments indicating that little had been learned by the Department or government as a result of the work of the Russell Committee. Matters of equity and equality were dismissed in one aggressive and blinkered paragraph in his presentation:

> We do not think of education in terms of social engineering, nor do we see it as an instrument to be wielded by governments or educators for the radical reconstruction of society. We have the more modest, liberal and realistic aim of providing a framework within which an independent teaching profession can offer to all, young and old, the best possible opportunities, within the resources available, to achieve self-fulfilment by the maximum enhancement of their individual capacities confident that they will themselves discover how best to make their own unique contribution to the renewal of society. We find the concept of recurrent education that has been put before us more confusing than clarifying.

With hindsight, it was perhaps a blessing that so few people active in adult education at the time were aware of the tone, language and contents of Weaver's presentation or, indeed, that he had spoken at all on the subject of adult learning. One of the unanswered questions is who, if anyone, briefed him or drafted his speech. The present author has seen a copy of the speech but there is no indication of its originator. Given that the government was soon to make clear its intention to take only limited piecemeal action towards implementing the Russell Report, it is possible to surmise that Weaver was offering a government snub to the committee and its report. Immediately following the completion of the Russell Report and of the reports published by UNESCO and OECD, there was a buoyant expectation that there might be significant positive moves despite the difficult economic conditions facing the government and the people. Weaver offered a 'wet blanket' observation that 'we have our own form of recurrent education'. Having made this provocative and wildly inaccurate comment, he then asserted that the terms 'further' and 'adult', as used by the Russell Committee, gave sufficient expression to recurrent education.

In reality, the systems of further and adult education in the UK, during the early 1970s, could not be said to be more than a limited gesture towards trans-lating the vision of recurrent education expressed in the 'Clarifying Report' into the reality of programmes and practices in the country. It was as if everything that needed to be said regarding legal guidelines for adult learning had been said in the 1944 Education Act and the Further Education Regulations of 1969, despite their obvious and acknowledged shortcomings. Weaver implied that the UK had nothing to learn from the experience of others and the considered ideas and arguments of the OECD and UNESCO reports: 'We cannot, therefore, readily accept that all these valuable diverse opportunities for self-realisation which we construe as impressive expressions of recurrency should be swept away in the name of a new and dubious interpretation of the word.' It was not clear who Weaver thought he was speaking for when he employed the word 'we'. Certainly the people active in adult learning development work in the UK, or participating in the work and debates of international organisations, or due to soon launch the Association for Recurrent Education (ARE), would not have wished to be associated with his remarks.

It was particularly regrettable that Weaver should have spoken in these terms when he must have been aware of the thinking of the Russell Committee and the contributions of Jim Simpson HMI to both the work of the committee and the Council of Europe's Council for Cultural Cooperation (CCC). Simpson was appointed to be an assessor to the Russell Committee and, although he retired from the Inspectorate in September 1971, he continued to serve with the committee until the report was completed. He had been actively involved in the work of the Council of Europe prior to the establishment of the Russell Committee and he was to continue working with the council for a further number of years. In 1966, the CCC's debate on developing educational policy had been marked by the introduction of the concept of 'permanent education'. As a contributor to the publication *Permanent Education* (Council of Europe Council for Cultural Coooperation, 1970), Jim Simpson had referred to the rela-tionship between 'permanent education' and community development, and this was reflected in the Russell Report two years later. Much of the work of the CCC revolved around the concept of 'cooperative monitoring', whereby small groups of experienced practitioners from different countries worked together, visited programmes and projects in a number of countries and produced reports comparing and contrasting methods and outcomes with a view to enabling providers to learn from each other across national borders. This system, had it been adopted in the UK, might have reduced the wasteful competition and point-less bidding by individual providers for short-term funds. Instead, it could have offered an opening to much more constructive cooperation and sharing, and a recognition that, in any given area, one provider was likely to be best placed to meet the learning needs of the target population, alone or in partnership with others.

Simpson's attitude towards liberal adult education was not shared by all of his HMI colleagues. The view that liberal adult education should be regarded as general, social and personal education, provided through whatever subject and activity it happened to use as a vehicle, was not supported by some more tradi-tionally minded HMI. It has been suggested to the present author by a retired HMI that inspectors with compartmentalised and somewhat reactionary and elitist attitudes held sway during the 1970s. The consequence was that, whereas many informal and developmental community-based adult learning initiatives were launched in different parts of the country, their legitimacy was called into question at the centre. Whatever may have been the truth and the significance of this alleged division of opinion within the Inspectorate, it became apparent during the period of ACACE's work (1977–83) that the arguments for advancing adult learning, within the Inspectorate as a whole and by the Inspectorate to ministers, were weaker than they should have been throughout the 1970s and the early 1980s.

The nineteenth session of the General Conference of UNESCO in 1976, held in Nairobi, moved international thinking and vision forward. The First UNESCO International Conference on Adult Education in 1949 had concluded that provision should be available and accessible to respond to all the many and various needs and aspirations of adults everywhere. The Nairobi General Conference took the matter further. In an implicit reference to human rights, as defined by the United Nations, the General Conference adopted the recommen-dation that 'the access of adults to education, in the context of lifelong educa-tion, is a fundamental aspect of the right to education and facilitates the exercise of the right to participate in political, cultural, artistic and scientific life'. The language of this recommendation was stronger than the Russell Committee would have used regarding the subject, and certainly stronger than any UK government would have endorsed.

The Fourth UNESCO International Conference on Adult Education was held in Paris in 1985. Since the Third Conference (Tokyo, 1972), there had been a major expansion in the provision of learning opportunities for adults in most parts of the world. This was in spite of the international political tensions of the time, and the economic crises and internal conflicts evident in many countries and many regions. Lifelong learning or lifelong education were becoming more widely used terms to identify programmes of learning activity. The Paris Conference was a milestone among UNESCO world conferences in a number of ways. Experience had shown that adult education, in its various forms, was an essential feature of social, cultural and economic policies and of wide-ranging development programmes in cities and countries of the developing and developed worlds. The conference reminded governments and national Responsible Bodies that a broad-brush approach to meeting the needs of entire cities, countries or regions must be tempered by a carefully focused regard to the learning needs of particular groups. Among those mentioned were women, the elderly, minorities, disadvantaged groups and migrant workers. The conference stressed the importance of countries learning from each other, and of UNESCO as an organisation able to facilitate international training, research and evaluation. In addition, the conference reminded all concerned that the effective delivery of learning opportunities called for the imaginative use of all structures and institutions, community settings and networks, the media and industry.

By the end of the 1985 UNESCO conference, there was a belief that many countries were ready to implement lifelong education policies, placing the responsibility for delivering learning on a variety of public, private and voluntary establishments and organisations, supported financially and in other ways by governments. Specialist adult learning organisations and institutions would become facilitators and advisers to other bodies in addition to being providers themselves. The UNESCO International Conference on Adult Education in Paris was the largest and most widely representative of the series of conferences launched in 1949. Among the delegates from the UK were members of the Russell Committee, its research assistant, members of ACACE, HMI and senior personnel of the DES, in addition to delegates from NGOs which had submitted evidence to the committee and to ACACE. The deliberations of the Paris Conference were informed by contributions drawn from the work and reports of the Russell Committee and ACACE. It was the biggest platform, to date, on which UK adult learning policy-makers and providers had been able to play a part.

Learning: The Treasure Within (The Delors Report)
In 1993, UNESCO decided to establish the International Commission on Education for the Twenty-first Century 'to study and reflect on the challenges facing education in the coming years and to formulate suggestions and recommendations in the form of a report which could serve as an agenda for renewal and action for policy-makers and officials at the highest levels'. This commission

was chaired by Jacques Delors, former French Minister of Economy and Finance and President of the European Commission. The Delors Report (UNESCO, 1996) sought to build on the work of the Faure Commission. It paid particular regard to the application of the two concepts, 'lifelong education' and 'the learning society' in the changed and dangerous world of the last few years of the twentieth century.

In common with a number of national and international studies and enquiries, including the Russell Committee, the Delors Commission reflected on the term 'lifelong education':

> Not only must it adapt to changes in the nature of work, but it must also constitute a continuous process of forming whole human beings – their knowledge and aptitudes, as well as the critical faculty and ability to act. It should enable people to develop awareness of themselves and their environment and encourage them to play their social role at work and in the community.

This was an inspirational expression of a commitment to move from damaging competition and separateness towards cooperation and partnership, from exclusion and elitism towards inclusion and mutual respect and, finally, from representation towards participation.

The commission's report famously suggested that education should rest on four pillars:

1. 'Learning to know', being the acquisition of a broad general education and in-depth knowledge in a few specified subjects.
2. 'Learning to do', the acquisition of competence based on a range of abilities and skills rather than an often narrow specialised vocational training.
3. 'Learning to be', being an enhanced self-awareness and dignity as an individual of actual and potential worth.
4. 'Learning to live together', the development and application of a range of social skills coupled with an understanding of the inestimable value of cooperative and supportive action based on sensitivity and concepts of mutual respect.

The sense of the commission's conclusions and recommendations was to create a framework for lifelong learning. This would touch all aspects of social living and personal development and incorporate the state and the component parts of economic, occupational, social and domestic structures as they evolved through time. Helpfully, the commission suggested that the term 'learning throughout life' should be used to apply to the continuity of learning opportunity and experience being advocated for all, from cradle to grave. The UNESCO debate had been firmly moved away from a narrow interpretation and application of the understanding of adult education. Adult learning as an element of personal, domestic, social and economic life, sometimes formal and structured, sometimes informal and developmental, became accepted as both normal and appropriate.

Writing in the *UNESCO Courier*, Jacques Delors (1996) identified what he believed to be four crucial issues arising from *Learning: The Treasure Within*. First, to what extent are education systems in the different countries able to be the 'key factor in development by performing a threefold function – economic, scientific and cultural'? By economic, he meant the creation and maintenance of a 'qualified and creative workforce'. Scientific was taken to mean the advancement of knowledge such that 'economic development goes hand in hand with responsible management of the physical and human environment'. The inclusion of a cultural function was to prove challenging and politically controversial in some countries within a few years. The commission asserted that 'education would be failing in its task if it did not produce citizens rooted in their own cultures and yet open to other cultures and committed to the progress of society'. Questions have been raised as to whether this was a role for the education system or not. In the context of rising ethnic and religious tensions around the world, some conservative interests have argued against the aim in principle, regarding moves towards embracing multiculturalism as undesirable.

Delors' second crucial issue was identified as 'the ability of education systems to adapt to new trends in society'. In his *UNESCO Courier* article, he stated that 'education must take into account a whole range of interrelated and interreacting factors that are always in a state of flux, whether it is dealing with individual or social values, family structure, the role of women, the status accorded to minorities, or the problems of urban development or the environment'. This was a firm demand for maximising flexibility in systems and procedures, for willingness to change priorities and acknowledge inequities in provision, and for an acceptance that providers of learning opportunities for adults should normally expect to be obliged to work in partnership with other organisations, services or agencies to enable many individuals and groups to achieve their learning goals.

His third point concerned 'relations between the education system and the state'. Circumstances will often differ greatly between countries and, consequently, setting an international blueprint becomes impossible. The Delors Report argued that in each and every country it was necessary to consider the most appropriate dispersal of powers, duties and responsibilities between the state and other bodies. These included regional and local authorities, public, private and voluntary promoters of learning programmes and activities, and individuals and groups seeking learning opportunities. This issue has proved to be politically crucial in many UNESCO countries. Political dogma and rhetoric have, at times, impeded or confused the process of decision-making which, ideally, should be informed by the best interests of learners. Throughout much of the period covered by this book, the policy and organisational changes in England and Wales appear to have been led more by party politics than by educational considerations. In turn, this has led to the education service being unreasonably and unrealistically expected, by governments, to deliver outcomes that have a curative affect on the nation's social and economic ills. An education service cannot be both true to itself and simultaneously act as a surrogate police force, ambulance service and job centre.

Delors' fourth issue was thought to be nebulous and inadequately explained or defined. He set education the task of promulgating 'the values of openness to others, and mutual understanding – in a word, the values of peace'. He asked whether education could create and use 'a universal language that would make it possible to overcome certain contradictions, respond to certain challenges and, despite their diversity, convey a message to all the inhabitants of the world'. It was soon evident that the first three of Delors' crucial issues were understandable, recognisable and susceptible to action by governments and nation states, separately or in conjunction with the multiplicity of education providers. The fourth issue was incapable of translation into an action plan beyond curriculum review in some aspects of learning.

EC White Paper *Teaching and Learning: Towards the Learning Society*

The European Commission (EC) White Paper, *Teaching and Learning: Towards the Learning Society* (European Commission, 1995), gave its backing to a concept of lifelong learning which would bring employment and economic policies closer to education and training. There was an acceptance that in any situation of social and economic change there would be winners and losers, and that the losers would require special programmes tailored to their needs. Hard political and moral arguments would ensue if a neo-liberal approach were to be adopted and applied with determination. Two fundamental questions demanding politically acceptable answers were expected to arise: (i) why should firms invest, through the taxation system or by direct payment, in lifelong learning that they judged they did not need?; and (ii) why should the state take corrective measures in order to secure access to lifelong learning to those whom the economy did not need? According to the White Paper, the response to the first question was that firms should be expected to demonstrate a social responsibility and that it would be in their interest to educate and train a reserve of skilled and flexible labour. In response to the second question, the state should expect to complement any contribution to lifelong learning made by firms and educational and training bodies, thereby raising the general level of knowledge, understanding and skill in the adult community in order to respond positively to future changes in the economy and in the workplace. In addition, the state should support and give access to groups in the population which, otherwise, might find themselves isolated and excluded from the mainstream of society, thus becoming increasingly vulnerable and likely to be in receipt of other, more negative, forms of public funds and services.

4
The Russell conclusions and recommendations

The value of adult education is not solely to be measured by direct increases in earning power or productive capacity or by any other materialistic yardstick, but by the quality of life it inspires in the individual and generates for the community at large. It is an agent changing and improving our society: but for each individual the means of change may differ and each must develop in his own way, at his own level and through his own talents. No academic subject or social or creative activity is superior to another provided that those engaged in it develop a greater awareness of their own capacities and a more certain knowledge of the totality of their responsibilities as human beings.
(Paragraph 6, General Statement opening the Russell Report)

As a commitment to the promotion of all forms of adult learning, the quotation at the head of this chapter could not be bettered. The General Statement, preceding the detailed recommendations listed at the beginning of the report, outlined the views of the committee regarding the best future arrangements for adult learning in the light of the political, economic and financial circumstances at the time. It confirmed the open, flexible and comprehensive nature of adult learning as adopted by the committee and expressed with clarity and firmness the progressive and enlightened view that adult learning concerns quality of life as well as standard of living, and the essential interests of individuals in addition to the wider interests of society. The General Statement explained that some of the recommendations 'are fundamental to the development of adult education in England and Wales'. These were summarised in paragraph 3.1–10 of the General Statement and have been discussed in Chapter 2 of this book. The committee explained that:

Underlying our Report and the recommendations that spring from it are the following key propositions:

On demand for adult learning
In our changing and evolving society the explicit and latent demands for all kinds of adult education have increased and will continue to increase.

Adults, in their own right, have claims for the provision of a comprehensive service which can satisfy these demands in appropriately adult ways: all areas of education will be enriched if demands for the education of adults are met.

On resources for adult learning
Within our community there exists an enormous reservoir of human and material resources: a relatively modest investment in adult education – in staff, buildings, training and organisation – could release these resources to adult education for the benefit of individuals and the good of society.

On leadership for adult learning
The successful development of adult education depends in very large measure on a consistent lead and direction being given by the Secretary of State. (Paragraph 2.1–2.3 of the General Statement)

The report listed 118 recommendations gathered under 38 different headings. Some of the recommendations were specific and narrowly focused while others were extremely general. The recommendations, as listed in the report, comprised a rich mixture of aspiration, hopes and urgent requirements. In this chapter, the committee's recommendations are considered under the headings used in the report, with the relevant paragraphs of the report noted for each heading. More detailed attention is given to issues emerging from the report's recommendations in the extended commentary on post-Russell legislation and development in subsequent chapters.

The general structure (paragraphs 148–54)
The committee considered the strengths and weaknesses of a number of different possible arrangements and arrived at the firm view that the existing structural pattern for adult learning was the most appropriate and should continue. The Russell Committee judged that the LEAs should continue to be the main providers in any given areas, and should 'take the initiative in co-operative planning' with other providers, statutory and voluntary. It was with this in mind that the committee attached great importance to adult education sub-committees being established by Regional Advisory Councils for Further Education, if they did not already exist, and, second, the creation of a Local Development Council for Adult Education in each LEA area (see below).

Government lead (paragraphs 155–60)
The committee recognised the lack of clarity given to adult learning within Sections 41 and 42 of the Education Act 1944. However, the report's recommen-

dation regarding the loose wording was particularly diffident, only suggesting that the two sections should be revised 'when opportunity arises' and that the 'Secretary of State should make an early statement of policy to local education authorities clarifying what is meant'. Unfortunately, the committee did not recommend that an explanation be given by the government as to how LEAs could be expected 'to secure the provision for their areas of adequate facilities for further education' without powers of direction, sufficient resources or guaranteed departmental backing. Nor did the recommendation specifically call for a definition of 'adequate facilities'. These unsatisfactory elements of the existing legislation were to continue to trouble individuals and organisations seeking to achieve appropriate and suitable provision.

A further point of confusion of intent, and lack of clarity of meaning, concerned the recommended creation of a Development Council for Adult Education for England and Wales. The recommendation spoke of such a Council being 'a national channel of consultation and advice' to the Secretary of State and that the 'title is chosen advisedly to indicate the purpose of the Council'. If the purpose was to be 'a national channel of consultation and advice', it was not evident from the wording of the report why the word 'development' was included in the title. The purpose of the council was certainly not evident from the suggested title to those deciding whether or not to accept the recommendation. 'Development' was not an acceptable word to Margaret Thatcher, who received the report and its recommendations, nor to her Labour successor, both of whom made clear their belief that consultation and advice should emerge from an 'advisory council'. Development, to the Secretaries of State and, even more, to the governments of the 1970s, conveyed a sense of expansion in funding and programming. When ACACE was established in 1977, it was in the light of this recommendation.

Regional cooperation (paragraphs 165–9)

In view of the importance of Regional Advisory Councils for Further Education (RACs) in respect of providing technical and vocational post-school further education, it was logical that the committee should recommend that those RACs which did not have 'sub-committees for adult education', should establish them. There was considerable variation in student fee policies and fee levels between providers within many of the regions. This, coupled with the difficulties often faced by potential students seeking to enrol outside the LEA area in which they lived, caused the committee to recommend that any difficulties arising from the acceptance of 'free trade' between neighbouring authorities should be resolved by regional consultation. However, RACs had neither over-riding powers nor sanctions. Despite the best efforts of many, when an LEA decided not to accept 'free trade', financial and/or administrative barriers prevented some potential students from enrolling where their best interests would have been met. Yet it is also possible to understand the point of view of local authorities where levels of local taxation were much higher than in neighbouring authorities, and it seemed logical to charge higher fees for students from the lower tax authority. The RACs disappeared as a consequence of the passing of the Further and Higher Education Act 1992, when further education colleges were removed from LEA control. This left matters of cooperation and joint planning of programmes, fee policies and fee levels to be determined on the basis of goodwill. Regional policy-making, to mirror the general mobility of adult students from place to place and home to work transport patterns, where it had existed, began to disappear in the early to middle 1990s.

Local Education Authority initiative in cooperative planning (paragraphs 170–2); Local Development Councils (paragraphs 173–5)

LEAs, as the main providers of adult learning programmes in most areas, were considered by the committee to be the appropriate bodies to lead any local coordinating arrangements involving different providers, adult learners and voluntary community organisations. The committee regarded LEAs as essential agencies able to ensure that national policy was applied to local areas in accordance with legislation. In addition to urging LEAs to cooperate with the range of local statutory and voluntary agencies with an interest in and/or a contribution to make towards the development and delivery of adult learning opportunities, the committee recommended that LEAs should provide support and/or grants to such organisations. The report made the point that 'many local education authorities already give support in this way to community associations, women's organisations, music and drama groups, old people's clubs and other social organisations, and we regard it as of prime importance that these groups should be brought into the local structures of adult education'.

The committee then recommended that: 'In every local education authority area there should be established a Local Development Council for Adult Education widely representative of those who have an interest in adult education as providers or users and students. The range can also be widened, especially in order to bring many more disadvantaged or handicapped groups into an integral relationship with the service.' The committee recommended that the Local Development Councils should have no financial or other powers. They should be consultative and advisory. As they were formed in different areas, they operated according to different constitutions. Some enjoyed a measure of financial and executive responsibility delegated by the LEA. Despite a 1980 ACACE report on the numbers, types and functions of the then existing Local Development Councils (see Chapter 6), gradually, during the ten years following the publication of the Russell Report, most Local Development Councils were wound up as the national economic squeeze exerted on adult learning was tightened.

Local Education Authority direct provision (paragraphs 176–203)

The committee made a number of recommendations to enhance the role and improve the ability of LEAs to lead the delivery of adult learning in their areas. LEAs were encouraged to develop and broaden the curriculum on offer to include opportunities for adults 'to complete formal general education'. Formal general education was defined as courses normally followed in school or college before completion of initial education. This was in recognition of the thinking, at the time, that adults should have a 'school-leaving equivalent' body of knowledge or qualifications, measured by examination successes. LEAs should assume the main responsibility for ensuring that sufficient appropriate opportunities would be available for sections of the population that, traditionally, had participated the least. LEAs were urged to target resources towards groups and individuals with particular learning needs or at particular risk of increased social and educational exclusion. It was recommended that this should be achieved by the LEAs extending cooperation with specialist statutory and voluntary agencies working with people with disabilities, refugees, homeless people, ex-prisoners and other groups. The committee was exercised by the problem of how best to improve the quality of staffing and increase the numbers of staff employed to organise and deliver the local adult learning programmes. To this end, the committee recommended that LEAs should create the equivalent of school and college governing bodies to oversee the provision in given areas. Until such time as the Secretary of State was able to introduce legislation granting delegated responsibilities to bodies created to oversee the management of learning programmes, LEAs should give them as much responsibility as legislation currently permitted.

The recommendations went on to argue for an increase in the number of professional and support staff to take forward the work of newly formed area organisations. Whatever may have been the merits of such developments, they were frequently delayed or greatly reduced as a consequence of budget reductions in the 1970s and 1980s. These same reductions, plus the view in some LEA areas that residential learning was not a 'value for money' response to identified learning needs, led to the closure of a number of LEA short-term residential colleges, rather than the increase recommended by the committee. Evidence submitted to the committee from a number of sources (universities, non-educational voluntary organisations, LEAs, broadcasting, WEA, hospitals and other agencies and establishments) all indicated that, for many people, the traditional course requiring attendance for a few hours each week for many weeks, was an entirely inappropriate way of learning. The committee urged LEAs to develop alternative patterns of delivery in addition to, or in place of, weekly classes, thus introducing flexibility and choice.

The Direct Grant principle (paragraphs 204–10)

The committee strongly supported the Direct Grant principle, whereby earmarked and ring-fenced funds were granted to named adult learning bodies. Generally, central government funds, channelled to LEAs and the University Grants Committee in accordance with formulae to calculate amounts for adult learning, could be transferred by the recipient bodies to other purposes on the basis of local decision-making guided by local determination of priorities. Earmarking or ring-fencing ensured that central government funds, once allocated for a particular purpose, would be devoted to that designated activity. Since the 1924 Board of Education Adult Education Regulations had identified particular establishments and organisations as 'approved associations', subsequently designated as 'Responsible Bodies', the DES and its predecessor departments had limited its direct earmarked aid to listed, named bodies. In 1954, the Ashby Committee published its report on funding for Responsible Bodies. Ashby had recommended continuation of the responsible body principle. Nonetheless, the Russell Committee recommended that 'the term "responsible body" should be discarded' and that there should be greater flexibility in the system. The committee argued that direct grant from the DES should be available to 'major providing bodies'. Universities and the WEA were the major providing bodies in the mind of the committee. However, the committee did not 'exclude the possibility that at some time in the future another body might qualify for the same kinds of grant, for a similar range of purposes'. In addition to the universities and the WEA, the committee recommended that direct grants should be made to the long-term residential colleges and to bodies undertaking general promotion of adult learning.

The universities (paragraphs 211–23)

While paying tribute to the long history of the contribution to adult learning by British universities, the committee stressed the importance of universities becoming more overt contributors to 'the public system of education'. It was thought that participation of universities in the membership and work of the National and Local Development Councils would assist this process. In addition, the committee made a number of specific recommendations as to the aspects of adult learning for which direct grant could be made, given the nature and history of universities as providers of particular types of learning opportunities.

Additionally, the committee identified a number of learning activities specifically meriting grant-aid. These included liberal studies of the traditional kind,

> 'balancing' studies of an academic character, designed to complement earlier specialisation in education', education programmes to provide background knowledge and intellectual skills related to the roles performed by adults in society, industrial education for workers from the shop floor to senior management, project work involving research or enquiry, and training for adult educators and development workers.

The final area recommended by the committee as worthy of development in the universities and of grant-aid by the DES was described as 'pioneer work' and included work 'of an informal or pioneer character with disadvantaged sections of the population, including the training or orientation of those working in such fields, especially voluntarily' and 'provision of adult access to graduation or other qualification at an advanced level'. All of these activities would bring universities into closer association with other local agencies, organisations and establishments. Individual universities and the UGC were urged to give consideration to making more funds available for the education of adults and to providing greater ease of access to university facilities and resources. The recommendations were far-reaching and had radical implications. Had they been received by the government and universities with imaginative goodwill, there is little doubt that learning opportunities for mature adults at higher education levels would have increased greatly in volume and variety. This was not to be. In the years following the report's publication, it was left to the determination and creativity of individuals or groups of colleagues within individual universities to make the desired progress, alone or in association with other agencies.

Following the publication of the Russell Report, the Vice-Chancellors' Committee (VCC) and the Universities Council for Adult Education (UCAE), separately, and subsequently jointly, gave consideration to the report. An undated memorandum for discussion, prepared by the UCAE, identified a number of issues for joint attention by the two bodies. The report had highlighted increasing demands for higher education opportunities for mature adults. Accurate statistics regarding mature adult students were not then available. Russell had appreciated that the OU would not be able to satisfy the increased demand, partly due to the special nature of OU degrees but also because the distance learning core of OU study was not suited to all people and all subject areas. Many adults wished to follow narrower courses more in line with the single-subject or combined honours degrees offered by the existing traditional higher education establishments. Adult students looked for a response to their growing call for qualifications and recognition at the end of courses of study. All concerned were in agreement that the wider age mix would be potentially beneficial to all students and to universities and teaching staff. Little was known about the strength and character of demand from mature adults for full-time and part-time study. The Robbins Report (1963) had urged universities in the larger cities to programme part-time evening degree courses. Four years later, the report on the 'Future of Birkbeck College in the University of London' expressed the hope that 'Birkbecks' might be established in major centres of population throughout the country. This did not happen.

In its paper for discussion with the VCC, the UCAE argued that 'part-time students would be members of the university in every respect, but would continue their employment while studying for degrees'. The paper did not refer to the requirements of unemployed people, or to the particular needs of women, many of whom were not in paid employment but had domestic responsibilities, often including caring for young children. Despite this omission from the paper, within a few years, crèches, nurseries and pre-schools were established on a number of university sites as support for the higher education of parents, guardians and carers. The national economic situation was such that the universities, through the VCC, did not wish to move ahead with any discussions likely to lead to greater financial commitment to mature adults when the overall budgets were at standstill, at best. In its observations to the VCC on the situation at the time, the University of Oxford commented, without explanation, that the provision of a 'Birkbeck-like' facility for mature students studying part time might be 'less appropriate in the Oxford context than in the larger civic universities'. Nonetheless, Oxford, in common with most higher education establishments, did welcome the potential benefit to universities and individuals of having a wide age mix among the student population. In keeping with the widely held view that priority should be given to young people, Oxford noted the uncertainty surrounding financial support for mature students and its wish that any improvement in the funding of mature students should not be 'at the expense of support for existing commitments nor by means of an ear-marked grant' which would reduce the university's financial flexibility.

Between the early 1970s and the end of the century, the number of people enrolled in higher education increased significantly. The proportion of the increased number who were 21 years of age or over also grew. By the year 2001/02, 90 per cent of part-time higher education students in England were categorised as adult students and approaching 30 per cent of full-time students were adults. Yet in many cases, such adult students were young adults under the age of 25 for whom entry to higher education had been deferred for a variety of reasons, and there was an uneven spread between the 'old' and 'new' universities, with the majority of mature students studying in the 'new' universities (ex-polytechnics). Despite the overall growth and the higher proportion of adult students, working-class participation had hardly risen during the period of 30 years. Indeed, during the last few years of the twentieth century, the proportion of mature students from working-class backgrounds fell. At the end of the century, less than 3 per cent of all higher education students were adults who had followed the route provided by access and similar courses. With the drive for higher numbers and the continued belief in the overriding value of the front-loaded model of education, calling for evermore investment in learning for young people, insufficient attention had been paid to the needs of potential adult students and the communities of which they formed parts. Greater collaboration between further education and higher education and greater understanding of the contribution of community-based adult learning, coupled with a support system for students designed to accommodate the needs of mature adults as well as teenagers, was urgently required and continues to be so.

The drive for greater participation by mature, working-class adults has had to confront one overriding danger, recognised as such since before the Russell Committee was appointed: while higher education may benefit individual students, it does not necessarily benefit working-class communities. As the most able, most assertive and/or most determined working-class individuals move into a higher education system, they may gain and develop values likely to lift them out of their communities. Thus, while the individuals may benefit educationally and economically from the experience, the potential of higher education to reduce social exclusion and disadvantage in society will not have been achieved. This remains an unresolved tension in access work.

The voluntary sector of adult education (paragraphs 224–5); The Workers Educational Association (paragraphs 226–41)

Despite receiving written and oral evidence from many significant local and national voluntary organisations, and visiting projects and organisations in Liverpool, Hertfordshire and Oxfordshire, the recommendations in respect of the voluntary sector, apart from those relating specifically to the WEA, were not strong. The committee acknowledged, in general terms, that 'voluntary organisations have an important role to play in adult education and their contribution should be safeguarded'. It was suggested by the committee that the voluntary sector was frequently well placed to advise and inform providing bodies regarding particular needs which might not have been articulated in terms understandable to LEAs, universities or WEA Districts. Although the voluntary sector itself was a large-scale direct provider of adult learning opportunities, it was not generally acknowledged as such. More often than not, the voluntary sector was thought of as a go-between for local people and learning providers or the interpreter of local community learning needs to the providers. The combined contribution of the then Pre-school Playgroups Association (now the Pre-school Learning Alliance), National Federation of Women's Institutes, pigeon fanciers' clubs, arts, crafts and sports organisations, large and small, was considerable. Published reports on the role and contribution of voluntary organisations in CDP neighbourhoods, EPAs and in conjunction with the national adult literacy campaign, in the early to mid-1970s, ensured a wider recognition of the crucial and, often, central importance of the voluntary sector in adult learning. This recognition was later reinforced by the work and publications of ACACE (see Chapter 6) and, later, by the activities of the Voluntary Adult Education Forum (VAEF) from 1985, and of the ECA.

Since its creation in 1903, the WEA had been, and continues to be, a unique voluntary organisation and mainstream provider of adult learning programmes. At meetings held during the Oxford Extension Summer School in 1903, Albert Mansbridge discussed with a number of Oxford academics his idea of a working-class movement for learning and change in the UK. In 1907, two important events took place. First, a conference considered 'What Oxford can do for Working People'. This was followed by the publication of *Oxford and Working-class Education* which established the pattern for WEA tutorial classes. For many years, the WEA has also been a promoter of courses for other providers. The Russell Committee judged that the WEA would continue to be a significant provider of learning for adults, thus meriting grant-aid from both central and local government. Having considered the evidence submitted by the WEA, universities, the TUC and a number of individual trade unions, and initiatives undertaken by some WEA branches and districts, the report recommended that the organisation should give particular attention to four specific areas of work (paragraph 232.1/4). To some extent, all were being undertaken by the WEA in the late 1960s. The WEA judged them to be priority areas and had identified them as such in its evidence to the committee.

1. *Education for the socially and culturally deprived living in urban areas.* The committee argued that such work would have to be experimental and often informal, usually undertaken in cooperation with other local agencies across a range of health, welfare, community, environmental and other services. The WEA was reminded that its involvement 'would have to be in a strictly educational role and closely integrated with the work of the other bodies'.

2. *Educational work in an industrial context.* This was an encouragement to the WEA to develop further its work with the TUC and individual trade unions related to courses for shop stewards and other workplace learning. Speaking to a WEA conference soon after publication of the report, Vic Feather, General Secretary of the TUC, referred to the expansion of interest shown by the TUC and a number of unions in developing educational programmes for shop stewards and branch officers to achieve greater competence and efficiency in carrying out their trade union duties.

3. *Political and social education.* Much of the work of the WEA had been designed to have the purpose of raising political and social awareness in addition to offering intellectual challenge. The committee urged the WEA to increase provision in conjunction with 'socially oriented organisations'. Oxfam and Shelter were mentioned in the report. In addition, the association was encouraged to expand its programme linked with ' "role education" for local public service workers, elected councillors and other people engaged in social and political activity'.

4. *Courses of liberal and academic study below the level of university work.* Traditionally, the WEA had been a strong provider of liberal and academic study below the level of university study, both as a lead into university study itself and as an appropriate form of study, in its own right, for many people. The organisation was recommended by the committee to continue with this work in close association with LEAs: 'It is an area in which the role of the WEA may gradually come to include a greater element of promotional work, encouraging and supporting balanced programmes by local education authorities as well as making provision of its own.'

In all aspects of its activity, the WEA was recommended to keep its policies and programmes under review in conjunction with local authority departments and appropriate national and local voluntary organisations, 'and to ensure that it does not use up its resources on work that could equally be done by others' (paragraph 233). The committee expected the links between the WEA and universities to become looser as the relationship with the LEAs became stronger. This expectation was not realised to the extent imagined by the committee. In many cases, the relationship between universities and local WEA Districts and Branches changed in character but remained strong. Very few LEAs established strong educational links with the WEA. Even the more enlightened LEAs, notably ILEA, only maintained a relationship based on enabling the WEA to use ILEA premises free of charge and for the WEA to receive grants, from time to time, for specific activities and programmes. A further recommendation of the committee, which reflected the wishes of the WEA itself, as set out in the association's evidence, was that the designation of each individual WEA district as a 'responsible body' should be ended. Direct grant, in respect of approved programmes, should henceforth be paid to the WEA centrally.

The long-term residential colleges (paragraphs 247–55)
It was recommended that the existing long-term residential colleges should continue to receive direct grant from the DES and that an additional college should be established in the north of England, to redress in part the geographical

imbalance. The committee acknowledged that many people had benefited from the full-time residential experience and that the demand and need for such learning experiences would continue. For many years, long-term residential colleges had maintained an outstanding record of offering alternative routes into higher education to those leading directly on from school. Indeed, some of the colleges had offered forms of recognised higher education to mature adult students themselves. Despite their evident success, residential colleges were held, by some critics, to be expensive and thereby to be employing resources that could serve a larger number of students in other forms of adult learning. By its very nature, residential full-time learning is bound to be more costly per head.

The committee was of the view that:

The colleges have a remarkable record of finding men and women from unpromising (sic) backgrounds and developing their intellectual capacities and personalities so that they have gone on to make important contributions to society. The colleges have done this by developing, each in its own way, an ethos which combines the traditions of liberal adult education with academically demanding courses and a strong community spirit.

While advancing the cause for a comprehensive and all-inclusive pattern of provision, the committee had no difficulty supporting the continuation of public funding for long-term colleges. The colleges were seen to have provided a route to higher education, designed primarily with mature adults in mind and, in particular, for mature adults from educational and social backgrounds largely untouched by the direct school to higher education passage. A comparison was drawn between the long-term colleges and the then colleges of education for people training to become teachers. Both were attractive to some mature adults. Both thereby served the needs of some individuals and the wider society. A large number of applicants for places at the long-term residential colleges lived in the north of England. The committee, noting this fact and acknowledging that there were approximately three firm applications for every place, recommended that a further college should be established in the north of England. The Northern College for Residential Adult Education (Northern College) was opened in 1978 in Wentworth Castle near Barnsley, and rapidly became an acknowledged and well-respected provider of residential adult learning.

Media: partners and supporters (paragraphs 256–62)

Written and oral evidence was submitted to the committee by the BBC and the ITA. Broadcast series on radio and television had been produced to aid the learning of individuals and groups. The evidence of benefit was clear. Experience gained from the work of the NEC and the College of the Sea and from ILEA's Educational Television Service all pointed towards the same conclusion: that the broadcasting media were likely to prove ever more important contributors to the nation's adult learning. The committee paid great attention to the 'application of educational technology and experiment with multimedia approaches to adult learning in association with more formal class growth'.

Respect was paid to the recently opened OU. At the time, the role and contribution of the OU was limited to degree courses, held to be outside the remit of the committee. During the early years of the OU, it was apparent that the existing universities and the extra-mural departments were unsure how they could and should relate to the new institution. The Planning Committee had been established in 1967 and submitted its report (Open University, 1969) to Ted Short, Secretary of State for Education and Science on 31 December 1968. Brian Groombridge, Education Officer at the ITA and, later, Head of the Extra-mural Department at the University of London, was a member of both the OU Planning Committee and the Russell Committee. Harold Wiltshire, Professor of Adult Education at the University of Nottingham, had been a member of the government's Advisory Committee on the University of the Air (DES, 1966b), which led to the decision to establish the OU, and was also a member of the Planning Committee. Roy Shaw, at the time the Director of Adult Education at the University of Keele, was a member of the Planning Committee and was later to become a member of ACACE from 1977 to 1980. Linkages between the different advisory and planning bodies continued in the 1970s and 1980s in much the same way as they had existed in the 1920s. There was a sense in which the 'great and the good' were being appointed. More charitably, and more helpfully, it could be seen that there was a useful continuity of thinking influencing decisions and planning across a range of adult learning initiatives.

The Times questioned, in an editorial (7 June 1968), the justification for creating the OU, well before the Planning Report was published, but coincidental with the appointment of Sir Walter Perry as the OU's first Vice-Chancellor. The editorial went so far as to demand that:

> It is time for the Planning Committee and Miss Lee [Jennie Lee was Minister of State at the DES responsible for the Arts and the OU] to convince us all that the University is something more acceptable, feasible and desirable than just an expensive memorial to one who may well be its original mentor, that most brilliant of self-educated men, Aneurin Bevan.

Jennie Lee was Aneurin Bevan's widow. In his personal account of the OU, Walter Perry (1976) outlined graphically the political and academic cynicism and suspicion at the time. The Planning Committee had been appointed by Jennie Lee. Perry records that:

During the life of the Planning Committee the Conservative Party never went on record with any public statement about their attitude to the Open University. Nevertheless, it was discovered later, any potential applicant for a job in the University who wrote to the Party for advice was, throughout the whole period, advised not to apply as the future of the institution was considered to be in doubt.

In a letter to the present author dated 18 March 2002, David Grugeon, Director of UK Partnerships in the Office of the Vice-Chancellor of the OU, wrote:

The OU was an extraordinary hybrid of adult, further, higher education and educational broadcasting and technology ... The wider world of adult education, in the continuing embattled state of UK adult education, was totally divided about the OU, as you recall, with some appalled and some excited. Those of us who joined in 1969 had to get our friends fast, to help set up the sophisticated regional support operation to assist tens of thousands of adults seeking university education (on open entry) to survive the rigours of distance education. I knew from my work for the National Extension College since 1963, and the BBC since 1964, that good learning materials were not sufficient: the regional and local support of the wider world of adult education (tutors, counsellors, study centres, day schools, summer schools, exam centres, special support for disabled students, prisoners, isolated, remote, shift workers, oil rig workers, carers, frail, etc.) would be critical to build the solid and interactive human network to keep people studying across the personal, domestic, vocational and locational vicissitudes.

The Committee of Extra-mural Officers of UCAE discussed the OU at a meeting on 3 November 1972. Minutes of the meeting record, unenthusiastically, that 'several members of the Committee expressed interest in recent reports about developments in the work of the Open University'. In the 1960s and early 1970s, it was generally assumed that pursuit of degree courses, whether through the OU or a traditional university structure, should relate to employment aspirations. This was government thinking. However, it is an interesting fact that during the following 30 years, it became increasingly recognised and applauded that many adults would choose to study at degree level for purely non-vocational reasons. Based on the OU model, the Russell Committee explored the need for similar forms of provision at other levels. The term 'analogues of the Open University' was used. The committee recommended the creation of analogues of the OU at a lower academic level and for a general increase in the amount of radio and television broadcast time for adult learning.

The committee deliberately avoided becoming involved in the debate in the early 1970s concerning the possible designation of a new radio and/or television channel as solely dedicated to education. This matter was left to be decided as one element of the country's future broadcasting policy. Although there was much debate at the time about the desirability of having a television and/or radio channel exclusively devoted to education, the Russell Committee concluded that to make a recommendation on the matter was to exceed its terms of reference. With the benefit of hindsight, it might be concluded that this was an error of judgement. In recommending an increase in broadcast time for adult learning and for the creation of 'what we have called analogues of the Open University at a lower academic level', the committee was moving safely with the mainstream of contemporary thinking among LEA and voluntary sector practitioners. Yet despite numerous attempts, no successful large-scale 'Open University analogue' has yet been created, although the OU model itself has been copied in many other countries, and the OU has made a modest contribution to continuing education at sub-degree level, as proposed by the Venables (1976) Report.

Despite the importance of the subject, the reluctance of the committee to make a firm recommendation reflected the minimal level of interest among some providers. Minutes of the meetings of UCAE's Committee of Extra-mural Officers are indicative of this widely shared attitude. At its meeting on 26 May 1972, it decided, in respect of its Broadcasting and Television Sub-committee: 'As there appeared to be no business for this sub-committee, and no desire to perpetuate it was expressed, the committee decided that it should be discontinued.' It was suggested, by the Russell Committee, that the recommended National Development Council for Adult Education should work with NIAE and bring forward proposals for greater cooperation between the media and adult education agencies. This suggestion was not followed up, in view of the deterioration of the economic climate in 1973, resulting from the international oil crisis, and the unwillingness of the government to establish the National Development Council.

Adult education in relation to industry (paragraphs 265–9)

In assessing the need for adult learning of many types, Part 1 of the Russell Report discussed the essential interrelationship between the foreseen changes in the patterns of work and non-work and the development of adult learning. While stressing the likely importance of work-related education and training, the committee emphasised the direct benefit to the individual of general and personal education and the indirect, but nonetheless significant, benefit to society and the national economy. All providing bodies were urged to give attention to increasing and targeting adult learning opportunities for management and shop-floor employees across the multifarious aspects of industrial relations. The Society of Industrial Tutors (SIT) submitted both written and oral evidence to the committee on this subject. The important contribution of the SIT to the development of adult learning in relation to employment and industry during the period following publication of the Russell Report is discussed in Chapter 8.

University extra-mural departments, the WEA and an increasing numbers of polytechnics and colleges had been promoting courses for shop stewards in cooperation with the TUC and many individual trade unions. This was in accordance with the terms of an agreement between the TUC and the CBI (TUC, 1968). The Code of Industrial Relations Practice encouraged trade unions and management to 'take all reasonable steps to ensure that stewards receive the training they require' and 'to seek to agree on arrangements for leave' in order that this training could be appropriately delivered. Expansion of this work would require the employment of more trained tutors. Given that much of the cost of shop stewards and other trade unionists would be met by employers in the form of paid leave from work, the committee argued that the same treatment should be applied to this form of 'role education' as to any other form integral to the fourth area of recommended WEA development. In 1967, the Central Training Council had encouraged industrial training boards to make grants available for this activity.

Educational leave (paragraphs 270–3)

That part of the Education Act 1944, providing for compulsory day or block release for set amounts of time for all young workers under 18 years of age, was never implemented. Such day and block release as was available in the 1960s was mainly associated with narrowly defined vocational study or the components of recognised apprenticeship schemes. There was a particular problem in relation to young women workers since very few entered employment fields in which apprentices existed. The committee noted that 'only 10 per cent of women employees under eighteen were taking day release courses in 1969, compared with 40 per cent of young men'. One of the few references to policies and practice in other countries in the report related to Paid Educational Leave (PEL). UNESCO had been pressing the need for PEL since its General Conference in 1964 and the International Labour Organisation (ILO) had been considering the subject since 1965. The committee expressed the hope that the TUC and CBI, in conjunction with government departments and adult learning providers, would move quickly to establish suitable arrangements in England and Wales. The fact that a number of West European countries had already incorporated UNESCO and ILO recommendations into their domestic legislation was mentioned as was the wish that 'we do not lag behind'. Despite the considerable interest in making progress, lack of political and industrial commitment and priority has meant that little has been achieved.

The broader education of workers (paragraphs 274–5)

In its evidence to the committee, the TUC stated that many people are brought into contact with adult learning programmes and possibilities by becoming involved in trade union education and training. The committee endorsed this point and recommended that providing bodies and the trade union movement should work together to strengthen the links between trade union education and training and the general provision of adult learning opportunities for 'industrial workers'. In this context, the committee drew attention to the extent to which the particular needs of 'women in industry' were not being met. The contrasting references to 'industrial workers' and 'women in industry' indicate the nature of the employment and economic scene in the early 1970s. It was to change so dramatically within a short time. There were some training opportunities for small numbers of women. Nevertheless, the committee observed that access to general education in working time for women was virtually non-existent. Particular concern was expressed by the committee about the position of working mothers for whom it was often impossible to find the time outside working hours for their own chosen personal and intellectual development through organised adult learning programmes. Providers were urged to seek the support of employers in developing programmes during the normal working day. At this period, there was no such successful model as the later UNISON 'Return to Learn' scheme (Kennedy, 1995) to which the committee might refer. Yet despite such initiatives, the development of broad learning opportunities for both men and women workers continued to lag behind provision for shop steward training throughout the period under consideration.

Education for retirement and for occupational change (paragraph 276)

Paragraphs 34–40 of the report set out the thoughts of the committee on 'Changes in Patterns of Work and Leisure'. Looking ahead to likely changes, the committee repeated the then common forecast, most of which was correct:

> Demand for skills of many kinds, including ever new kinds, is expected to increase steeply with consequent requirements for training and re-training; but the place of the unskilled labourer is diminishing. Many people are thought likely to move from production to service employment, for among other things the growth of leisure will add to the demand for services; but such employments often involve a direct personal and moral relationship between worker and client, and there will be a need for education of a kind that fosters inter-personal skills. (paragraph 34)

Yet it was to be the return to mass unemployment in the late 1970s and 1980s, rather than the recommendations of the Russell Report, which led to action by government on training and retraining issues. Education for occupational change became a growing element of adult learning programmes during the 1970s and 1980s, due largely to the commitment of government funds to work-related education and training and programmes for unemployed adults. Much of this provision was made by organisations other than LEAs, universities and the WEA. This aspect of adult learning in the post-Russell period is discussed in Chapters 7 and 8.

Having made the general point about the link between learning and changes in people's life-patterns, the committee showed its concern to set preparation for retirement within the totality of adult learning, establishing the relationship between that part of life dominated to a great degree by the need to obtain, secure and retain paid work on a regular and continuing basis and life as a whole. The committee recognised the value of pre-retirement learning as advocated, encouraged and facilitated by the Pre-Retirement Association (PRA). The particular difficulties faced by small firms in providing opportunities for staff to be released for sessions prior to their retirement dates were noted in the report. Within less than ten years of the publication of the report, the employment scene had changed so dramatically and disturbingly that many employees, at all levels in industry and commerce, were faced with unexpected redundancy or early retirement at short notice with no opportunity to participate in any form of planned and structured programme of preparation for retirement learning. Ironically, and worryingly, those in employment worked, on average, a longer working week than their opposite numbers on the continent of Europe, despite the increase in unemployment. This was at a time when a reducing number of workers enjoyed job security. Such problems were viewed in the 1980s as issues to be solved by 'market forces' rather than an approach that stressed the ethical responsibilities of both employers and government. The latter approach emerged to prominence during the 1990s in debates about the social policy to be pursued by the EU.

Adult education and the disadvantaged (paragraph 277–85)

Thirty years after publication, terminology employed in the report may now be considered in some respects dated and even inappropriate. However, in considering the recommendations of the committee, years after they were written, attention should not be diverted from issues of principle and policy to a discussion about semantics and the ever-changing language. A discourse of social inclusion or human rights does not necessarily result in more government action or professional commitment than a discourse of disadvantage. 'Disadvantage' was taken to apply to people who, for whatever reason, 'cannot easily take part in adult education as normally provided'. The study conducted by the Research Assistant to the committee identified a wide variety of learning needs (Clyne, 1972). It confirmed the widely held opinion that employing general words, like 'disadvantaged' or 'deprived', did not offer sufficient guidance as to the nature of learning opportunities required by groups and individuals, and increasingly provided both within and outside the mainstream of adult learning provision.

Suitably designed, structured and delivered learning programmes were called for by the committee for the many people excluded from social and community life by virtue of their disadvantage. Increased collaboration between education bodies and voluntary and statutory health, welfare, housing and social services was recommended in the report. This collaboration was thought to be essential in recognition of the fact that, very frequently, meeting the learning needs of some groups and individuals called for experience, knowledge and under-standing unlikely to be found in an adult learning organisations alone. Such organisations were likely to have white staff, to be headed by male senior staff and to have few, if any, disabled or disadvantaged people in decision-making positions. Following the conclusions of the research study, the committee identified 'the test of disadvantage . . . to be the extent to which such integration into active society is prevented' by a number of factors (paragraph 279):

- personal capacity (including physical and mental conditions)
- social disadvantage (including geographical isolation, poverty and social deprivation)
- educational disadvantage (including the lack of basic education, sensory impairment and lack of English language).

The committee acknowledged that the three factors interact and overlap. For example, an adult with a physical disability might also live in poverty and have been prevented from participating fully in initial education.

Specific action was recommended by the committee (paragraph 280.1–280.4):

- Provision for individuals and groups with particular learning needs consequent upon their identifiable disadvantage. It was thought that, at times, these people could be accommodated in general programmes and courses with additional support. For others, separate and special provision would be necessary.
- Training for staff working in an educational context with excluded and/or disadvantaged people.
- Educating the public about exclusion and disadvantage. For this important aspect of adult learning, the committee stressed the potential contribution of the mass media.

- Training and orientation of people supporting those with particular learning needs. The committee had in mind family members, employers and work colleagues, and carers.

The committee recognised and commented on the particular importance of mental stimulus and activity for older people, many of whom were likely to find themselves increasingly lonely and on the margins of society. Adult learning opportunities often provided older people with significant social as well as educational benefit and contributed greatly to enhancing the dignity of older people in their families, neighbourhoods and communities. Greater acknowledgement of the learning needs of older people and their requirement for easier access to facilities and programmes was evident in the work of many providers after the publication of the report. A particular challenge to adult learning provision, which could not have been foreseen by the Russell Committee or by ACACE, was the rapid incorporation of use of the Internet into learning programmes for groups and individuals. Much of this growth has taken place outside the period covered by this book. Development of much teaching and learning outside and inside formal school and college programmes has depended on access to the Internet. Office of National Statistics data indicate that the proportion of households with access to the Internet in the UK was 10 per cent in 1998, rising rapidly to 46 per cent in 2002 but then stabilising. By the beginning of 2003, 95 per cent of people aged 16–24 years had accessed the Internet but only 15 per cent of people aged 65 years of age and over had ever done so. The gap between younger and older adults has been widening since such data were first collected and analysed, while the proportion of older people in the total population has been growing and their desire and proven ability to learn for their own benefit and the advantage of others have also been growing.

Just as the gaps between the younger and older in society, however defined, widened as the years passed by, so it was evident at the time of Russell, and continues to be the case, that the gaps between the 'haves' and 'have nots', however defined, have also widened. This is the sense in which the report employed the word 'disadvantage'. In *The Disadvantaged Adult* (Clyne, 1972, p. 127), the present author argued that: 'Adult education is an essential service which, as a community provision, seeks to offer men and women the opportunity to improve their physical and mental welfare. In this way, as the personal satisfactions of individuals increase, so the quality of community life generally will improve.' Yet it was also clear that certain individuals and, in some instances, groups have particular needs and make particular demands. Thus providing a service for the whole community meant taking account of difference: 'Disadvantaged adults do not form a uniform group, identified by their common difference from the norm, however normality may be defined. Each minority group, within a wider category of the disadvantaged, expresses particular demands and makes apparent specific needs' (p. 128). The conclusion was that, 'The efficient administration and organisation of an adult education service depends upon many varied organisations and individuals. Co-operation and consultation is essential before the specific needs of disadvantaged adults can be recognised and met. Adequate provision may depend on joint staffing and/or joint financing between departments of a local authority or between statutory and voluntary bodies' (p. 134). Yet provision and facilities for disadvantaged adults, despite the instances of good practice recorded, were shown to be patchy. In response to a circulated questionnaire from the committee's Research Assistant, one disarmingly frank Chief Education Officer stated, 'I have to inform you that no special provision is made on the education side for the people you describe though, of course, their health and welfare is the concern of the County Borough Health Department.' The extent to which provision increased and improved in the years after 1973, in response to the report and its recommendations, is outlined in Chapters 7 and 8.

Second chance: adult access to qualification (paragraphs 286–99)

Courses variously titled Second Chance, New Horizons and New Opportunities for Women (NOW) were established in the 1960s and 1970s by LEA establishments, WEA branches and universities. At the time the report was written, the term 'Second Chance' was taken to be both acceptable and accurate as an indication of the purpose of the course. Such courses increased in number during the 1970s, by when it was freely acknowledged that, far from offering second chances to many students, the courses were, in fact, offering a first chance. For a multiplicity of reasons, large numbers of adults had not achieved what they hoped for as teenagers or young adults, or the school system had failed to accommodate their individual needs. It was not universally accepted that courses to prepare adults for higher level study or to test their capacity to undertake advanced study, fell within adult education as defined for the purpose of the committee's remit. The committee asserted that such courses and such aims and intentions 'formed a valid and important part of adult education' (paragraphs 286–7). Access courses, in their various forms, increased greatly in number during the middle to late 1970s and in the early 1980s. Some courses were of a general nature. Some were linked directly with designated higher education establishments and offered guaranteed entry to those completing the access courses. Certain courses were designed specifically with the needs of women in mind. Others were targeted towards ethnic minority communities. ILEA, through the development of Open Colleges covering all 12 boroughs of inner London and the City of London, was in the vanguard of this growth.

Flexibility and creativity were the watchwords for the committee in setting out its recommendations calling for further work on reviewing the examination systems and the unnecessary rigidity of the full-time requirement for most higher education courses. The committee also urged universities and polytechnics to consider ways of introducing a credit transfer procedure and the possibility of combined courses with the OU. Such flexibility would assist mature adults, whose commitments often extended across home and work, in addition to their commitment to the study upon which they were embarking. These recommendations were designed to increase accessibility and acceptability. For many individual adult educators and staff teams, the Russell recommendations gave the necessary impetus to bring about creative change. Initiatives designed to introduce Accreditation of Prior Experiential Learning (APEL) and Credit Accumulation and Transfer Schemes (CATS) were indicative of greater flexibility in the system. APEL established the means of recognising and respecting adult learning wherever and however it takes place: in the home, at work or in the community. CATS acknowledged the fact that the mobility of adults, often for family reasons, means that study started in one place may have to be completed in another.

Student support (paragraphs 300–6)
The committee acknowledged that many adult students, at different times and in different circumstances, may require financial support to meet the costs of residential or correspondence courses, travel, textbooks and other materials. With the aim of ensuring that adult students would be treated no less favourably than young people leaving full-time initial education, the report recommended that changes should take place in arrangements for student support. Having made the general point that adults should be entitled to 'the necessary financial assistance' during periods of full-time or part-time study (paragraph 300), the committee recommended that students accepted on one-year or two-year courses at long-term residential colleges should be entitled to mandatory awards. As implementation of such a recommendation would require a change in the applicable legislation, the report recommended that the government should establish interim arrangements until legislative changes could be made. The interim arrangements would take the form of funding being channelled through the existing local authority funding system. The government accepted this recommendation. A further recommendation was that the number of State Scholarships for Mature Students should increase to ensure that each and every mature adult completing a course at a long-term residential college and transferring to an undergraduate course would receive a scholarship.

Students' contributions (paragraphs 308–14)
Having considered the case, the committee was not persuaded that student contributions (fees) should be abolished. It was thought that such a proposal

would be politically and financially unacceptable to the government. Unlike schoolchildren, the majority of adult students would have disposable income from which they could reasonably be expected to pay fees or contributions. The committee considered, but rejected, the case for charging students the full economic costs of their courses. Advocates of this case asserted that adult learning should be regarded as a luxury for which consumers should pay in full, unless the potential students were found to be totally dependent on low fixed incomes derived from pensions or benefits. Correspondence between Cabinet Ministers, discussed in Chapter 5, indicates the strength of this political view in the Conservative Government in 1973/4. By contrast, the committee regarded 'adult education as an important social service and an integral part of the educational system which it is entirely legitimate to subsidise from public funds, both national and local' (paragraph 311).

'Fees' was not an attractive word to the committee, which preferred to think in terms of 'contributions', indicating that no student should be expected to meet the total cost of the teaching and tuition made available. The committee suggested two general points to guide providers in determining the cost to students. First:

> Adult education should be readily available to all who wish to take advantage of it: therefore, student contributions should be set at such a level as would not discourage any significant number or category of people from making use of the provision and special arrangements should be made for those who might be deprived of the opportunity to attend classes because of their inability to pay. (paragraph 312.1)

Second, all areas of study should be considered of equal worth and opportunities should be available for minority interests to be studied. There should be no hierarchy of subjects or levels of study delineated by the level of contribution called for from the students.

In the years following publication of the report, due to the lack of strong guidance from central government and the very different policies of providers, the level of student contribution set varied considerably from place to place for the same or similar courses of study. As will be noted in Chapters 7 and 8, governments in the post-Russell years did not accept the recommendation of the committee that all areas of study should be considered of equal worth. A hierarchy of study areas, giving precedence to qualification-bearing courses and work-related training, was introduced. Students were expected to make greater contributions towards the cost of courses that were deemed to support their leisure and cultural interests, rather than improve their position in the labour market.

Accommodation and equipment (paragraphs 315–31); Building programme (paragraphs 332–9); Resources (paragraphs 342–54)

The 20 recommendations listed under these three sub-headings ranged from the very general to the very specific. The committee was concerned that much adult learning was taking place in inappropriate accommodation, often backed with inadequate or insufficient equipment and support resources. Nevertheless, an apparent paradox was outlined in the report, indicating that much of the expansion in adult learning programmes evident in the 1950s and 1960s had been 'conducted in premises likely to deter rather than attract potential students' (paragraph 316). The expansion in programmes was due to the increase in interest in adult learning aroused by greater use of the media for provision and publicity, development of community school and community college projects, growth of learning in the community and the expansion of work-based and work-related learning for those in employment. In addition to maximising the use of existing educational premises, mainly schools and some colleges, adult learning providers were urged to seek ways of delivering learning programmes and activities in premises conveniently located from the point of view of potential students. Greater use of community halls and centres, village halls, libraries, museums and galleries was to be encouraged. Not only was the provision of more and better accommodation recommended by the committee, but the need for greater provision of suitable childcare premises for young children was identified to enable young mothers, in particular, to join classes during the mornings or afternoons.

The DES and local authorities were urged to be more attentive to the needs of adult students when considering building programmes, minor works funding allocations and equipment allowances. At the same time, providers of adult learning were expected to be sensitive to the problems arising from the dual use of buildings and teaching spaces and the additional wear and tear costs of equipment, cleaning and maintenance. In every area, there should be a designated centre for adult learning in which classes and other activities promoted by universities, WEA and other bodies might take place alongside provision by the LEA. This recommendation largely arose from the well-argued evidence submitted by the Association for Adult Education (AAE). Indeed, Howard Gilbert, one of the leading members of the AAE at the time, Principal of the North Havering College of Adult Education and a member of ACACE from 1977 to 1983, has advanced the opinion to the present author in a letter of June 2002, that 'the key finding for adult education organisation from Russell was the proposal for effective Centres'. He remains of the view that the Russell recommendation regarding area centres gave the necessary impetus and encouragement to imaginative individuals in many parts of the country, in educational arrangements as different as adult education institutes, colleges of further education and arts centres to establish multi-faceted learning centres for adults, often modelled on the community-based and community-managed settlements of the late nineteenth and early twentieth centuries. In the years following Russell, this concept was moved forward by the ECA.

The committee recommended that aids to learning for adults, including audio-visual equipment and books, should be more widely available. Library, museum and gallery authorities should be enabled to increase their contribution of books and other resources to assist the teaching and learning processes. This plea for course programmes to be appropriately located in suitable and accessible premises, supported with equipment and facilities designed and provided for adult learning, did not meet with a positive response in most areas of the country. Accommodation newly made available for the exclusive use of adult learners was likely to be unimproved or unsuitable rooms or buildings declared surplus to the requirements of schools. Funds were not generally made available to improve and equip premises for adult use. Adult learners were not given the consideration recommended by the committee. The picture was not uniformly bleak. There were exceptions. The committee's recommendations gave the necessary impetus to some LEAs to improve and adapt existing buildings, or to establish purpose-designed, well furnished and well equipped centres, including the Sutton College of Liberal Arts and the Longford Street Centre for the Central London Adult Education Institute.

Staff (paragraphs 355–417); General local education authority staff (paragraphs 356–78); Administrative and advisory staff (paragraphs 379–80); Ancillary staff (paragraphs 381–4); Staff of other major providing bodies (paragraphs 385–94); Part-time staff (paragraphs 395–402); Training (paragraphs 403–17)

The committee viewed staffing as a crucial issue. Indeed, the first of the 25 recommendations concerning staffing was: 'The provision of staff of good quality, in sufficient numbers, with the necessary training and wisely and economically deployed is critical to all the developments in adult education which we recommend and should be regarded as the first priority' (paragraph 355). Employers of adult learning staff had applied whatever part-time and full-time salary arrangements and scales they chose. Sometimes existing national scales were applied or adapted to meet local circumstances. In some areas and organisations, locally determined salary levels were defined and applied. With regard to LEA staffing, the committee recommended that the Burnham Further Education Committee, responsible for determining appropriate scales for full-time principals and other professional teaching staff, should review the salaries of those employed in the LEA adult learning sector. Such a review should also provide the basis for an assessment of the components and levels of salary for part-time teaching staff in LEA adult learning. LEAs were urged to appoint sufficient administrative, advisory and ancillary staff. For universities, the WEA and other major bodies providing adult learning programmes and employing staff for the purposes of organising and delivering the programmes, the committee recommended that the DES should grant-aid programme providers in respect of such posts. This grant should be in addition to the grant for direct teaching staff salaries.

Staff training was seen by the committee to be a critical matter for all providers. It recommended that the changing needs for training should be constantly reviewed by all bodies involved in adult learning: the DES nationally, each Local Development Council and providing bodies individually and collectively. The successful completion of training, coupled with an assessment of the levels of teaching and learning and the specialist nature of some minority learning activities, should make it possible to offer salary enhancement for certain individuals. Newly appointed 'heads of area adult education organisations' should have the opportunity to attend full-time training for which they should be released on full pay during normal working hours.

The number of full-time organising and teaching posts increased greatly in the 1970s, particularly in the LEA sector. However, nationally, there were comparatively few ancillary and support staff appointed and very few new development workers employed to liaise with other agencies and community organisations to create new programmes in new locations. ILEA was determined to build on the already strong teams of staff located in the area adult education institutes and central support units. During the 1970s, it led the way in terms of the expansion in the number of staff and the special responsibilities of the staff. In addition to the growth in the number of subject organisers and teachers, by creating development posts including community education and outreach workers, specialist staff to work with parents and families, media resources officers and technicians, the authority displayed its commitment to adult learning as an element of a comprehensive education service. In response to the staffing recommendations, many providers of adult learning programmes and specialist organisations increased the range and volume of training opportunities. There was no uniform pattern to the training nor was it universally available. Some providers paid their part-time employees for time spent participating in training courses. Others did not. Some offered training in-house. Others commissioned training from universities and other bodies.

Statistics (paragraphs 418–25)

Available statistics in respect of adult learning provision by the WEA, universities and long-term residential colleges were found to be entirely unhelpful to the committee in its work. The DES figures in respect of LEA provision were quite inadequate, being both incomplete and inaccurate. For the major providers, other than the LEAs, comprehensive data were required for the purposes of calculating the annual grant. The report set out, in some detail, the issues arising from the fact that available statistics were neither complete nor consistently recorded (paragraphs 421–4). In the judgement of the committee (paragraph 420), essential fields of information comprised:

- the numbers of students in classes provided respectively by the LEAs, universities and WEA
- the numbers of academic staff employed by these bodies, in different categories
- the types of courses offered by these bodies within broad categories.

The Russell Committee lacked information about the size and make-up of the student population, the range and nature of the courses followed and the extent and manner of the movement of students from course to course and level to level. In conjunction with ACACE, NIAE undertook a comprehensive nation-wide survey of participation in adult learning. From the late 1970s, comparative statistics became available. Yet information on progression routes remained difficult to obtain. For example, the degree to which adult students have used liberal and non-vocational courses as a springboard towards vocational, professional and qualification-bearing education and training remains largely unknown. Anecdotal and incidental small-scale information has proved of interest and, often, convincing to professionals, but less compelling to those responsible for making decisions about the allocation of resources to adult learning.

The committee confirmed the experience of the Pre-school Playgroups Association, repeated in the work of the EPA teams following the Plowden Report's conclusions: parents who participated in adult learning programmes were likely to increase their interest in and influence on the education of their children. The social and civic value of adult learning was clearly indicated. As an element of neighbourhood and community work with residents of an outer Liverpool housing estate, the present author managed a number of small-scale surveys which were used for multidisciplinary staff training purposes but not published. Having sought to record the experiences, attitudes and behaviour of two sets of residents, one of which had participated in adult learning courses and the other had not, a clear set of differences emerged, despite the fact that in all other respects the two sets of residents were similar. These differences indicated that residents who attended courses on a regular basis, and undertook the course work conscientiously, were more likely than the other group to pay their rent on time, support their children's school activities, including attendance at parents' evenings, and participate in local voluntary and community activities. In addition, they were likely to visit doctors' surgeries and hospital outpatients' departments less frequently than those who were not attending courses.

The National Institute of Adult Education (NIAE) [since 1983, the National Institute of Adult Continuing Education (NIACE)] (paragraphs 426–30)

While recognising the important work undertaken by NIAE since its creation in 1949 as a result of a merger between the National Foundation of Adult Education and the British Institute of Adult Education, the committee judged that the role and the contribution of NIAE could and should be considerably enhanced. To this effect, it was recommended that the DES and NIAE should agree a five-year development programme, the initial funding of which would be undertaken by the DES. Suggested areas of expansion included: enabling the institute library to develop into a major library, archive and resource centre containing material from other countries and international organisations as well as domestic information; increasing the range and size of the programme of conferences and seminars; regular surveys of take-up and participation and one-off focused enquiries; a wide range of general and specialist publications and additional journals; and an abstracting service to enable practitioners, researchers and others to gain access to adult learning literature, current thinking and practice in other parts of the world. Over the years following the publication of the Russell Report, and with an impetus driven by the work and legacy of ACACE, NIACE expanded considerably in size, scope of workload and impact on the national and international adult learning scene.

5

What happened next? How was the report received?

I have arranged for the immediate publication of this Report because of the importance of the subject, and the great interest with which the Report is awaited, particularly by the organisations directly concerned with adult education. The Report makes many recommendations of considerable importance which will need to be studied very carefully by the government and by the many other interests concerned.

The educational world owes a debt of gratitude to Sir Lionel Russell and his colleagues who have carried out such a thorough and comprehensive study of adult education in a changing society.

(Margaret Thatcher, Secretary of State for Education and Science
in the Foreword to the published Russell Report, 1973)

The post-Russell context

The amount of time and detailed attention devoted by providing bodies, professional associations, voluntary organisations and students to the report confirmed the importance attached to it. There was the hope and, indeed, expectation that, following acceptance by the government of most, if not all, of the recommendations, future arrangements for adult learning would be much improved. The present author, having been closely associated with the work of the committee and personally involved in much of the follow-up activity documented in this book, remains convinced that the report was a significant and forward-looking document, in tune with a practical assessment of the political and financial realities of the time. Many creative initiatives and positive changes, launched in the years following 1973, were directly linked to the report, its commentary and recommendations.

The 1919 Report, in tune with contemporary thinking, was based on the premise that adult learning should be seen as a movement for change with a social purpose – a movement not a service. This fundamental aim influenced much thinking about adult learning throughout the twentieth century. Consideration of the Russell Report and its impact on the shape of adult learning provision took account of the motives of individuals and the broader interests of society as discussed in the report. Adults pursue learning for a variety of reasons, including personal ambition, need, aspirations and dreams. Simultaneously, policy makers and major providers will be motivated by the need to strive for equity in society and for the broad acceptance of liberal values within a framework of citizenship and social responsibility. The report's argument that adult learning alone cannot deliver the desired changes was generally accepted. Adult learning plans, programmes and policies are most effective when advanced in conjunction with a wide range of community services and activities, private and public.

Writing in *The Guardian* on 5 July 2002, Polly Toynbee discussed the social and economic changes of the previous 25 years, in the light of the national 'Social Trends' statistics published in 2002. She noted that: 'A healthier nation is living longer. A richer country has more foreign holidays, lap-tops, mobiles, multi-channel TVs.' She concluded that 'the 1977 mass working class, with two-thirds of the people in blue-collar jobs, had shrunk to one-third, while the rest migrated upwards into a 70 per cent home-owning, white-collar middle class'. Yet 1977 was the year that Britain was more equal in how income was shared than at any time in its history. Since 1977, we have gone backwards. The widening gap between the 'haves' and the 'have nots' has become increasingly evident. Much as her predecessors in the early years of the twentieth century argued, Toynbee called for an adult learning movement with a social purpose, striving to achieve social change. Arguments and debates have continued about the extent to which publicly funded adult learning programmes should be instrumental in intention.

The government response to the report

The encouraging words of Margaret Thatcher's Foreword to the Russell Report sat uncomfortably next to the dismissive treatment of adult learning in the White Paper *Education: A Framework for Expansion* (DES, 1972a). This was published in the same month, December 1972, in which the Russell Report was submitted to the Secretary of State. Thatcher's White Paper was designed to be a development plan for education with an emphasis on five government designated priorities: nursery education; school building; staffing in schools; teacher training; and higher education. Given that the Secretary of State would have been briefed on the likely conclusions and recommendations of the Russell Report as the White Paper was being drafted, it was a major disappointment to those awaiting Russell to read the comments on adult learning in the White Paper. There was only one specific, and entirely inadequate, reference to adult education:

> 'Adult Education' recalls first and foremost the pioneering efforts of the Workers' Educational Association, the extra-mural boards and the residen-

tial colleges to expand the opportunity for university education to working men and women. Its boundaries, however, have been so enlarged by subsequent work of local education authorities and others as to make it almost coterminous with a large part of 'further education'. The government propose to give it careful study in the light of the forthcoming report of the Committee on Adult Education which was appointed in 1969 under Sir Lionel Russell's chairmanship thoroughly to review the whole field. (paragraph 104)

On 25 January 1973, a few weeks after the Russell Report was submitted to Margaret Thatcher and two months before it was published, the Prime Minister, Edward Heath, addressed a meeting of the Society of Education Officers (SEO). The SEO was the professional body to which LEA Chief Education Officers belonged. John Henry was a member of the Russell Committee and a senior member of the SEO. He would have briefed his SEO colleagues on the contents of the report. Similarly, the contents of the report would have been known to the Prime Minister's office. Heath's speech was positive and encouraging. At one point, he diverted from his prepared text to stress the importance of embracing permanent education, actually using the French term, *éducation permanente*. He made clear that his support for adult learning derived as much from his personal experience as from educational or political judgement. His listeners, and those who read reports of the speech or the speech itself, were left with the impression that the Heath government would support the reasonable and realistic recommendations of the report. The year 1973, however, was to prove a rocky year for public services, including adult learning. The government called for restraint across all services and urgent and immediate budget cuts in certain areas of provision. Regrettably, Heath's fine words counted for nothing when budget, policy and priority decisions were taken in the months ahead. Nevertheless, it is worth being reminded of some of his observations as an indication of his good intent:

> Now, as never before in the past, individuals are able to contribute to society their own special gifts – be they intellectual, artistic or practical – thereby bringing something unique into the world. I often think of this when I am enjoying the two leisure activities which most appeal to me, namely music and sailing.
>
> Not long ago, these were both activities confined in practice to a small minority with the time and the money which were then required to enjoy them . . . but today music and sailing are simply examples of a wide variety of activities, which include drama, art, literature, languages and sport, to name but a few, all of which are available through our local education authority provision to the man (sic) in the street.

There are two final thoughts which come immediately to mind once we begin to reflect seriously on education and society in modern Britain.

The first is that it is becoming increasingly absurd to think of education as a process which stops at the age of 16, or 18 or 22. Indeed, the more we improve the methods and the institutions for educating the young, the greater the need, and the demand, for continuing education later on.

The massive expansion of further education, now enjoyed by nearly four million students, shows that substantial provision already exists. The development of the Open University, for example, shows that it is possible to take quite new initiatives: I was particularly pleased to note the successes of its first graduates. Our post-school education system is already a powerful and flexible one. We must use it to the full . . .

Immediately following the publication of the Russell Report on 27 March 1973, the pressure for a much-needed, supportive and early acceptance of the report and its recommendations by the Conservative Government was considerable. Organisations and individuals, many of whom had submitted evidence to the committee, lobbied Members of Parliament (MPs) and ministers. Spirits were raised and then dashed in turn as the spring and summer of 1973 passed.

In a House of Commons debate on 10 April 1973, Norman St John Stevas, Under-Secretary of State for Education and Science with the brief for adult learning, commented encouragingly: 'We are entering into a situation in which education will and must continue throughout life . . . it is meeting a moral crisis not by negative prescription but by seeking to provide positive good for people's minds and thoughts.' Within a few weeks, the government had announced expenditure cuts in response to the world oil crisis. During a May 1973 debate in the House of Lords, Lord Belstead, Parliamentary Secretary, said, in reply to a plea for government action on the recommendations of the Russell Report, 'I cannot, at this point in time, give your Lordships answers to the recommendations in the report; and I am bound to say that I am not entirely convinced that it would be desirable.' Lord (Edward) Boyle, previously Conservative Secretary of State for Education and Science, at the time Vice-Chancellor of the University of Leeds, contributed to the debate and urged the government to act: 'The money is small.'

In its first issue on 30 March 1973 following publication of the report, *Education* carried the banner headline 'Russell – it's realistic, so why not apply it?' In the same issue, Sir William Alexander (elder statesman of LEA work and ex-editor of *Education*) made a number of strongly supportive observations on the report's recommendations, including endorsing the proposals that there should be a centre for advice and help in each LEA area, that adult education should equip people to earn a living 'but, perhaps more importantly; to equip them to live fuller lives and play their part in their community'. This was again an echo of the 1919 Report. Alexander had been a member of the Planning

Committee of the OU (1967–9). He continued by asserting that participants in adult learning programmes should be full participants in the control and management of those programmes. Addressing a conference of the East Midlands Institute of Adult Education soon after publication of the report, Vic Feather, General Secretary of the Trades Union Congress, endorsed much of the report and urged action by the government and others 'to remedy the lack of opportunity for personal satisfactions experienced by most working people'. He called for a statutory duty to be placed on LEAs, to include an obligation to assist 'recognised voluntary bodies' in financial and other ways.

Elsdon *et al.* (2001) suggest that 'the failure to press on to a quick completion and publication of the Russell Report, before it could fall victim to political change following the defeat of the first Wilson government' was a critical mistake. This is an unrealistic and unreasonable hindsight judgement. It would not have been possible for the committee to have completed its work, produced and submitted its report to the Secretary of State and for her to have had time to persuade the Cabinet to put through the necessary legislation and make decisions on funding, all within a matter of 12 months. The committee was appointed in 1969. The general election, bringing a change of government, took place in 1970. Elsdon, sounding a note of desperation bordering on resignation, commented that: 'Publication [of the report], in practice, marked the end of a period of hope and expansion for adult education, and not the dawn of a new and happier era which its initiation had seemed to inaugurate.' Roger Fieldhouse *et al.* (1996) have argued, with little more enthusiasm, for a restrained acknowledgement of the usefulness of the report in writing:

Nevertheless, despite the Report's limitations and the failure to support its recommendations with a modest increase in public expenditure, it did help to re-focus adult education, encouraging it to concentrate once more on socially committed, political work with disadvantaged groups, and to devote more resources and energy to the needs of the 'adult education untouchables' (sic).

Anne Corbett (1978), at the time a leading education journalist, wrote later of the report 'as a mountain which had laboured long and brought forth an over-weight mouse, the Russell Report was not able to escape the slur of being altogether too modest'. In their wish to appear to be alongside impatient critics, seeking a radical and immediate change in the world order, some commentators lost sight of realities. The Russell Committee saw the report as a call for change and improvement, despite the known limitations and restrictions inhibiting early action. Negotiations for membership of the European Common Market, the world oil crisis, budget cuts at central and local government levels and planned reorganisation of local government to take place in 1974 were all challenges to the UK government. They were among many reasons why the title of the report, *Adult Education: A Plan for Development*, was a fair indication of how the report should be used. It proved to suit its purpose. The report and its recommendations formed an invaluable reference document and a guide to change, whenever the time was more propitious than it was in 1973. Eventually the challenge of modernising social and economic structures would have to be met, and adult learning would be a key tool in that process. The report transcended the immediate constraints of the time of its publication.

In March 1973, shortly before the publication of the report, the Secretary of State submitted a paper to the Cabinet Home and Social Affairs Committee (HSAC) alerting her Cabinet colleagues to its impending arrival and suggesting a subdued government response to its expected contents and recommendations. This was consistent with the language employed in the brief reference to adult learning in the White Paper, *Education: A Framework for Expansion*, quoted earlier in this chapter. Although the White Paper did not purport to cover all aspects and phases of education in equal detail, it was illuminating and disappointing to people awaiting the publication of the report to learn of the government's partial, unhelpful and belittling view of what constituted adult education and that it did not feature among the government's priorities.

However, within little over four months, Margaret Thatcher's view of the report and adult education generally seems to have changed. On 27 July 1973, she wrote to Robert Carr, the then Home Secretary who chaired the HSAC, stating that she intended to bring a paper to a meeting of the Cabinet Committee due to be held in the early autumn of 1973. She copied her letter to all members of the HSAC. In the letter she fairly reflected the general view about the Russell Report:

> The document is, in many ways, conventional and moderate; and there has been widespread public pressure for its implementation. The strength and unanimity of support in the educational world has been exceptional; indeed the only area of debate has been whether the report's proposals go far enough.

She continued by reminding her Cabinet colleagues that she was 'publicly committed to consultation with the local authorities and other main interests in this field and it would be difficult and undesirable to delay beyond the autumn'. She expressed her conviction 'that consultation should take place on the basis of a more constructive and imaginative stance by the government' than was implied in her earlier paper to the HSAC.

Using terms that would have been welcomed by adult educators at the time, had they known of the exchanges between the Secretary of State and her Cabinet colleagues, Margaret Thatcher made a number of further observations:

I believe that here there are very real opportunities for social benefit and an improvement in the quality of life as well as for credit and goodwill to the Government . . . I shall therefore wish to come to Committee with proposals for a forward-looking consultative document based on a commitment to both qualitative and quantitative development of existing provision and a firm lead from the Government.

Referring to the local authorities and other providers of adult learning programmes and services, she wrote: 'I would need to be able to assure them that, if they responded to my initiative, the necessary additional resources would be forthcoming.' As a separate point in the same letter, Margaret Thatcher commented on the implications of the UK's membership of the then European Economic Community (EEC), now the EU, and asserted unequivocally: 'Moreover, there is no doubt that our membership of the EEC will progressively involve central government in a much more dynamic attitude towards this area of education; all our developing contacts in the European setting illustrate the strength of the present preoccupation with "permanent education" and "recurrent education".'

In contrast to the positive and progressive tone and language adopted by Margaret Thatcher, the response she received to her letter from Patrick Jenkin, Chief Secretary to the Treasury, was both cold and dismissive. His retort, copied to all members of HSAC, foreshadowed Prime Minister Thatcher's own posture, words and actions of the early 1980s, when he wrote in his letter of 1 August 1973:

I must say at once that I am dismayed that you are contemplating any addition, even a minor one, to the programme for public expenditure on this service. Surely adult education does not have the sort of social priority which would justify a further increase in public expenditure at a time when we are actively seeking savings?

He reminded the Secretary of State that, at the March 1973 meeting of the HSAC, he had said:

Adult education was a field where there might be good grounds for looking to those who used the service to pay a substantial contribution towards the cost of providing it, perhaps by way of a succession of phased increases in fees. I am sure that we should consider the scope for self-financing before we contemplate any further expansion of this service.

Margaret Thatcher's reaction to the letter from Patrick Jenkin was short and to the point. Having read the letter, she noted on 3 August 1973 for her Private

Office staff: 'Advice please – the Treasury seem to be getting somewhat hysterical.' Having received the advice she had sought, she wrote again to Patrick Jenkin on 10 August 1973, copying it to all members of the committee. In an effort to keep the temperature down, she opened her letter by saying: 'I find it difficult to understand why my letter of 27 July should have aroused such alarm at the Treasury.' She admitted to having modified her previously held view on the 'scale of the response we should make to the Russell Report, but this is not surprising since important new evidence is now available, in the shape of the strong and widespread public reaction in favour of the report, and I must clearly take this into account'. While accepting the financial restrictions and disciplines placed on spending departments by previously taken Cabinet decisions to seek reductions in public expenditure, she, nonetheless, was clear that if the government were to merely provide for a continuation of funding for adult education at the same level, it would not have been seen to have responded adequately to a report calling for modest growth. She concluded, 'we must instead respond more positively to the report's main recommendations'.

Eventually, a paper headed 'A Policy for Adult Education' was presented to the HSAC by Margaret Thatcher on 7 December 1973. In the paper, she argued that, by stretching the report's suggested timetable for growth to some 12 years instead of the seven years recommended in the report, the financial impact would be less and would be seen to be acceptable to the government and its supporters. Nonetheless, she repeated her conviction that

> . . . the Government should take an imaginative and constructive approach to the Report. This conviction results from a more detailed appraisal of the Report in the light of the strong and widespread support given to its recommendations by educational bodies and individuals; from Parliamentary pressure for their adoption; from my acceptance of the need to satisfy both the manifest and the latent demands for non-vocational adult education; and from my belief that the Report provides a good opportunity at very small extra cost for furthering one of the Government's main objectives – an improvement in the quality of life.

Therefore, she sought to persuade her Cabinet colleagues that she should enter consultations with the adult education organisations and local authorities indicating the government's acceptance 'of the report's major recommendations about the growth of the adult education service'. By this, she meant doubling the number of students between 1968/9 and 1981/2 and substantially increasing the number of full-time staff. She also proposed to double the government's contribution to adult education building programmes. While accepting that she was advocating growth in expenditure on adult education at a time of severe restraint imposed by the government, she argued that 'this increase in expenditure in an area of education which has received little support from successive governments is very modest compared with the savings I have offered to achieve in other areas'.

In her paper, she tackled the matter of fee increases as proposed by Patrick Jenkin in the HSAC meeting of March 1973 and repeated in his letter to her of 1 August 1973. While accepting that some increase of adult education fees might have proved acceptable, provided all further education fees were seen to be equally increased, she cautioned her colleagues to recognise that there is a point when increasing fees has a damaging effect on the service and its development. On the matter of finance generally, she clearly stated that it would be principally for the local authorities to use any extra resources according to their own local priorities. Therefore, it might well have been the case that her wishes would not have been implemented across the country in an even manner. Her final plea to Cabinet colleagues was to confirm her view that the cost of her proposals was modest but 'the minimum necessary for a strong and healthy service . . . to do less would invite strong and widespread criticism'.

Throughout the period of 12 months, between the publication of the report and the February 1974 election defeat of the Conservative Government, Thatcher's evident personal commitment to action was not generally known. Her commitment was not articulated in parliamentary debates nor in the platform statements from her ministerial team. Publication by the National Archive of some of the 1973 ministerial and Cabinet correspondence, in advance of the normal 30 years embargo, leads to the conclusion that adult learning has not been considered sufficiently important, in political terms, for disagreement between ministers to be maintained as confidential for as long as legally possible. Margaret Thatcher did not conduct her proposed consultation. The funds she had requested were not made available. It has been generally accepted that a principal reason why the necessary modest funding was not forthcoming was the oil crisis and consequent economic problems which hit the country at the end of March 1973, precisely when the report was published. It has also been suggested, by Fieldhouse et al. (1996), that the Treasury view that the extra funding for adult learning should be allocated to the OU in 1974, meant that no monies were to be available for other aspects of adult learning provision.

Universities Council for Adult Education (UCAE)

In common with many other organisations responding to the recommendations of the report, the Universities Council for Adult Education (UCAE) gave the report a general welcome but regretted the understatement of the need for additional resources for providing organisations. This point was given extra urgency in view of the ease with which Edward Heath, in his speech to the SEO on 25

January 1973, had made no reference to extra public funding when he said he would wish to see LEAs providing more learning opportunities for adults. The UCAE, WEA and TUC were all concerned that the report's recommendations did not sufficiently recognise that academic costs include more than tuition. Abandoning the concept of 'responsible body' and urging the DES to grant aid a wider range of institutions, as recommended in the report, was welcomed by the UCAE provided extra resources were made available.

Adult learning organisations became increasingly frustrated as the months passed after publication of the report. Whereas the government had promised to circulate a consultative document, no document appeared. Towards the end of 1973, NIAE, WEA and UCAE prepared a joint letter to the Secretary of State. The minutes of the UCAE Executive Committee meeting, held on 15 February 1974, reported that 'the Secretary of State had replied to the letter ... the reply seemed to imply that consultations would have taken place but for the General Election. In view of this, it was agreed that the matter should be taken up as soon as the election was over.' At the following meeting of the UCAE Executive Committee, held on 25 March 1974, it was minuted 'since the Election period was now over, it was agreed to write to the DES after Easter urging that consultations should now begin on the Russell Report'. Bearing in mind that more than one year had elapsed since the publication of the report, and that parliamentary debates had been held on the report and its recommendations some months previously, the expression of concern was mild in the extreme. Concern among adult educators that the report might be shelved, in view of the financial difficulties facing central and local government and, hence, most providers, led to demands for action being somewhat subdued.

The reception in Wales

Local government reorganisation in England and Wales took place one year after publication of the Russell Report. In an extended letter to the present author, Doug Jones, who had worked as the senior LEA officer responsible for adult education in the county of Glamorgan before reorganisation and, after the changes, in a similar post in the new Mid Glamorgan, explained the situation in Welsh LEAs from the point of view of an intimately involved committed enthusiast who made a lasting impact on the nature and quality of LEA provision. Arrival of the report at this time was a challenge for many LEAs in Wales and England. Reorganisation hindered 'its proper consideration and implementation'. One of the consequences of budget reductions in Mid Glamorgan and other LEAs in 1974 was that the appointment of full-time staff, already agreed by the planning committees for some of the new LEAs, and recommended by Russell, was 'abandoned'. Jones wrote:

It could be argued that had it [the Russell Report] been published two years earlier, it might have formed the basis of policies that could have been devised by the old authorities ready for implementation by their successors. Published two years later, it could have been used by the new authorities to plan their policies in a time of financial constraint and accelerating social and economic change . . . However, it did eventually prove to be a useful weapon in protecting the good practice and provision already in place, against determined attempts to trivialise and curtail adult education.

Tom Ellis MP, a member of the committee, prepared an addendum to the report giving particular attention to adult learning needs in Wales. This is considered further in Chapter 8.

Workers' Educational Association (WEA) and the Trades Union Congress (TUC)

The TUC had submitted written and oral evidence to the committee. At its conference in Blackpool, in September 1973, it expressed regret that the government had not responded to the report and its recommendations. In the conference debate and the associated conference papers, the TUC welcomed the report's observations on the WEA and the suggested priority areas for development of its work. It considered that additional funds should be made available to enable central and local government to give more support to providers. The proposed National Development Council was welcomed. However, the TUC did not see the need for Local Development Councils in each LEA area when strengthened Regional Advisory Councils could and should assume the proposed role and duties. Not surprisingly, the TUC regretted the weak references to paid educational leave and the absence of a strong recommendation on staff training and teaching materials for trade union education. The continuation of an obvious vocational/non-vocational division was strongly regretted.

Evidence submitted by the WEA had made a great impression on the committee members not only in respect of what the evidence said about the vision of the WEA for its own future but also in respect of the relationship between the WEA and other providers and organisations. At a WEA conference soon after publication of the report in 1973, Vic Feather, General Secretary of the TUC, urged the association to move forward with confidence. He argued that if the WEA did not exist, it would have to be invented. This was justified as more than simple public platform rhetoric by his further comments about the special and particular work of the WEA. In his view, it existed:

• to secure the future of working-class adult learning

- to secure the support and cooperation of trade unions to enrich the lives of workers who should be seen to be playing a greater role in society
- to offer learning opportunities to people whose school experience was seriously inadequate, to enable working men and women to come to terms with changes in work and society more generally
- to offer chances of personal fulfilment missing from the 'socially destructive environment of boring jobs and trivial recreation dominated by commercial concerns', and
- to help people to control their working conditions and contributions to industrial democracy as well as political democracy.

Optimism and eager anticipation in the months following the publication of the report turned to feelings of rejection as neither the Conservative nor the Labour Government that replaced it in February 1974 showed any sign of pushing for progress in adult learning. In October 1973, the WEA National Planning Committee minutes recorded the association's assumption that the Secretary of State would wish to see an expansion of the work of the WEA. The National Planning Committee recorded its wish to bring WEA districts together in a cooperative effort to plan future growth and development of the association and its work. In March 1978, five years after publication of the report, and after ACACE had started work, a draft document was produced by the WEA National Office for discussion within the association. It recorded that 'there has still been no definite government response to the Russell Report. All major decisions relating to the Russell recommendations appear to be shelved.' The annual conference of the London District of the WEA, held in October 1978, considered a report which included the statement: 'The Russell Report has never been implemented. The current grant arrangement shows little real increase in support and indeed introduces the concept of a definite cash limit in any one year.' Reference was made to the priority areas for WEA develop- ment recommended by Russell (paragraph 232.1–4) and endorsed by the Conservative and Labour governments but without commensurate additional funding. Regret was expressed at the London District conference that the DES had asked the WEA to move away from the fourth priority, 'courses of liberal and academic study below the level of university work' (paragraph 232.4) and concentrate on the first three: 'education for the social and culturally deprived living in urban areas', 'educational work in an industrial context' and 'political and social education' (paragraph 232.1–3). A move such as this was thought by the report to the conference to amount to putting the traditional liberal educa- tion base of WEA adult learning at risk. The strength of pessimism within the association could be judged from the conclusion of the London District, recorded in the report to the conference, that 'in these uncertain circumstances, the production of a detailed long-term plan is of doubtful value and we have made no attempt to devise one'.

Adult learning and community development

In language reminiscent of the 1919 report, the Russell Report strongly commended community-based and community-led adult learning with overt social purpose. People actively involved in social and community action and development in educational priority areas, Home Office-funded Community Development Projects, outreach and community education work in inner London, the valleys of South Wales and elsewhere took great encouragement from the report. The Russell Committee was clear and firm in its expressed view that such activity was correctly identified as an important form of adult learning with a particular social and community purpose in addition to delivering benefits to individuals. The opening of the Preface to *The Disadvantaged Adult* (Clyne, 1972) indicated the strength of the relationship between community development and adult learning:

> Adult education is a community service which can effectively bridge the gap between education and social services. Although an educational service, it is not necessarily provided by readily identified educational agencies. In its historical role, it can be seen as a liberalising influence in a world brutalised by crude and unrestrained industrial and commercial expansion. In its contemporary role, it must be seen as one feature of an all-embracing *éducation permanente*.

Tom Lovett, WEA tutor-organiser attached to the Liverpool EPA and later to be Professor of Community Education in the University of Ulster, urged adult educators and community leaders to recognise the conclusion of Russell that community adult education must be an active agent for change. He further suggested that the opportunities open to adult educators who adopted a community approach could not be exaggerated (Lovett, 1975). As early as 1970 Lovett's colleague Keith Jackson (1970) had published an influential paper called simply *Adult Education and Community Development*. Many of those working at the intersection of adult education and community development were represented in Jane Thompson's (1980) edited volume *Adult Education for a Change*. When referring to the later work of Tom Lovett in Northern Ireland, Eldwick Research Associates (2001) asserted dogmatically that:

> The link between community education and community development has not been widely appreciated until recently. Those trained in traditional adult education methods, where the emphasis is on the class and the

academic development of the individual student, have little understanding of the lifelong learning process involved in community development, where the emphasis is on individual and collective development and the achievement of certain social, economic and cultural objectives.

That such an erroneous statement could be included in a commissioned piece of research in 2001 was an indication of the lack of background knowledge and understanding of the researchers. The reference to Tom Lovett did not acknowledge his major contribution to the practice and understanding of the relationship between community education and community development since the 1960s. In addition, the researchers could also have referred to the Russell report evidence, the ample ILEA/LCC records on community development and education going back to the late nineteenth century, the 1919 Report and the origins of the WEA and Ruskin College.

Another response to the Russell view that adult learning should be seen, in many situations, as an activity with a social purpose was offered by Doug Jones in his extended letter to the present author. His experience in South Wales led him to conclude that

... most people feel unwilling or unable to try together to influence the shape and direction of developments of any kind – at least in Wales. It seems to me, therefore, that although adult education provision and the activities of community groups greatly enrich the quality of life in communities, they are not necessarily instruments for creating social change or for resisting imposed and unwelcome change. This is even more noticeable in deprived communities, of course, where participation in learning is low and demoralisation, a sense of helplessness and even alienation are endemic.

An alternative and more positive view of the relationship between adult learning and community development in South Wales can be found in Chapter 8.

Gerry Fowler MP and the 1974 Labour Government

Without any doubt, as Minister of State, Gerry Fowler was the most effective and informed advocate for adult learning of all responsible ministers in the period covered by this book. He was largely instrumental in the decision to appoint the Russell Committee in 1969. He successfully argued for the initial funds to launch The Adult Literacy Resource Agency (ALRA) in 1975 and he was the driving force behind the creation of ACACE in 1977. He was perhaps unique among the succession of responsible ministers, many of whom were only in post for very short periods of time, in having first-hand experience of the world of adult learning and having the ability and personal attributes to enable him to maintain close working links with 'the field' on the basis of shared experience and understanding.

In 1976, he addressed the annual conference of SCUTREA and two years later, after being replaced by Gordon Oakes in the ministerial team at the DES, he was a keynote speaker at the annual residential conference of NIAE. His two speeches highlighted many of the issues central to the debates of the 1970s. While acknowledging the particular economic constraints, understandings and language of the time, the speeches remain relevant today. In addressing priorities in adult learning at the SCUTREA conference, Gerry Fowler advanced and developed two propositions. First, 'the general pattern of educational provision within the country, and in most developed countries, will less and less embody the end-on [front-loaded] apprenticeship principle and more and more embody the recurrent or continuing principle'. In saying this, he was strongly endorsing the OECD view of adult learning within the scheme of educational provision (see Chapter 3). His second proposition was that 'we shall have to think less and less in terms of adult education as a defined sector of provision, distinct from other areas of post-compulsory provision'.

By way of elaboration on these propositions, he discussed the increasing importance of PEL. The Russell Report (paragraphs 271–3) paid attention to educational leave and referred to the conclusion and recommendation of the UNESCO general conference of 1964 'to grant workers leave, paid if possible, necessary for training in the framework of permanent education'. This was followed, in 1974, by the ILO convention, to which the UK is a signatory, calling on all states to create and introduce a policy of PEL as one element of an employee's right to further education and training. Despite the frequent representations to both Conservative and Labour governments since 1973, no coherent national PEL scheme is in operation more than 30 years later. The PEL campaign was relaunched in the UK in 2002. Fowler argued that day release for young workers, featured in the Education Act 1944 but never fully implemented, was a form of PEL and that the time would come when there would be regular release from work for educational purposes. He suggested that education must be seen as a continuing process from initial education through working life and 'even perhaps the period of retirement'.

Fowler could be excused for not being able to foresee the implications of the dramatically changing age profile of the population towards the end of the century and the impact of the expansion of part-time work and early retirement on the balance of life and on lifestyle changes. He expected to see major changes in further education colleges. He recognised that the colleges would move away from a narrow focus on 'immediate post-school age groups' and 'may in future have to cater for all age groups'. This was in the expectation that PEL would lead to a growth in the numbers of older adults attending further education colleges.

He did not envisage the situation towards the end of the century when the majority of further education students would be mature adults, when he said 'there will doubtless always be a weighting towards the lower end of the age spectrum'. Gerry Fowler, despite being a well-informed and well-briefed minister, was clearly unaware of predictable demographic changes over a matter of one-quarter of a century, reflecting a decline in the birth rate and an ageing population. The SCUTREA conference was reminded of one of the earliest and most important policy and funding changes he had introduced in 1974: the creation of a system of mandatory grants for students at long-term residential colleges and an entitlement to a mandatory award for anyone admitted to a full-time degree course after successfully completing a course at a long-term residential college. Many adults benefited from these changes, which had been called for in the Russell Report.

Fowler's concluding points to the SCUTREA conference were precise and accurate but, unfortunately, neither shared nor noted by governments for the remaining years of the twentieth century: 'There are fallacious but popularly held beliefs about education: for example, that it could provide the solution to social problems and that investment in education would solve the country's economic problems.' This statement was an endorsement of the opinion of the Russell Committee that education and training initiatives alone will never prove sufficient. Yet it appeared to cut across the assertion of Prime Minister Callaghan in his Ruskin College speech of the same year that educational expenditure must produce economic outcomes. The view of the Russell Report was that adult education policy must coincide with other policy (and budgetary moves) to lift individuals, families and communities out of poverty, whether it is poverty in the sense of shortage of money or poverty in terms of unmet essential basic needs and absence of entitlements. This was expressed in the recommendation that Local Development Councils for Adult Education (paragraphs 173–5) be created and the recommendations regarding improving and increasing learning opportunities for 'disadvantaged' people (paragraphs 277–8). The need for what became known much later as 'joined-up government' became ever more obvious but the practice of 'joined-up government' continued to be elusive.

In 1976, the DES issued a discussion paper following initial consultation held in the spring of that year. The government's declared intention was to establish a national Advisory Council for Adult and Continuing Education. The Russell Committee (paragraphs 160–4) had recommended that the government should create a National Development Council. The challenging economic situation at the time caused the government to back away from employing the word 'development' in the title of the proposed new body for fear that its expansionist connotations would excite unrealisable expectations. The Advisory Council would have an operational link with NIAE to enable the accumulated knowledge, experience, network of contacts and resources of NIAE to be accessible to the council. In his speech to the 1976 SCUTREA conference, Fowler insisted that there would have to be closer cooperation and collaboration across sectoral boundaries and, second, that the long-held wish to have coherent policies and promotion of learning for adults would be realised as a result of the work of ACACE. With regard to his first point about closer cooperation and collaboration, the competition encouraged by the post-1979 Conservative governments, and the organisational changes they introduced, increasingly drove providers and organisations apart. Calling for coherence in policies and promotion, following the work of ACACE, proved to be equally unduly optimistic.

The 1976 discussion paper confirmed the government's view that: 'The main function of the council would be to advise the Secretary of State, both continuously on general questions of national policy for adult education and occasionally on specific questions referred to it for consideration.' The paper continued: 'It is envisaged that two early tasks for the council would be to advise on methods of organisation and priorities so as to achieve the best results in the current period of economic stringency, and to plan ahead for changes in strategy and policy once the resources are available for a future expansion of the service.' The Secretary of State who had appointed the Russell Committee and agreed its terms of reference in 1969 was Shirley Williams. It was Shirley Williams, again, who was the Secretary of State responsible for establishing the membership and terms of reference of ACACE in 1977. As the responsible junior minister, Gerry Fowler had been largely instrumental in consulting interested bodies in the field of adult learning and preparing for the creation of ACACE. At a time when organisations and individuals concerned with the range, nature and volume of adult learning opportunities had been expressing disappointment about the modest action taken by governments following the publication of the Russell Report, the discussion paper acknowledged the need for more resources but indicated that they would only be available at an unspecified future date. It was not clear why the Advisory Council was to be expected 'to plan ahead for changes in strategy and policy' when the Russell Report, less than four years old and still on the table of the Secretary of State, had documented a major review exercise, with a total of 118 recommendations for change and improvement. In the event, when ACACE started its work in 1977, it largely operated without any reference back to the Russell Report or the evidence submitted to the Russell Committee. ACACE was able to define and, in so far as it was possible, to quantify unmet needs and to advise accordingly. It was for governments to determine whether or not the necessary public resources were available for the purposes.

The *Times Higher Education Supplement* (THES) carried a major article by Gerry Fowler, now relieved of ministerial responsibility, on 15 April 1977. In it, he dramatically stated that 'Adult education is in a parlous state'. He confirmed that the general terms of Section 41 of the 1944 Act meant that it was virtually impossible to enforce the Act against any LEA appearing to fail to fulfil its duty to secure adequate provision of education for adults. ACACE was to give attention to the definition of 'adequacy'. Yet no parliamentary action was taken to bring firmness and clarity to legislation before the changes introduced in the Further and Higher Education Act 1992 which divided adult learning in a most unhelpful and damaging way (see Chapter 7). Fowler set out ways in which specific features or elements of adult learning provision had been improved since 1973. Nearly four years after the Russell recommendation that a set of four priorities should be adopted by the WEA, extra funding was added to the annual DES grant. Funds had been released to underwrite the creation and operation of ALRA, to meet the cost of TUC trade union studies as well as enabling mature students to obtain grants at long-term residential colleges as of right. None of this strengthened or expanded the mainstream of adult learning, in particular the LEAs. Most mature students on degree courses gained mandatory awards following the Education Act of 1975. The OU was protected during the mid-1970s against most cuts and restraints, although student fees at the OU increased in line with inflation. There had been no movement on PEL.

In his April 1977 article, Fowler reasserted the Association of Recurrent Education/OECD policy line: 'instead of asking whether there is a fundamental design flaw in our educational model, we subject its workings to an almost morbid scrutiny to see if tinkering with the engine will make it perform more effectively . . . there is of course an alternative model'. The arguments against merely adding to initial learning in early childhood and teenage years, up to and including direct access to further and higher education, have continued. Fowler's comments in 1977 remain true in the early years of the twenty-first century, despite the fact that many more young people now stay on at school after 16 years of age, and/or continue to further and higher education. Those who stay at school and college after 16 attract a greater share of resources than those who leave and this increases the longer they stay in education. Fowler suggested that expenditure was not related to learning need or learning potential but rather it was being increasingly concentrated on the 'most able and often the most advantaged'. He observed that once people had fallen behind in the learning process, especially in basic skills, they are likely to have fewer and fewer chances of gaining access to education resources. He concluded that 'at a time when technology, industry and society are changing more rapidly than ever before, it is nonsense to seek to transmit in 11 years of schooling the knowledge and skills which must serve for nearly 50 years of working life, and beyond into retirement'.

One thread of Fowler's article, which linked the Russell Report and ACACE, was his discussion of the need for 'citizen education'. He argued that the National Development Council (the soon to be created ACACE), as proposed by Russell, should pay regard to the importance of achieving greater measures of democratisation and public accountability in public services. This topic was addressed by ACACE in its publication, *Adult Political Education* (1983). The 1919 Report had paid regard to the same issue.

National Institute of Adult Education Conference 1978

The 1978 NIAE annual residential conference was a milestone. A number of contributions marked out crucial issues for the attention of ACACE, for adult learning organisations and providing and funding bodies, including departments of government. Contributors highlighted matters requiring both immediate and long-term action. In doing this, they drew attention to matters considered by the Russell Committee and to recommendations included in the report. Although the NIAE conference took place five years after the publication of the report, the keynote presentations to the conference indicated how the report had been received within the world of adult learning. Neither the 1970–4 Conservative Government nor its Labour successor had issued a statement of commitment by the government to implementing the recommendations in the report. The report was still considered to be a current document and a statement of unfinished business.

Fowler, who had been succeeded as Minister of State by Gordon Oakes, reminded the conference of the long-standing recommendation by the OECD that all countries should establish a strategy for continuing education throughout working life – not 'throughout life' but 'throughout working life'. The previous Conservative Government had outlined a possible limited form of PEL in 1972. At the time, it was expected that the government's view on PEL, to some degree, pre-empted the recommendation of the Russell Committee on the subject. However, the Conservative Government had not implemented its own limited scheme, nor had the Labour Government, after 1974, taken up the matter. Fowler called for a comprehensive PEL, to include 'housewives and the disabled'. PEL was both an economic and an educational need. He reflected on the changes which had been evident since the publication of the Russell Report in 1973, outlined the increase in the number of learning opportunities for disadvantaged groups and noted the acceptance of 'participation' as a watchword in education, social and community work. Picking up one of the early lessons of the Community Development Project (CDP) and EPA schemes of the late 1960s, he warned that, at a time of financial cuts, there was a danger of increased and improved chances of learning in poorer areas removing 'working class leaders to middle class jobs'. He reminded the conference that the financial cuts, coupled with increases in student fee levels, was leading to the creation of a middle-class service with an expanded service for educationally and socially disadvantaged people running alongside. The coherence sought by Russell and emphasised in the discussion paper, circulated by the DES prior to the establishment of ACACE, was not being achieved. Adult education remained an undefined and inadequately protected statutory service.

Rendel Jones, Chief Education Officer of East Sussex and, at a later date, Treasurer of NIACE, in a hard-hitting, honest but somewhat pessimistic presentation, reminded the conference that government pressure on LEAs and other bodies, in recent years, to raise the level of student fees had led to a great reduction in enrolment numbers. Despite the offer of concessions to people on low incomes, the fall in student numbers was often greatest among those with the greatest learning needs who were deterred by the published basic fee levels and were reluctant to be seen or heard asking for reductions. More often than not, he said, increasing individual fees led to a reduction in the gross fee income to the LEA. It has frequently been argued that it rarely makes financial sense, let alone educational sense, to increase fees for adult learning. Adult learning is extremely price sensitive. Raising fees usually conflicts with efforts to widen access and participation. Rendel Jones stressed that adopting short-term expedient actions, including raising fees or closing classes or centres would often lead to major reductions in provision which would take considerable time to re-establish. This lesson was not learned. In inner London, ILEA had remained committed to a policy of low fees and generous concessions. After the dismemberment of ILEA in 1990, many centres were closed, buildings were sold for conversion to luxury apartments and local programmes and special projects were simply terminated. Within a very short space of time, capital assets and learning programmes, carefully nurtured over more than 70 years, were lost to the people of London. Rendel Jones urged the conference, ACACE and the government to realise that 'many local authority officers knew little and cared less for continuing education'. His message was well taken. For some time, confronted by legislative change, financial stringency and general insecurity, many adult educators felt there was an absence of committed and well-informed people to argue the case for adult learning wherever and whenever policy and financial decisions were to be taken. Jones was speaking for many people, in LEAs and elsewhere, when he suggested that the insensitive and entirely negative approach that he had outlined was bound to make it more difficult, if not impossible, to adopt and implement the primary thrust of the Russell Report: the recognition of adult learning provision as a significant activity towards achieving a fairer and more equal society.

At the time of the 1978 NIAE Conference, Allan Rogers was District Secretary of the WEA in South Wales and a member of ACACE. He was also a local councillor and was soon to be elected as an MP. Rogers drew a parallel between the idealism of the post-1945 era, with the development of the welfare state, and the concern in 1978 for personal, social and political education. His contribution to the conference was an important reminder that adult learning programmes and activities have formed an invaluable element of an integrated approach to relieving suffering from current problems and, at the same time, finding a way through those problems to a better future. The Russell Committee received evidence of much of this activity. Recommendations in the report encouraged organisations, universities and LEAs to give greater attention to provision through partnership between educational and non-educational social agencies.

A major influence on adult learning and its social and political importance throughout much of the second half of the twentieth century was H. D. (Billy) Hughes. As a member of both the Russell Committee and ACACE, chairman of ALRA, national elected officer of the WEA, leading member of NIAE and the Residential Colleges Committee, his accumulated knowledge, experience and wisdom were well employed. Once the report had been published, Hughes was one of the most active people pressing for early action, using his links with Parliament and the political networks to good effect. Soon after publication of the report, he had urged Margaret Thatcher to open consultations on the report, presumably unaware of the block to progress being exercised by the rest of the Cabinet. In a letter to Gerry Fowler, Minister of State in the Labour Government, dated 20 March 1974, Hughes mentioned that:

> Mrs Thatcher, in almost her last act as Secretary of State [before the February 1974 General Election], indicated that she was considering opening consultations with the major Adult Education bodies which have been promised since the publication of the Report over a year ago. It is understood that the Department was about to publish a consultative document last December [1973], when the 'economy cuts' intervened.

The letter went on to suggest to Fowler that national consultation should start on the details of the recommended National Development Council and that LEAs could be encouraged to establish Local Development Councils for their areas to coincide, where necessary, with the reorganisation of local government boundaries due in 1974. In his reply, dated 22 April 1974, Fowler stated that 'we have, of course, some ferociously difficult problems to face during these early weeks in office'. Nonetheless, he continued by saying 'we are however keen to make progress'. A meeting was held on 3 July 1974 between some members of the committee (Sir Lionel Russell, Billy Hughes, Henry Arthur Jones and John Henry) and Gerry Fowler. It failed to move the process forward.

In his contribution to the 1978 conference debate, Billy Hughes described the unsatisfactory legislative status for adult learning arising from the still unamended Education Act 1944. He argued that, without new legislation, LEAs would continue to be pushed towards a narrow non-vocational view of adult learning, while university extra-mural departments and the WEA would be enrolling mainly the relatively well-educated. He then made a number of observations on matters which would preoccupy conferences, councils and committees for years to come. While the Russell Report had urged providers to give greater attention to meeting 'the needs of the educationally disadvantaged', he asserted that the experience of the literacy campaign and the three years of ALRA's work (1975–8) showed that broader basic education within the overall pattern of adult learning provision was essential. He was an early believer that literacy and numeracy should be seen to be two components, among many, forming a comprehensive body of adult basic education (ABE) or adult basic skills. There was a 'growing realisation that youth and adult unemployment might well be a continuing problem in the new age of technology'. Partnerships, cooperation and collaboration were called for to bring together labour market agencies and services and education services to provide for integrated education and training services. He described how the experience of the OU had led to the creation of open colleges and open college networks and, finally, he called for an expansion of access and foundation courses for adults wishing to enter higher education. This last point was directly related to the Option E in the DES discussion document on higher education (DES, 1978). Option E, commended to the conference by Hughes, foresaw a drop in the number of 18+ entries into higher education and suggested that 'surplus capacity might well be absorbed by mature students, qualified by motivation and experience'. Hughes's presentation was primarily based on recommendations of the Russell Committee, many of which had not yet received the attention he and others thought they merited.

Hughes and Jones were the only members of both the Russell Committee and ACACE. Christopher Rowland HMI was, initially, the Secretary to the Russell Committee. Then, after 18 months, he became an assessor to the committee. He was an assessor to ACACE. Having been Research Assistant to the committee, the present author was later appointed to be a member of ACACE. Other important links between national committees of the period were provided by Brain Groombridge and Roy Shaw. Groombridge had been a member of the Open University Planning Committee from 1967 to 1969 and was, subsequently, a member of the Russell Committee. His experience as Deputy Secretary of NIAE and Head of Educational Programmes at the Independent Broadcasting Authority greatly strengthened his contribution to the pressure being exerted on governments for action on the Russell recommendations. Roy Shaw was a member of the OU Planning Committee. At the time, he was Director of Adult Education in the University of Keele. Later, from 1977 to 1980, he was a member of ACACE during his time as the chief officer of the Arts Council of England.

The 1978 NIAE conference took place early in the life of ACACE. It was an excellent platform for advancing and sharing topics considered by the Russell Committee but requiring further attention from ACACE and, in the light of advice from ACACE, attention, endorsement and action by the government. In his presentation to the conference, Gordon Oakes, as Minster of State, sought to reassure those attending the conference and others that the government was sensitive to the difficulties facing adult learning. Since the oil crisis of 1973, the Conservative and Labour governments had found the economic climate intimidating and threatening to any policies and programmes dependent on growth in public funding. He repeated the well known, but much feared, central government perception that adult learning actually meant, primarily, work-related and vocational education and training. This was not encouraging to an audience convinced, as the Russell Committee had been, that the benefits to individuals and the community of liberal, non-qualification-bearing courses and activities would be at risk if the government were to establish a hierarchy of learning. Later in his speech, he confirmed the government's acceptance of the Russell Report's assertions about the equality of learning and the primacy of the motivation of the learner.

Gordon Oakes was also sensitive to the political importance of acknowledging the growing and changing aspirations of women in the fields of education, training and work. He made the further point that 'there will be the need and the opportunity to make it possible for more men and women to continue their education and be trained and retrained throughout their working life. In all this, the emphasis must be on quality, relevance and adaptability'. This was probably the first acknowledgement, in a government statement on adult learning, of the needs of both women and men to gain access equally to learning opportunities. His use of the phrase 'throughout their working life' disappointed his listeners. They had hoped to hear him speak of opportunities throughout life, thus recognising lifelong learning in its full meaning. The comments on quality, relevance and adaptability were well received and marked an early indication of governmental interest in these professional concepts. Hitherto, it had been expected that governments would restrict their interest to the quantity of provision rather than quality. Quality was left to the teaching and training establishments and organisations with the support and advice of HMI and others. Oakes defended and then praised the traditional offer of learning programmes arranged by LEAs:

> There is always some Smart Alec around who tries to put adult education down by sneering about winemaking, do-it-yourself and suchlike. That to me is a sort of illiteracy of the imagination – and damned impertinence into the bargain. Making things and doing things are important for three good reasons – they are worth doing in themselves, they get adults into educational buildings, achievement in one field can lead people to try other courses . . . There is enormous potential for promoting social harmony by increasing mutual understanding. And not least, there is the right of all citizens of this country to enjoy the benefits of publicly funded services.

Unfortunately the fine-sounding conference rhetoric, welcomed by the conference as an acceptance of the Russell view of adult learning, was not matched by subsequent policy, programmes, funding or action.

The Minister suggested that the three-year funding arrangements for the Adult Literacy Unit (ALU), which followed the ALRA in 1978, was

> ... proof that it [adult literacy] is now regarded as fully entitled to a proper place in the educational scheme of things, which means making it a local responsibility. The Government has borne this in mind in settling the level of the Rate Support Grant for this year, although as always, it is up to the LEAs themselves to make decisions on actual expenditure.

Oakes seemed to be unaware of a continuing problem throughout the period covered by this book. Local decision-making by elected local councillors, in the light of local circumstances, was, in principle, welcomed as an essential element of the democratic system and the balance between central and local government. However, the absence of 'ear-marked' funding for adult literacy and the lack of guidance from the DES about the expected quantity and nature of provision led to uneven levels of provision. Leaving decision-making to individual LEAs could and did mean that some LEAs used the element of the Rate Support Grant, identified for adult literacy work, for other purposes. The extent to which an individual LEA was prepared to protect that part of the Rate Support Grant, initially granted by the government for literacy or any other aspect of adult learning, was a transparent indication of the priority given to adult learning by the LEA. With regard to adult literacy, ILEA and a small number of other LEAs had established systems and appointed specialist staff at the time of the Literacy Campaign and then immediately following the publication of the Russell Report.

Oakes disagreed with Hughes' understanding of one important point in the DES 1978 discussion document on higher education. Whereas Hughes identified opportunities for mature adults in Option E, outlining the consequences of a projected decline in the numbers of 18 + -year-olds, Oakes was of the view that this did not concern adult education. Adopting a compartmentalised and blinkered view of adult learning, Oakes insisted that the discussion paper dealt with higher education which, in his view, was quite different from, and not to be described as, adult education. One of the principal messages of the Russell Report, that all types of adult learning should be seen to form a coherent whole rather than an assembly of strictly distinct and separate penny packets of provision, was not recognised by the Minister. It was clear that differences of perspective were more than simply semantic differences. At the end of his presentation, during which he cannot have failed to have become aware of increasing unease, he led with his chin by saying: 'I hope it is not too much to say that if all goes well, 1978/79 could prove to be a turning point for adult education.' It *was* too much to say. Budgets were being squeezed. Despite the early work of ACACE, which had been created by the government in 1977, adult learning had become marginal to government planning. There was an evident lack of determination and action to match ministerial statements. Within a short time, the election of 1979 was to bring about the defeat of the Labour Government and the return of a Conservative Government led by Margaret Thatcher. Thus within two years of the establishment of ACACE, a new government with a very different agenda was in office. Margaret Thatcher, who, as Secretary of State, had been supportive in much of her behind-the-scenes lobbying of her Cabinet colleagues in 1973, became Prime Minister in 1979. As Prime Minister, she adopted a totally different approach to publicly funded and publicly provided public services, including adult learning. As policies changed during the post-1979 period, competition became more common than collaboration or cooperation and fragmentation and separateness characterised the scene.

6

The Russell Committee, ACACE, UDACE and REPLAN: The struggle for coherence

Everyone has the right freely to participate in the cultural life of the community, to enjoy the arts and to share in scientific advancement and benefits.

(Article 27, Universal Declaration of Human Rights)

Terms of reference

All government inquiries and all government-funded bodies are bound ultimately by their terms of reference. During the twentieth century, there was a constant tension between government concern to ensure that public expenditure was directed at urgent social and economic needs, and the professional adult education concern to develop a comprehensive service that would serve adults in all their roles. It is useful in this light to review the terms of reference and practice of the Russell Committee, the Adult Education Committee that produced the 1919 Report, and the bodies which were consecutively charged with advising and developing the field of adult learning in the 1970s and 1980s – ACACE, UDACE and REPLAN. Both the Adult Education Committee (AEC) which produced the 1919 Report and the Russell Committee were charged with paying regard to the current provision and both were restricted to what was generally described as non-vocational adult education, thus seeking to exclude attention to work-related education and training and higher education. As was mentioned in Chapter 1, the Board of Education fought against the creation of the AEC. The AEC was established as a sub-committee of the Reconstruction Committee, over which the Prime Minister, David Lloyd George, presided. When the committee was ready to report, the chairman of the committee, A L Smith, felt obliged to write to the Prime Minister in the covering letter accompanying the Final Report: 'As there has been no appointment of a Minister to succeed Sir Auckland Geddes, and as the matters raised by our terms of reference are not within the scope of any single Department of State, this Report is presented to you as head of the government.' This was the first and the last time that a national report on adult learning, from a body established by the government of the day, reported directly to the Prime Minister. It was noteworthy that the Chairman of the committee partly justified this reporting route by commenting that 'the matters raised by our terms of reference are not within the scope of any single Department of State'. This was an early example of a plea for 'joined-up' government, which foreshadows more recent pleas for adult learning policies which transcend departmental borders between, for example, health, social services and education. The Board of Education was concerned that the committee was being invited to move onto the board's territory, and these sensitivities explain the explicit exclusion (albeit in parentheses) of 'technical' and 'vocational' education. Technical and vocational education were held by the board to be 'serious' learning after school age, whereas the programmes for adults promoted by universities, the WEA and other voluntary bodies were not granted the same level of respect by the board.

One of the principal recommendations of the Russell Report (see Chapter 4) was that the Secretary of State should 'establish a Development Council for Adult Education for England and Wales'. Given the weak position of adult education within the DES, this was seen as an important method of ensuring that the 'Russell agenda' would be carried forward. Yet it is also clear that, given the deteriorating economic circumstances of the mid-1970s, neither the Conservative Government, nor its successor Labour Government after the two general elections in 1974, was willing to accept the designation 'Development Council', since the word 'Development' implied or assumed growth in volume and expenditure. Within government, the most effective conduit for lobbying on this issue came from the Minister of State, Gerry Fowler. Eventually, Shirley Williams, as Secretary of State, succumbed to the demands and pressure from individuals and organisations involved in adult learning and, in particular the persuasion of her Minister of State, subject to the word 'Development' being replaced by 'Advisory'. The Advisory Council for Adult and Continuing Education (ACACE) was established in 1977, with a three-year remit:

> To advise generally on matters relevant to the provision of education for adults in England and Wales, and in particular:
>
> (a) to promote cooperation between the various bodies in adult education and review current practice, organisation and priorities, with a view to the most effective deployment of available resources; and
> (b) to promote the development of future policies and priorities, with full regard to the concept of education as a process continuing throughout life.

The issue raised in (a) of effective use of resources takes up a theme stated in the terms of reference set for the Russell Committee, in 1969 ('the most effective and economical deployment of available resources'). In clause (b) the word 'development', with its obvious resource implications, does appear. Yet it is here qualified as referring to 'policies and priorities' rather than the actual mechanisms which might bring any such policies and priorities to fruition.

In his *Times Higher Education Supplement (THES)* article of 15 April 1977 (referred to in Chapter 5), written after leaving government office, Gerry Fowler explained the background to the terms of reference and initial agenda set for ACACE. He had started to explore the possibilities of implementing the Russell recommendation to create a National Development Council in 1974 and picked up the subject again in 1976. On 26 April 1976, the Minister of State met representatives of a number of organisations involved in adult learning to discuss the Russell recommendation. A note of the meeting states that 'the Minister of State said that there seemed to be general agreement on the need for a centre for innovation and planning which might appropriately be called the national advisory council for adult and continuing education'. The agreement to which Fowler referred may well have applied to ministers and staff within the DES. Among practitioners and interested parties in adult learning, the view was that the new body should have development roles and responsibilities. Indeed, reference to innovation in the note of the meeting led some people to believe, optimistically, that ACACE would have a stronger and more interventionist brief than acting solely as an advisory council. There had been disagreements between government departments concerning whether or not the council should be a free-standing body, separate from NIAE, and whether it should have executive powers including resource allocation. LEA and Treasury hostility soon ended consideration of the council having executive powers including the allocation of public funds. ACACE was established separately from NIAE but shared its premises in Leicester.

Fowler was keen that ACACE should be charged with the responsibility to watch and comment on learning provision and changes and to report, advise and recommend as it judged appropriate. He particularly wished ACACE to advise on the potential use of non-traditional locations for learning including community centres, libraries and other neighbourhood settings. Fowler was consistently seeking to act on conclusions reached by the Russell Committee and implement the recommendations in the committee's report. At his April 1976 meeting, he was at pains to stress the importance of the new advisory council operating in a reasonable and realistic manner given the economic situation. The note of the meeting reports his view that:

> Its functions would be to develop ideas so that when the country's economic circumstances permitted a development of adult education, this would be on the lines of an agreed strategy rather than simply providing more of the same: in the short term too, it could have useful

things to say on the best way of handling adult education in a period of contraction.

At a time when there was a uniformly shared belief among providing bodies that adult learning, in all its many forms, was grossly underfunded, it was dispiriting to know that the most supportive of Ministers of State was speaking the language of cuts. The critical reference to 'more of the same' was a stark warning that even in improved economic circumstances, adult education would be required to seek out new constituencies and meet changing needs. It is instructive to look at the various publications of ACACE in this light – on education for the adult unemployed, adult education for the black communities, basic education and educational guidance. Following the April 1976 meeting, the DES circulated a discussion paper called 'Setting up of a "National Advisory Council for Adult and Continuing Education"'. The paper suggested that including the term 'continuing education' in the title 'takes account of the developing appreciation of adult education as part of a process which extends from the immediate post-statutory education period throughout life. It also indicates an awareness of developments in adult education in the context of UNESCO and the OECD, in which this country has much to both learn and to contribute.' The paper did not elaborate on which UNESCO and OECD developments were in the minds of departmental officials and/or ministers, nor did it explain what should be learned and contributed. It is reasonable to assume, nevertheless, that DES thinking was influenced by the UNESCO concern with Basic Education and, in particular, OECD's interest in how adult learning could support the project of economic change and modernisation.

Gerry Fowler's comments, in the *THES* article, on the programme of work for ACACE were clearly made without thought of the political implications for adult learning that might follow from a possible change of government in 1979:

> This may seem an ambitious programme. So it is. But it is an agenda for years, not months, of deliberation. When it is again possible to increase educational investment, in new directions, we must be prepared. Otherwise, we shall merely repeat the mistakes of the past. That is why the new council, the birth of which is imminent, may win for itself an influence unimagined by those concerned only to restrict its remit.

Interestingly, Fowler did not spell out what he considered to have been the mistakes of the past which he did not wish to see repeated. It is reasonable to conclude, however, that these included the rapid expansion of LEA provision of 'leisure' courses in the late 1960s and early 1970s. ACACE had an initial life of three years, 1977 to 1980. Despite the apparent lack of interest in general adult learning, on the part of the recently elected Conservative Government, ACACE was granted a second three-year term in 1980, principally because more time was required to complete work on specific remits of the government. It was less charitable when the time came to consider appropriate arrangements for the period beyond 1983.

Membership of ACACE

The Russell Committee comprised the appointed Chairman, Sir Lionel Russell, plus thirteen members broadly representative of adult learning interests and bodies. Due to the small number of committee members, further reduced when two were obliged to leave through ill health, the membership was drawn from a narrow spectrum. The shortage of contemporary experience of the voluntary sector, apart from the WEA, was regrettable, as was the absence of current knowledge and recent experience of the broad range of cultural, community and social services within which adult learning operated. Important developing work by, with and for ethnic minorities was not represented nor was there representation of any of the adult learning work of significant women's organisations. Committee membership did not include anyone appointed specifically because he or she was an adult student. ACACE started its work with the distinct advantage that its membership comprised the Chairman, Richard Hoggart, and 24 council members. Within this larger number, ACACE was able to profit from wide experience across relevant activities and services. The gaps evident in the collective knowledge and experience of the Russell Committee members were not as evident in ACACE. Given the wide remit of ACACE, it was invaluable to the Chairman that the experience of council members was so broad. Within the first year of the life of ACACE, Shirley Williams wrote to Richard Hoggart (19 May 1978) stating: 'The Secretary of State for Wales and I fully agree with the Council that there should be no unnecessary barriers between adult and other further education, especially at a time when the concept of continuing education and other trends point to the need for a closer relationship.' She continued by saying that: 'Local authority associations all subscribe firmly to the view that adult education is and should remain an integral part of the education provision made by a local authority.'

At the end of the first three-year term, seven members were not reappointed; seven new members were appointed by the Secretary of State. Unfortunately, the changes caused a loss to the council of the knowledge and experience of a senior public librarian, and of a member who had been both General Secretary of the Arts Council and head of a university extra-mural department. At the same time, there were also important continuities. The Chairman, Richard Hoggart, the present author, and Professors H. A. Jones and Naomi McIntosh remained members of ACACE through until 1983. In addition, ACACE benefited from the work of John Taylor as Secretary to the Council until May 1983. The council was also able to establish sub-committees for particular pieces of work, which drew on a wider field of professional expertise. For example, the Political Education publication (ACACE, 1983) was preceded by the setting up of a sub-committee including Gilly Greensit from the British Youth Council, and three prominent academics, including Walter Perry of the OU. In some cases this work led to publications which were seen as statements of ACACE views, in others to reports held to be of interest and importance but not committing ACACE to particular conclusions. Thus *Links to Learning* (ACACE, 1979b), the influential report on educational guidance services of 1979, represented ACACE policy, while *Case Studies in Educational Guidance for Adults* (Butler, 1984) was a research report by Linda Butler and colleagues published jointly by ACACE and NIACE. While some areas of enquiry took up themes present in the Russell Report, others (in relation to, for example, work with unemployed adults, adult education for ethnic minority communities and educational guidance) corresponded to major social and economic changes that took place, or were more fully recognised, after 1972.

Activities of ACACE: research or enquiry?

The Russell Committee was established by the Secretary of State as an official government committee of enquiry to be served and supported by the DES. From the outset, as explained in Chapter 2, the committee was not supported with sufficient backup administrative and research staff. The only piece of commissioned research was contracted with the University of Leicester and related to the educational and social needs of disadvantaged minority groups (Clyne, 1972). The Russell Report records the committee's frustration that, having identified the shortcomings of available statistics particularly in the LEA sector, their own enquiries did not yield complete information (see Appendix B of the report). In paragraphs 418–25 the report made detailed recommendations as to the categories of statistics that the DES might collect through the LEAs in the future.

The position of research in ACACE was more complex. At the 1982 annual conference of SCUTREA, John Taylor, Secretary to ACACE, described the ways in which ACACE operated. He explained that ACACE was not 'primarily a research body'. He continued: 'In essence, the Council exists to advise; enquiries are necessary in the preparation of advice; the Council's reports are based on those enquiries; and consequently the enquiry and associated publishing programme make up a large part of the Council's work.' In other words, ACACE sought to provide evidence as a basis for policy development. Taylor went on to explain the relationship between enquiry, advice and publication. In contrast with the procedures followed by the Russell Committee, determined according to the strict guidelines of a formal government committee of enquiry, ACACE operated within the public arena. During its life of six years, ACACE completed 36 enquiries, all of which were published and widely used. Russell reflected on the past, commented on the present and made recommendations as to the future. ACACE, by contrast, concentrated on contemporary policies and provision and advised the Secretary of State and the professional community as to the best way forward in terms of programmes, priorities and practices. Taylor and ACACE membership were of the view that, by publishing information and analysis of the contemporary state of adult learning, it was possible to begin to tackle immediate problems and determine future developments on a firmer basis. In his SCUTREA presentation, Taylor made the obvious, but often ignored, point that:

> It might be argued that, irrespective of the long-standing debate about whether a national council for adult and continuing education should be an advisory or development body, there is a straight forward need for this service of information and analysis. With the present Council's remit expiring in October 1983, this at least might be one of the arguments for a successor body, if only because information and analysis needs to be continually brought up to date.

It is clear from the enquiries conducted by ACACE that there was increasing divergence in the field between organisations alike in name but different in their approach to their work. Thus the rather traditional 'liberal studies' approach of some university extra-mural departments might be contrasted with the innovatory 'pioneer work' at the University of Leeds (Ward and Taylor, 1986). This took up the theme of 'disadvantage' from the Russell Report and led to important work with disadvantaged individuals and communities in West Yorkshire, which continued through the 1980s and 1990s. In the case of LEA work, political control in local government was an additional, complicating factor. Those LEAs in which political control matched the national Conservative Government (from 1979) were more likely to give priority to reducing expenditure (by cutting classes or increasing student fees) and, therefore, local taxes, than attempting to improve adult education participation rates. In inner London, the situation was complicated by the existence of ILEA as the LEA for inner London, separate from the Borough Councils. Thus in some boroughs, ILEA found itself in potential conflict with not only central government but also individual Borough Councils. Government determination to reduce the level of spending on education (including adult education) in London was an important motive for the abolition of ILEA (Cushman, 1996).

Michael Stephens, Professor of Adult Education in the University of Nottingham, commented on trends in research in adult education during the period 1970–81, in his presentation to the SCUTREA conference in 1981

(Stephens, 1981). Having observed that it was possible to read the famously influential 1919 Report and 'believe that the concept of research had not yet been invented' and then to note that Robert Peers, the world's first professor of adult education, could write about his first 15 years at the University of Nottingham without mentioning research, Stephens drew attention to references to research in the Russell and Alexander Reports. As mentioned in Chapter 4, the Russell Committee made specific recommendations regarding future research (recommendations 26 and 116–118). The Alexander Report, in paragraph 142, stated: 'We therefore recommend an expansion of research into aspects of adult education.' Stephens then asserts the importance of ACACE's 'surveys and pieces of research'. Whereas ACACE preferred to apply the word 'enquiry' to much of its work leading to reports and publications, Stephens is comfortable describing the programme as being 'research'. Yet again, we are made aware of the use of different terminology applied to the self-same processes.

In his survey of research during the period 1970–81, Stephens makes only a passing general reference to research, survey and enquiry work undertaken by or on behalf of the broadcasting authorities, trades unions, LEAs, international organisations and voluntary organisations, other than that work undertaken by NIAE and one minor reference to the Educational Centres Association (ECA). The evidence available to ACACE from its numerous enquiries was that much research work had been undertaken during the 1970s, although it was usually small-scale due to the difficulty of obtaining funding for the activity. Throughout the years since the creation of the Russell Committee, too little regard was paid to the MA and PhD theses, usually unpublished, produced by adult learning practitioners. These formed a rich but neglected body of material, produced not by academics but by practitioners, many of whom were conducting research alongside their responsibilities of organising, teaching and learning in communities and neighbourhoods. Mention should also be made of the combination of innovatory practice with research and writing by university adult educators such as Mary Hamilton, Keith Jackson, Tom Lovett and Jane Mace.

The major part of the work of ACACE was the completion and publication of 36 enquiries, each of which was derived from survey and research and included an element of consultation with practitioners. Enquiries fell into three different categories: (i) policy and organisation at all levels; (ii) curriculum and programme development; and (iii) fact-finding. Many of the enquiries related to topics highlighted in the Russell recommendations itemised in Chapter 4. The government directly commissioned ACACE to report on adult basic education and on education for unemployed adults. Both topics were central to the conclusions and recommendations of the Russell Committee, but given new urgency as economic conditions deteriorated, many unskilled jobs were lost, and unemployment rose towards a peak of over three million. The ACACE reports, *A Strategy for the Basic Education of Adults* (ACACE, 1979d) and *Education for Unemployed Adults* (ACACE, 1982a) carried forward consideration of these two subjects by the Russell Committee, leading to policy and programme developments initiated by the DES and Welsh Office. It is not possible in this book to give an exhaustive account of the research conducted by ACACE, but some of the highlights are drawn out in the next three sections.

Educational guidance for adults

In 1979, ACACE published *Links to Learning*, a report on educational information, advisory and counselling services for adults (ACACE, 1979b). In doing so, it highlighted an important, developing area of work. The OU, from its earliest days, had been keen to make its courses available to people from as wide a range of backgrounds as possible. This meant that many of the students coming into the university were rather ill-equipped for the rigours of studying at university level. In addition to employing full-time and part-time tutorial staff at a regional level, the Open University also appointed staff with a specific responsibility for 'counselling' students. 'Counselling' issues included preparedness for study, study skills, balancing study and other demands on an adult's time, dealing with doubts and uncertainties that might inhibit an adult's study progress, and referring adults facing particular difficulties to more specialist counselling agencies.

Within the OU, some staff viewed the development of educational guidance (a term deemed more appropriate than counselling, which is just one activity among a number of guidance activities) as a more general requirement in a society where education was seen as a recurrent or continuing activity through adult life. In 1976, as the OU prepared to develop its own non-degree continuing education programme, the report of the Committee on Continuing Education of the OU had stated:

> Information on the range of adult education opportunities, locally and nationally, needs to be coordinated, presented attractively and disseminated widely throughout the community. However, information alone is insufficient. Adults require access to advice and counselling on educational opportunity ... in such advice, educational and vocational implications will be frequently interrelated. The systematic monitoring of adult needs and demands would be likely to ensure a more responsive provision to meet them. (Open University, 1976, p. 101)

It was this last sentence that was to prove of particular interest to LEAs keen to expand the range of students in their adult education provision to better reflect the communities they were serving. In addition to *Links to Learning*, ACACE usefully produced directories of educational guidance services for adults in 1981 and 1982. By the time of the 1982 survey, the number of services had increased to 46. Simply by documenting this growth in local responses, ACACE gave added incentives to LEAs to either establish new services or maintain existing ones. In a highly decentralised situation, in times of economic hardship, the very existence of such publications served a useful function.

Organisation and structure

Russell recommended that the partnership between statutory and voluntary bodies should continue and that LEAs should be the main providers and lead bodies in local cooperative planning. The strength of this recommendation depended to a great extent on the effectiveness of the national and local Development Councils for Adult Education as recommended by Russell. ACACE undertook a number of enquiries, building on the work undertaken by Russell, in respect of the general structure for adult learning, the leadership role of the government, and the potential of regional and local cooperation. Among the publications, linking the work of Russell and ACACE in respect of the organisation and structure of adult learning, were *Protecting the Future for Adult Education* (ACACE, 1981), which concentrated on the issues facing LEAs, and *Towards Continuing Education* (ACACE, 1979c), a wide-ranging discussion paper. This latter publication led on to *Continuing Education: From Policies to Practice* (ACACE, 1982a). This latter publication was a most significant council report and was hailed by Fieldhouse (1995, p. 66) as:

> the most important adult education publication since the Russell Report: 'a milestone document' . . . it proposed a radical shift of emphasis for the whole post-school sector, abandoning the boundaries between education and training or between vocational and general adult education in a comprehensive, integrated system of continuing education. Its priorities were very similar to the Russell Report's emphasis on the disadvantaged.

Fieldhouse also records the concern of other adult educators at the time that, in the absence of increased resources, 'policies to practice' might divert resources away from liberal education into a more vocational direction.

If *From Policies to Practice* had the feel of an official report on 'the field', other documents produced by ACACE were more in the way of discussion documents, intended to stimulate debate and promote experimentation. *Political Education for Adults* (ACACE, 1983) contained nine short papers on the theme, framed by the 'Introduction and Conclusions' of a committee convened by H. D. Hughes. The present author contributed a paper offering an LEA perspective, and emphasising that political powerlessness was a further aspect of disadvantage:

'Those people who, by whatever definition, feel themselves to be or are objectively powerless, seek the means whereby the information conveyed to them can be used in the pursuit and obtaining of power' (p. 34). In the face of possible criticism from local councillors, the author continued: 'I would contend that political action, per se, is no part of adult education; but quite definitely, the preparation of materials and information used in political action and the organisational arrangements of political action can reasonably be based in a political education activity' (p. 35). This statement would have also served as a justification for the sometimes controversial outreach work with community organisations taking place in inner London at the period.

Fact-finding exercises undertaken by ACACE or commissioned by the council touched on a number of the issues raised by the Russell Committee's recommendations. Russell urged RACs to establish adult education commit-tees where they did not already exist. ACACE published a report *Committees Responsible for Adult Education in the Regional Advisory Councils* which acted as a guide to those RACs which did not have adult education committees. *Local Development Councils for Adult Education* (1980) was a survey report detailing the numbers, types and functions of Local Development Councils in existence in 1979. Interestingly, ACACE used the word 'development' whereas the DES and most LEAs had made it clear that the word 'advisory' would be more accept-able. Only a small number of LEAs had established Local Development or Advisory Councils in accordance with the general brief suggested by Russell. Of those that were established, many had a short life. At a time of financial restraint and, indeed, cuts in the late 1970s, there was a shortage of developmental oppor-tunities. This point can be illustrated by reference to the consequence of fee increases in the LEA sector. In association with NIAE, ACACE surveyed LEA fee levels and student enrolments in November 1980 and November 1981. The surveys showed that between 1979 and 1980 fees rose by an average of 37 per cent and enrolments fell by an average of 11 per cent. The comparable data for the change between 1980 and 1981 were an average increase in fees of 25 per cent and a decrease of 3 per cent in student enrolments. In this situation, most providing bodies were concerned to protect programmes against further erosion, rather than plan new developments. Following the Russell recommendation that '"free trade" should be established between neighbouring authorities and any difficulties ensuing from this policy should be resolved by regional consultation', ACACE published its report on 'Inter-authority Free Trade and Fee Recoupment Arrangements for Non-vocational Adult Education' in 1980. Had the report been published two years later, it would have indicated that many LEAs, confronting budget cuts, had opted out of free trade arrangements as a means of achieving modest savings.

Probably the most extensive and significant of the developments launched by LEAs was *An Education Service for the Whole Community* (ESWC), promoted by

ILEA (1973). This argued for an innovative education service in which better use could be made of existing educational resources in inner London. ESWC, as it came to be known, pointed out, for example, that 'the service exists for the individuals and for the community, not for its own sake' (p. 5). Subsequent developments in inner London and elsewhere owed much to this report.

The extent and scope of adult learning

In 1973, the year of publication of the Russell Report, the Council of Europe published a *Feasibility Study in the Collection of Adult Education Statistics* (Simpson, 1973). Simpson was influential in the Council of Europe as a nominee of the DES and HMI and, at the same period, he was also an assessor to the Russell Committee. Paragraphs 418–25 of the Russell Report dealt with statistics. The report recommended that the DES should consult with the appropriate adult learning providing bodies and improve the coverage of collected statistics. There is no reference in the report to the material being collected by the Council of Europe or of the work being undertaken by Simpson. In his Council of Europe report, Simpson drew the sad conclusion, in respect of many countries, that 'everywhere an obstacle is encountered in the sheer lack of reliable statistical information about the education of adults. By comparison, the planning of other sectors of education is statistically well informed.' The OECD published a participation study in 1977, the UK part of which was produced by Maureen Woodhall. The same author was later commissioned by ACACE to produce *The Scope and Costs of the Education and Training of Adults in Britain* (Woodhall, 1980). In this second study for ACACE, Woodhall documented the changes from the early to the late 1970s. She thus covered the period from Russell to ACACE and recorded the fact that public expenditure on the education and training of adults, across all types of institutions and learning systems, had hardly changed over the years, while the number of adults studying had increased. This increase from the beginning to the end of the 1970s obscures the considerable decrease at the end of the 1970s caused by the large rise in student fees, particularly in LEAs.

In an effort to gain a detailed understanding of the complexity of adult learning provision, ACACE commissioned Keith Percy of the University of Lancaster to produce an area study of northwest England (Percy *et al.*, 1979). Unsurprisingly, the study brought to light many learning situations similar in kind to those identified by Russell in the paragraphs relating to community-based work and work with disadvantaged adults. Percy identified a wide range of voluntary organisations, many of which would not have described themselves as having a primary purpose related to education or learning but which nonetheless provided learning opportunities for their members and for local communities. Included in this category were pigeon-fancying clubs, horticultural associations and model engineering clubs. The Russell Report stressed the importance of the role and contribution of voluntary organisations in adult learning, based on the experience derived from:

- initiatives and programmes included in the EPA schemes launched following the Plowden Report of 1965
- the Home Office Community Development Projects
- community development activities promoted by a number of LEAs in the late 1960s and early 1970s.

Both ACACE and the Russell Committee gave attention to the potential of broadcasting and other media in the overall provision of adult learning. Two policy and organisation reports, *Local Radio and the Education of Adults* and *Distance Learning for Adult Students* were published by ACACE. The OU accepted its first students as the Russell Committee was sitting. As the OU was predominantly working at degree level, which in the view of the Russell Committee fell outside its remit, it was inevitable that ACACE, with a much wider remit, should give greater attention to distance learning. Both Brian Groombridge (in Fieldhouse *et al.*, pp. 365–6) and John Robinson, in *Learning Over the Air* (Robinson, 1982, pp. 182–3) highlighted the impetus given to adult learning and broadcasting by the Russell Report. Groombridge modestly omits to mention his own important contribution to the deliberations and conclusions of the Russell Committee, of which he was a member while employed as Education Officer with the ITA.

One of the joint authors of *Adult Students and Higher Education* (ACACE, 1979a) was Arthur Jones, who had been the principal author of the Russell Report. ACACE shared the concern of the Russell Committee that many mature adults wishing to pursue study in higher education establishments were prevented from doing so by one or more of many problems: financial, geographical, timing and pre-entry qualifications. These issues were explored further in the ACACE report on the future development of a system of continuing education in England and Wales, *Continuing Education: From Policies to Practice* (ACACE, 1982a). The Russell Committee's general pleading for flexibility and imagination in programming and providing opportunities for adults was endorsed by ACACE. Russell had recommended that opportunities for adults to study part-time should be expanded. ACACE, in conjunction with Birkbeck College and others, undertook a study into part-time study in higher education, published in 1982 as *Part-time Degree Level Study in the UK* (Tight, 1982).

Picking up a theme from the Russell Report, Harold Marks HMI, in a lecture to adult educators attending a training course at Avery Hill College in London, in July 1977, suggested that the development of the concept and practice of recurrent education 'will involve us in much closer cooperation between institutions'. He foresaw the local Development Councils, as recommended by Russell and later surveyed by ACACE, establishing both the necessary ethos and mechanism to enable cooperation to be maximised. Within a few years, the combination of public expenditure cuts, bearing unreasonably on adult learning, and the government's restructuring of education and training for adults, led to greater competition between providers rather than more cooperation and, at the same time, led to the demise of most of the Development/Advisory Councils created after Russell.

REPLAN (1984–91)

A major force in adult learning in the 1980s was Noel Thompson, Under-Secretary with responsibility for this aspect of education at the DES. The strength of his interest, coupled with his determination to push for positive change and improvement wherever and whenever possible, gave much encouragement to activists. It was largely due to his efforts that a number of initiatives were launched, many of which carried forward points raised by Russell and ACACE. These included PICKUP, REPLAN, UDACE, Enterprise in Higher Education and the Technical and Vocational Education Initiative (TVEI). At the same time, the MSC, responsible to the Employment Department, was launching its own 'New Training Initiative' (Fieldhouse *et al.*, 1996, pp. 69, 347). This situation, in which two government departments shared responsibility for learning at and for the workplace, continued into the 1990s.

Following the recommendation of ACACE, in the seminal report *From Policies to Practice* (ACACE, 1982a), the government established REPLAN in 1984 to promote educational opportunities for unemployed adults in England and Wales. In February 1985, Peter Brooke, Parliamentary Secretary of State for Education and Science, said: 'There is at one end of the spectrum vocational education and training, which will be more or less job-specific. But the frontier between education and training is notoriously difficult to map and it does no service to the unemployed to engage in theoretical argument on where precisely to draw the line.' This was an honest and accurate report of the situation as experienced by individuals, groups and organisations working with and for unemployed adults. The same message had been received and understood by the Russell Committee and ACACE. Both bodies, therefore, recommended flexibility in planning and programme provision.

The three principal elements of the REPLAN programme were:

- a major programme, managed by NIACE, comprising a network of eight regional centres, staff development and local development projects

- central government grants to more than 90 LEAs in England and Wales between 1985/86 and 1988/89 to assist with meeting the costs of local staffing and programming
- curriculum development work at the Further Education Unit (FEU) related to the organisation, delivery and experience of new learning activities for unemployed adults.

It was not the purpose of REPLAN to organise job training or job placement, although an unemployed person might well have benefited in these ways from participation in REPLAN learning activities. Tony Uden, manager of REPLAN during its five years of life, summarised the basic principles guiding REPLAN's operations in *A Passion for Learning* (Gilbert and Prew, 2001, pp. 87–92). First, the success of REPLAN should be judged according to the extent to which adult learning providers changed policies and systems to accommodate the needs of adult unemployed students. Second, he argued that the ideas and working practices adopted by REPLAN should be accepted as relevant to meeting the learning needs of working-class students generally. In other words, he was arguing that the educational needs of the employed and unemployed were similar, at a time when funding was almost entirely targeted at the unemployed. Uden argued that working-class students, whether or not unemployed, who might have learning difficulties, suffer forms of discrimination, or who were excluded from the social mainstream in any way, would be better placed to gain from learning opportunities as a result of the efforts of REPLAN and its staff.

At the beginning of 1991, the government decided not to extend the life of REPLAN beyond October 1991. In his letter of 23 January 1991 to senior personnel at NIACE and REPLAN, informing them of the government's decision, Tim Eggar, Minster of State at the DES, wrote: 'I believe REPLAN has provided a solid base on which LEAs, education institutions and voluntary organisations can now build in continuing to improve education and training provision for the adult unemployed.' The government's decision marked an explicit and significant change in emphasis and focus. Whereas the brief of REPLAN had been 'to promote educational opportunities for unemployed adults', the DES made clear that the successor initiative would be 'the provision of literacy and numeracy skills' and would 'be targeted at unemployed people and at those in work who cannot progress without improved basic skills'. This amounted to a fundamental move away from the conclusions and recommendations of the Russell Report and ACACE, both of which had stressed the desirability of ensuring that work with and for unemployed adults should ideally be broad based and national in coverage. The concentration on training for work, as opposed to broader provision of learning opportunities for unemployed adults, was underlined: 'Basic literacy and numeracy skills underpin most activities in our lives. They are the foundation for further education and training and are essential for most jobs. There are far too many people who cannot gain employment or improve their prospects at work because their basic skills are inadequate.' While this was self-evidently true, the DES position ignored evidence about a wide range of other educational needs that might have inhibited adults in gaining or keeping jobs.

The reaction of providers throughout the country and of NIACE, as the national coordinating body for adult learning, was expressed by Sir Roy Harding, President of NIACE, in a letter to Tim Eggar dated 27 January 1991:

> I feel I must say that I am astonished that you do not believe there is a need for a successor programme of general promotion and support for providers of education and training which would give a national focus to the learning needs of unemployed and underemployed adults. This is entirely contrary to what we have found in our wide consultations about 'People, Learning and Jobs' [REPLAN Committee and NIACE proposal to build on the success of REPLAN]. As well as many others in close contact with local needs, every college principal, both in urban and rural areas, with whom we have talked has strongly endorsed our arguments for such a national focus concerned with fostering motivation and readiness to learn amongst the unwaged and unskilled, as well as helping in the development of access to guidance and assessment services.

In a letter of 4 February 1991 to Tim Eggar, Professor Paul Fordham, chair of the NIACE REPLAN Management Committee, confirmed the main points made by Harding. While he welcomed the creation of the Training and Enterprise Councils (TECs) and the basic skills initiative to launch a number of local projects developed by LEAs and TECs, he added that:

> (T)he REPLAN experience also shows how important it is for individual motivation and readiness to learn to match the training programmes which both Government and employers see as necessary ... REPLAN's great strength is in understanding that successful training must meet both the needs of employers and also develop the aspirations and skills of individual learners from the point where they can begin to realise their own potential ... I share the dismay of many to whom I have spoken that the boldness and imagination we saw in 1983 seems somehow to have been abandoned for the 1990s.

In 1982, the present author undertook a study of education and training for unemployed adults in five European countries. Two reports were produced and submitted to the funding bodies (DES, Anglo-German Foundation and the European Commission). With the agreement of the funding organisations, copies of these two reports ('Education and Training for Unemployed Adults: Policies and Practice in five European Countries' and 'Policy Responses to Long-term Unemployment') were presented to the OECD. Policies and practices in Denmark, the Federal Republic of Germany, the Netherlands, Sweden and the UK were reviewed. The reports were not published but were used as background reference documents for policy development by the organisations and governments in the countries mentioned. Quoting two paragraphs from the first report and one from the second illustrates the extent to which problems remain basically the same, more than twenty years after the reports were written. Early in the first report, the point was made that:

> Throughout the last ten years [since 1972] considerable attention has been paid in Western Europe and North America to the economic and social implications of rising unemployment amongst young people. Concern has led to action and, in some countries, to a radical re-appraisal of the nature of curriculum and organisation of school education. However, there has been little attention paid to the education and training needs of the mature unemployed adult or the effects of unemployment on the family and neighbours of the unemployed adult or on society in general. Social and family stress in inner city areas has been compounded during the last few years by the increased evidence of physical decay and the reduction, in real terms, of the capital and revenue investment in inner city areas on a pro rata basis to meet the rise in needs and the increasing number of problems. The spiral is downwards. Unemployment amongst the adult population only increases the rapidity with which that downward movement continues. The population profile of inner city areas has changed. In general, there is an increase in the proportion of the population made up of young, independent-living people who, for one reason or another, have become separated from their families. There has been an increase in the proportion of single parent families in most major cities of Western Europe and, thus, the consequences of such units within society become disproportionately great. Our benefit systems are rarely designed to respond to society as it is. Instead, they respond to society as it was thought to have been a number of years ago.

The concluding paragraph of the first report addressed the issue of terminology. Having explained that the two words 'education' and 'training' were, at the time, variously used in the five different countries studied, the paragraph continues:

> And yet, in terms of meeting the needs of unemployed adults, the words could and should be interchangeable. The time is past when we can assume that the educated and trained adult will secure a permanent job.

Increasingly, acceptance is being voiced by employers' organisations, unions and lastly, governments, that the continuing high levels of unemployment require society to offer education and training opportunities for adults which will enable them to improve their own levels of understanding, awareness and skill to confront the problems which they, as citizens, meet from day to day. It is neither evasive nor politically irresponsible to talk of education and training as alternatives to unemployment or employment during different phases of the working lives of large numbers of adults. If we are to seriously consider this issue, we are obliged to look wider than labour-market policies and look at the broader spectrum of social policies, national and international.

In an early paragraph in 'Policy Responses to Long-term Unemployment', the present author reminded policy-makers in December 1982 that lessons appeared not to have been learned. It might suggest to policy-makers and practitioners of the early twenty-first century that radical action is still awaited.

In looking at the education and training needs and opportunities of long-term unemployed people, national and local governments throughout most developed countries have fallen into the trap of pouring more resources into traditionally structured services. There is no automatic link between equality and expansion when expansion means extending the existing structures and provision when those selfsame structures have been seen to have failed to provide appropriate support and opportunities for a significant section of the population.

It was not, therefore, surprising to note that there was a perceptible move in the approach of providers in the late 1980s and early 1990s. This shift in emphasis was from job or work-related training towards skills for employment as an element of lifelong learning. In the UK, this did not gather pace until the incoming Labour Government, in 1997, expressed the twin aims of achieving equity in learning, throughout the country, and economic success in world markets.

Governments, over many years, failed to give the necessary urgent attention to changing the structures so clearly incapable of delivering appropriate learning opportunities in the numbers required. There has been a heavy emphasis on work-related training and, even more narrowly, on job-related training. Throughout much of the 1980s and the early and middle 1990s, governments were content to create employer-led systems. As a result, little effort was made to ensure that education and training programmes for unemployed adults and for adults, in work but with low skill levels, related to an informed vision of the likely changing patterns of employment. Increasingly, it was evident that, whereas learning programmes often included the development of computer-related skills, they did not pay sufficient attention to the development of essential generic skills including numeracy, reading, spoken communication, written communication and team working. There was a tendency to neglect the basic principle of ensuring that students and trainees had the opportunity to acquire those necessary skills to enable them to 'learn how to learn' and to appreciate the significance of learning as a social activity. Changes in the balance of industries within the national economy, with growth in the personal service and business sectors, gradually highlighted the overall importance of employees being able to work as members of a team in a changing work context. This assessment of the importance of generic skills is a reminder of the points made in both the Russell Report and the 1919 Report that adult learning, however the outcomes might be applied, should be firmly rooted in the whole life of the adult concerned. The adult is more than a worker.

Unit for the Development of Adult Continuing Education (UDACE)

Having considered reports and recommendations from ACACE, which had been disbanded by the DES in 1983, the department proceeded to propose the creation of two major projects. Both were to be overseen and administered by NIACE. The brief and history of REPLAN have been outlined above. Coincidental with the timetable for the creation of REPLAN, UDACE was created. Initially, the DES proposal was to establish a Continuing Education Development Unit. In the outcome, the unit was entitled the Unit for the Development of Adult Continuing Education, thus mirroring, in terminology, the scope of NIACE itself. It was noted that the title included the word 'development', which had been recommended by Russell within the context of a National Development Council but rejected by both Conservative and Labour governments. Important though UDACE proved to be, its brief fell short of the suggested outline advanced by Russell. Activities to be undertaken by the unit fell into three principal areas:

1. UDACE was expected to collect and disseminate information regarding efficient, effective and innovative practice.
2. UDACE was to examine, by means of establishing 'expert working groups', specific policies and practices, and to make recommendations to the government and/or providers with a view to ensuring further development and improvement in adult learning.
3. UDACE was expected, with the agreement of the DES, to participate in any aspects of future research and/or development initiatives to the benefit of adult learning.

During the ten years between the publication of the Russell Report (1973) and the winding up of ACACE (1983), it had been hoped by many that NIACE itself would be able to assume a greater developmental function, through expanded information, research and publications facilities. In this way, it would carry forward a number of the recommendations of both Russell and ACACE. Others argued that such a change would be unhelpful, in view of the likelihood that the institute's ability to bring together disparate providers, as a neutral coordinating body, would thereby become lessened. Debates about the most acceptable and positive role for the institute became largely academic when it became apparent that direct funding to NIACE, from the DES and the Employment Department, would not be forthcoming to meet the cost of significant expansion in role and activity.

Individual projects carried forward by UDACE were proposed by ministers or agreed by the DES after the recommendation of the UDACE Steering Committee. The UDACE programme was extensive and vigorously advanced by the Head of the Unit, Stephen McNair. Both McNair and Uden, Head of REPLAN, had the status of Associate Directors of NIACE. Both remained as senior members of staff with NIACE after the closure of the short-term programmes, thus giving important continuity. Major themes tackled by UDACE through their programme of research and publications included access courses, open colleges, partnership working between institutions, and briefing on important matters such as the 1988 Education Reform Act (ERA). The work on educational guidance was of particular significance, and produced many publications. Unfortunately, it was not matched by major advances in resources available for educational guidance. Indeed, in 2003 the National Association for Educational Guidance for Adults (NAEGA) took the unusual step of reprinting, with a commentary (Brown, 2003), the influential UDACE (1986) report *The Challenge of Change: Developing Educational Guidance for Adults.*

The UDACE Steering Committee encouraged and supported a number of initiatives designed to improve and increase progression in learning for adults. The Russell Report had accepted that what largely determines whether a course of study should be designated vocational or non-vocational 'is the student's motive for taking it', commenting that: 'We therefore see no virtue in attempting a sharp line of division anywhere across this spectrum, but have taken our terms of reference as being simply a convenient way of indicating that we should exclude the major areas of higher, technical and art education' (paragraph 4). Despite this statement of limitation, the report did pay some attention to adult access and progression in higher education, primarily by urging higher education institutions to be more flexible and responsive to the situation confronting adult students who, for very good reasons, were unable to accept the structures, timetables and administrative arrangements largely designed for teenagers. By the late 1980s, access and progression had become major issues within adult learning.

Access courses were launched by ILEA in conjunction with the inner London polytechnics, further education colleges and adult education institutes. The initiative derived from the experience of the ESWC programme, consolidation of the authority's equal opportunities commitments and the experience of early examples of 'second chance' courses, especially the Fresh Horizons course at the City Lit. Funding was made available by the authority through the ESWC programme for learning activities linking establishments across the phases of education or which linked voluntary and statutory providers of education with other public services. Equal opportunities policies, as applied to adult learning, required all ILEA adult learning institutions and other providers funded by ILEA to ensure that their organisational arrangements and practices included action to reduce and eventually remove discrimination in learning, according to gender, ethnicity and age. Access courses were designed to enable adults to progress up the academic ladder as far as they desired, subject to satisfactory completion of each stage in the process. Successful completion guaranteed progression. Where ILEA had led the way, other LEAs and establishments followed. Experience during the 1980s provided clear evidence that, unless courses were both designed and targeted for particular groups and individuals (gender, class, ethnicity and disability) recruitment varied little from the open recruitment for mainstream courses. Having appreciated the need and begun to learn about possible ways of meeting that need, public funding for the necessary advising and support of students became more difficult to obtain, despite active support from UDACE. The abolition of ILEA in 1990 caused the loss of many access courses.

The closure of UDACE in 1991 was mitigated to some degree by the continued relevance of its many publications and by the contributions made by ex-UDACE staff in the new posts they occupied. Indeed, in respect of the staff of both UDACE and REPLAN, it should be acknowledged that their ability to take experience, knowledge and creative confidence, gained through working in the projects, into other positions, ranked as an outcome of lasting importance. In a similar way, expertise built up in ILEA was made available across the country as staff were absorbed into jobs in other organisations. REPLAN had succeeded in bringing LEA adult and further education establishments closer together in a shared understanding of the need to remove barriers to learning facing unemployed adults. Gradually, during the life of REPLAN, it was recognised that problems facing unemployed adults concerning access and progression were problems confronting working class people in general. In this regard, REPLAN, consciously or unconsciously, embedded in its practice a number of the points made in the Russell Report (paragraphs 187/88 and 277–85) and in the related recommendations.

When we speak of a comprehensive service however we mean one that caters for all the people, including those hitherto untouched by adult education. Many of them are handicapped or disadvantaged in various ways, discouraged from participating in existing provision by their own limitations and circumstances, by unsuitable premises, by a sense of their own inadequacy, by the fear of an unwelcoming bureaucracy in the administrative arrangements, or simply by the language we commonly use in describing the service. (Paragraph 187)

Similarly, UDACE, in its work concerning access and progression in relation to higher education for mature adults and the further development of open college systems, sought to inform, assist and encourage institutions to be open and flexible in serving the needs of people who previously would have faced barriers to progress. Both REPLAN and UDACE urged providers and funders to think more widely, to review policies and practices and to acknowledge that traditional agendas and priorities were unlikely to be satisfactory responses to existing demands, let alone to new challenges.

7

Russell to the National Advisory Group: Legislation and government action

The value of adult education is not only to be measured by direct increases in earning power or productive capacity or by any other materialistic yardstick, but by the quality of life it inspires in the individual and generates for the community at large.

(Russell Report, General Statement)

The man who views the world at fifty the same as he did at twenty has wasted thirty years of his life.

(Muhammad Ali)

What did we learn from the Russell Report? This chapter identifies a number of governmental and other statutory influences on the character and organisation of adult learning during the post-Russell years. The legislative backcloth against which the Russell Committee conducted its work was largely determined by the Education Act 1944, with echoes of the Education Act 1918 still being heard. Although the 1918 Act had given LEAs responsibility for adult education in their areas, this element of the Act was never implemented by governments. The 1944 Act established 'a national system of education in England and Wales, locally administered by LEAs responsible for primary, secondary and further education'. To the extent that publicly funded adult learning was covered by legislation, it was generally subsumed within the terms further, technical and higher education.

Between the appointment of the Russell Committee, in 1969, and 1997, when the newly elected Labour Government established the National Advisory Group for Continuing Education and Lifelong Learning (NAGCELL), organisations and individuals involved with adult learning were obliged to come to terms with a glut of legislation, circulars, White and Green Papers. These documents impinged on adult learning, often in very different and conflicting ways. The period under review was typified by an absence of consistency in thought and action. The succession of short-term initiatives was indicative of a lack of agreed purpose and vision and an unwillingness to learn from past experience. It proved to be largely a time of missed opportunities when it would have been possible, given governmental imagination and determination, to place adult learning within the framework of comprehensive, coherent and forward-looking legislation.

The Redcliffe-Maud and Bains reports on local government (1969 and 1972)

Two reports on the future of local authorities, published during the time that the Russell Committee was deliberating, had a considerable impact on the role and responsibilities of local government in the years ahead. In 1969, the Redcliffe-Maud Committee report (HMSO, 1969) recommended a pattern and structure for local government, with individual authorities of sufficient size and strength to be in a position to provide the full public education service required by the 1944 Act. LEAs would be expected to be able to attract good quality elected councillors and appointed officers and, thereby, act as a democratic counter-weight to the power of central government. This vision of local government was not shared by the government of the day nor by any subsequent government. The Bains Report (Bains, 1972) dealt with the management of local authorities. Acceptance of one of its principal recommendations, that local authorities should act at all times corporately, brought LEAs firmly inside the broad struc-ture of local government alongside other local public services. This led to a perceived decline in the status and power of LEAs, many of which had previously appeared to operate in a semi-detached manner, straddling the local authority and the DES. As the years passed, the decline in status of LEAs became more evident as governments increasingly ignored them when launching new initia-tives. Rightly or wrongly, governments expressed the fear that the often sluggish and bureaucratic tendencies of the corporate local authority machine would impede progress and implementation. By the end of the century, very few major adult learning initiatives were controlled and administered by local government.

There is no evidence from published material or the archives that the Russell Committee considered the implications of the Redcliffe-Maud Report, nor did the committee submit evidence to, or hold a meeting with, the Bains Committee. The decline in power and status of LEAs following the implemen-tation of corporate structures and management for local authorities can be traced back to the Bains Report. Adult learning was not the only aspect of education provision at risk of marginalisation. If the Russell Committee had been in tune with the thinking of the Bains Committee, it is possible that consideration might have been given to the position of adult learning within the corporate structure. The benefit of hindsight suggests that the Russell Committee might have paid more attention to the possible structural links between adult learning and other elements of local government provision. Russell had recorded and welcomed the fact that much adult learning was funded, programmed and delivered by public services other than the LEAs. The committee also recognised the contribution of the voluntary sector, some of which was funded by grants from council Recreation and Social Services Committees.

In the years that followed, particularly at the time of the Save Adult Education Campaign of the post-1979 period, some attention was given to the advantages and disadvantages of bringing together adult learning with other services into a coherent and broadly-based community learning service. But such attention was local, ad hoc and limited. Potential partners included, for example, museums and galleries, in-house staff training, community development, sports and arts development and elements of social and recreation services. Consequent upon missed opportunities for a fundamental review of local government struc-ture and relationships in 1969–73, a number of local reorganisations took place in LEA areas in the following years. Uncertainties continued. Changed arrange-ments frequently had short lives. Adult learning failed to achieve a central position of agreed importance within corporate authorities despite the fact that much, and sometimes most, of what was recognisable as adult learning in a given area was not provided by educational bodies or institutions.

The DES White Paper *Education: A Framework for Expansion* (1972)

After reviewing the education service during the preceding two years, the government published its White Paper 'designed to provide a framework for future action' (DES, 1972a). This made clear that the government's priorities in education were nursery education, school building, staffing standards in schools, teacher training and higher education. The White Paper tended to be dismissive of adult learning, suggesting that the government proposed to give 'careful study [to it] in the light of the forthcoming report of the Committee on Adult Education which was appointed in 1969 under Sir Lionel Russell's chairmanship thoroughly to review the whole field'. The White Paper was published in the same month as the Russell Report was sent to the Secretary of State. Undoubtedly, the Secretary of State would have known of the general conclusions and recommendations already reached by the committee. It was a matter of considerable regret and disappointment to adult educators, at the time, that no appropriate attention was given to adult learning in the White Paper, which purported to provide 'the general direction of a ten-year strategy for the education service'.

The White Paper noted that the terms further, advanced, higher, adult, tertiary and recurrent were in use, 'but by no means self-explanatory . . . the divi-sions indicated by these definitions [i.e. the above terms] are artificial in that they present different faces of a broadly organised effort to enable all members of society, with their widely differing aspirations and capacities, once they have left school behind to learn where, when and what they want in the way that best suits them'. However, the White Paper qualified this all-inclusive statement by observing that the government wished to see progress across the spectrum of post-school learning subject to the limits of available resources and priorities determined by the government. In the years that followed the production of the White Paper, it became obvious that government priorities centred on work-related and job-specific education and training, and study leading to qualifications. The only exception to this general rule was the increased funding and support for adult literacy and broader basic education.

Employment and Training Act (1973)

In 1972, when the government announced the proposed formation of the MSC to coordinate employment and training services nationally, the Russell Committee was still at work. The MSC was formally established by the Employment and Training Act in 1973 and it started its operations at the beginning of 1974. UK membership of the EEC, now the EU, was endorsed by a majority vote in the first national referendum in UK history, held in 1975. At the time of the UK entry, the second phase of the EEC Social Fund was 12 months old. It continued until 1977, to be succeeded by further funding mechanisms. Through the Social Fund and its successor funds, the UK government was enabled to meet much of the cost related to work-related training and vocational education for young people and adults. Examples of elements of adult learning partly funded in this way included a number of the MSC programmes (e.g. Training Opportunities Programme) and the Home Office Urban Programme.

Establishing the MSC within the Employment Department was a partial recognition and acknowledgement that concentrating skills training and related education on young people was unlikely to produce sufficient skilled workers. Such an approach would also condemn older workers to greater frustration and low-skilled employment. The point was elaborated in *A New Training Initiative* (MSC, 1981) and further developed in *Towards an Adult Training Strategy* (MSC, 1983), when attention was particularly focused on the work-related education and training needs of adults with disabilities, and language and basic skills needs. This latter publication set out the justification for the creation of national and local services offering comprehensive and good quality information and advice to assist adults in making their decisions about education and training. It repeated and reflected on aspects of the Russell Report in its references to the particular learning needs of disadvantaged individuals and groups. It also used information, advice and recommendations emerging from an

ACACE study on educational information, advisory and counselling services for adults, published as *Links to Learning* (ACACE, 1979b).

DES Discussion Paper *Higher Education into the 1990s* (1978)

After a number of years of uncertainty and insecurity, this discussion paper appeared to offer new possibilities to higher education establishments in the field of adult learning. The Russell Report, in common with the Alexander Report in Scotland and the earlier Ashby Report of 1954 on the financing of responsible body adult learning, had concluded that this area of work should be seen as one element of the seamless total of adult learning provision. Russell stressed this point in its observations on the major potential contribution that university adult education might have to offer to the recommended national and local Development Councils for Adult Education. *Higher Education into the 1990s* led to extensive debates based on a fundamental false premise that completely invalidated its ambitious title. The paper expected a fall in the numbers of 18-year-olds admitted to higher education. It was thought that gaps in numbers could, would and should be plugged by the admission of more mature adults: but the anticipated decline in numbers of young people did not take place. Instead a higher proportion of a falling age cohort entered higher education at 18 plus. The central government drive for higher education to focus increasingly on work and job-related education and training was strong. It had been foreshadowed by the Conservative White Paper of 1972, *A Framework for Expansion*, and continued by the post-1974 Labour Government and the post-1979 Conservative Government.

Universities were urged to consider incorporating their adult and continuing education programmes into the mainstream subject-oriented departments. This change, evident in some higher education institutions, led to a dilution of the adult and extra-mural effort, dispersal of focused adult learning staff and disengagement of much higher education adult learning from local, regional and national networks of adult learning providers. At a time when ACACE was underlining the value of maintaining a comprehensive, all-inclusive pattern of adult learning, and with the firm recommendations of the Russell Report and other reports still recent, it was more than disappointing to be obliged to respond to a discussion paper so clearly moving in the opposite direction. The prospects of higher education increasing its provision for sections of the population with the greatest learning needs were reduced.

Advisory Committee on the Supply and Training of Teachers (ACSTT) reports (1975 and 1978)

One of the principal general recommendations of the Russell Report concerned the recruitment and training of sufficient full-time and part-time staff:

There should be a planned increase in the number of full-time staff employed in adult education, particularly in the local authority sector where as quickly as possible numbers should increase substantially, suitable career and salary structures should be introduced and opportunities for training and staff development should be extended. The service should, quite properly, continue to rely heavily on part-time teachers and more opportunities should be created for them to undergo training, while their salaries should reflect the extent of their training and their accumulated service and experience. (paragraph 3.5 of the General Statement preceding the Recommendations)

The 1972 *James Report* on teacher education and training (DES, 1972b) had commented on the training needs of full-time staff in further education and on the role and contribution of the four specialist further education staff training colleges. Part-time further education staff hardly featured in the report. The James Report did not detail the special, separate, but additional training needs of those further education teachers, full-time and part-time, working in the field of adult learning. Following the publication of the James Report, the ACSTT was established. In response to the conclusions and recommendations of the James and Russell reports with regard to training for adult learning staff, and building on training activity in a number of universities, colleges of education and LEAs, a further education sub-committee of the ACSTT was created. The ACSTT produced three reports relevant to adult learning: *The Training of Teachers in Further Education* (ACSTT, 1975) was followed three years later by *The Training of Adult Education and Part-time Further Education Teachers* (ACSTT, 1978a) and *Training Teachers for Education Management in Further and Adult Education* (ACSTT, 1978b).

ACACE (1982a) suggested that the fact that these reports were produced gave encouragement, status and legitimacy to the expansion in the volume of training available to adult learning teachers and organisers, although the DES had not accepted and commended the ACSTT proposals in their entirety. John Lowe (1975) discussed the moves towards more staff training in Britain within the global context. He noted that training developments elsewhere had preceded the creation of the ACSTT. The European Bureau of Adult Education (EBAE, now the European Association for the Education of Adults, EAEA), had organised a conference on training as early as 1961 and the Council of Europe had arranged an international meeting and issued a report, *Workers in Adult Education: Their Status, Recruitment and Training* (Council of Europe, 1965). From the 1960s, as far as training for part-time teachers was concerned, apart from local initiatives programmed by individual establishments, LEAs and, occasionally, by RACs, the principal method employed was to use the City and Guilds of London Institute (CGLI) Further Education Teachers Certificate, Course No. 730. Course 730 was usually delivered by further education colleges for part-time staff employed by LEAs and occasionally, by voluntary organisations grant-aided by LEAs.

In its evidence to the Russell Committee, ILEA had stressed the importance of staff training at all levels. Based at the City Lit, ILEA had already established an Adult Education Training Unit, staffed and funded to offer training to the authority's adult learning staff and staff employed by voluntary organisations and other bodies grant-aided by ILEA. In addition, the authority opened its training programme to staff employed by outer London boroughs. By agreement with the then Extra-Mural Department of the University of London, the authority annually funded a number of senior adult learning staff to follow the course leading to the acquisition of the Diploma in Adult Education (later Diploma in Adult Continuing Education). Some outer London boroughs and surrounding County Councils also paid for staff to attend this course. In advance of the recommendation of the Russell Report that staff should be paid for time attending approved training, ILEA and its institutes had made such payments as of right.

New Training Initiative (1981)

Within the range of MSC programmes, the New Training Initiative, launched in 1981, was important in marking a break from previously strongly embedded practice. From the time of its creation in 1973, a guiding feature of education and training promoted by the MSC had been the belief that progress, standards and qualifications should be based on successful completion of set training courses. The New Training Initiative aimed to increase the opportunities for young people and adults to train and retrain throughout their working lives and to be assessed according to their abilities and competences, however and whenever acquired. This was in keeping with the view widely evident in adult learning circles, and recognised as important by the Russell Committee, that students/trainees should have past learning achievements respected and recognised. APEL and CATS were flexible and appropriate methods of recording adult learning progress, especially in higher education. In urging higher education establishments to be more amenable to potential mature adult students, the Russell Report argued that the example of the new OU should be followed: 'The credit system that it operates is appropriate to the circumstances in which adults study, especially as it allows for certain prior study elsewhere to count for credit . . . a credit structure that allows for transfer of credit has the flexibility that adult students require' (paragraph 296).

Throughout the years after the publication of the Russell Report, Conservative and Labour governments frequently changed policies and priorities concerning work-related education and training. Funding systems changed. From the MSC to the Learning and Skills Councils (LSCs), via the

TECs, organisational arrangements changed. Nonetheless, certain issues remained central to the thinking of central government. The 1944 Education Act called for continuing education for school leavers moving from school to work. This was never implemented to the extent and in the manner set out in the Act. The second ever-present core issue was meeting the basic literacy, numeracy and English language needs of adults, as urged by the Russell Committee and others in the late 1960s and early 1970s. Third, despite the willingness of governments to pay lip service to the belief that all types of learning should be valued and the learner, not the provider, should make the valuation, governments have tended to give greater attention and greater financial support to qualification-bearing learning. As recently as 2003, the government indicated that public money would be available from 2005 to fund adults pursuing a Level 2 qualification (five GCSEs grade A to C, or the equivalent), with a consequent reduction in funds available for other forms of adult learning. This harks back to policies adopted in many countries in the 1950s and 1960s to offer adults school-leaving equivalency qualifications without reference to their relevance and suitability, and without paying regard either to the motivation of the adults concerned or the appropriateness of an assessment and examination system, primarily designed for young people, being applied to mature adults.

Strategy for Higher Education in the Late 1980s and Beyond (1984)

This report (NAB/UGC, 1984), produced by the joint National Advisory Body for Public Sector Higher Education (NAB) and the Standing Committee on Continuing Education of the Universities Grants Committee (UGC), followed much of the thinking of the Robbins Committee and echoed the wishes of the Russell Committee to see higher education accepted as being both for individual and collective economic gain and for personal and societal development.

> Continuing Education needs to be fostered not only for its essential role in promoting economic prosperity but also for its contribution to personal development and social progress ... in short, both effective economic performance and harmonious social relationships depend on our ability to deal successfully with the changes and uncertainties which are now ever present in our personal and working lives. That is the primary role which we set for continuing education.

Unfortunately, the general thesis of the NAB/UGC report was not incorporated in the policies and priorities of governments throughout the 1980s. They argued that only purposeful adult learning to enhance employment-related skills and qualifications was to be considered worthy of support with national public funds.

National Council for Vocational Qualifications (NCVQ)

National Vocational Qualifications (NVQs) and General National Vocational Qualifications (GNVQs) were launched by the government as a means of ratio-nalising and harmonising a multitude of often misunderstood and outdated vocational qualifications. NVQs were mainly intended for those in employ-ment or on adult retraining schemes, while GNVQs were pre-vocational courses directed at young people in school and college. By the introduction of what was intended to become a national framework of vocational qualifica-tions, adult students and trainees became involved in a scheme seen to have advantages and disadvantages. On the positive side, standardisation led to unquestioned acceptance of learning outcomes across different institutions and different parts of the country. These outcomes were defined in terms of compe-tence – the ability to complete a vocational task satisfactorily. The ease with which the arrangement was understood meant that employers' organisations and unions, in conjunction with education providers, were of one mind with regard to the two new forms of qualifications. On the other hand, many providers of learning programmes and many students who hitherto had been wedded to the flexibility introduced by credit accumulation and the negotiated curriculum sensed that the new arrangements would restrict options. There was particular concern about the extent to which NVQs/GNVQs might qualify students for admission to vocational higher education courses. There was also criticism from both students and employers of the expensive and bureaucratic assessment procedures.

In establishing the NCVQ, the government insisted that the initiative should be led by employers, who would dominate the newly created Industry Lead Bodies. By concentrating on vocational qualifications and work-related skills and knowledge, the NCVQ was moving against the flow of the conclusions and recommendations of the Russell Committee and ACACE. A potentially damaging rift was being created between different forms of adult learning. General education was moved further behind forms of prescriptive training in the queue for public funds and governmental recognition.

Education Reform Act (ERA) (1988)

With regard to post-school education and training, this Act introduced the most fundamental and comprehensive change to the existing public education and training services since the 1944 Act. The most significant consequences of ERA for adult learning were the removal of polytechnics from LEA control, the abolition of ILEA and the creation of 13 new successor LEAs in inner London. Reducing the powers, duties and responsibilities of LEAs in this way was a firm indication that, henceforth, the DES would be driving and controlling education policy for England and Wales from the centre. Arrangements for post-school education and training, as set out in the 1944 Act and subsequent legislation and regulations, were fundamentally altered by ERA.

Recommendations of the Russell Committee, and the conclusions and priorities for action set out in *Continuing Education: From Policies to Practice* (ACACE, 1982a) to the effect that the current and potential contributions of voluntary organisations to adult learning should be both recognised and supported more strongly, led to representations being made to the Secretary of State for Education. It was hoped that ERA might correct omissions from the 1944 Act and place a specific duty on LEAs to support voluntary organisations in delivering adult learning and for hypothecated funds to be available from the DES for the voluntary sector. These representations were not successful, although the DES Circular 19/89, 'Adult Continuing Education and the Education Reform Act, 1988, Planning and Delegation Schemes', did require LEAs to consult 'local voluntary providers', i.e. existing, recognised providers, often already in receipt of central or local government support. This was a far cry from the opinion of both the Russell Committee and ACACE that voluntary organisations, whose prime purpose was not obviously the provision of learning opportunities for adults, should be respected as important partners of mainstream educational bodies in the total provision of adult learning. An important NIACE discussion paper on continuing education, *Learning Throughout Adult Life* (NIACE, 1990), noted that: 'At a time when, for the first time, adults constitute a majority of the participants in post-school education, and when polytechnics, colleges and now also universities are encouraging mature student participation, the Act is almost silent on the needs of adult learners.' The Act concentrated on structures. Even so, the government was not clear and consistent in delineating the roles and responsibilities of the DES and the Employment Department for adult learning.

Although the Act itself was disappointingly weak in respect of adult learning, the DES Circular 19/89 was more encouraging and all-embracing in its clear statement that

> Adult continuing education serves the needs of adult learners. It covers a wide variety of educational and training opportunities which include general education, whether for personal, professional, recreational and other purposes; second chance education to promote access to further education and training, higher education or employment; and continuing education to up-date skills and knowledge. It is provided in different kinds

of institution, including adult education centres, adult education institutes and colleges, community schools and community colleges, colleges of further and higher education, polytechnics, universities and a wide variety of voluntary and other bodies. (DES, 1989)

However encouraging this statement was thought to have been, it failed to acknowledge that a significant element of the total adult learning provision was community-based and community-led. The definition in the circular concentrated on buildings and institutions, stating as it did: 'It is provided in different kinds of institution, including ...' The circular did not refer to learning frequently being provided by or supported by institutions of education, but being held in a variety of community settings. To this extent, the definition did not move the understanding and acceptance of the dimensions of adult learning as far as the Russell Report and the 1919 Report, before it, had recommended. In one other major respect the circular was disappointing. After ERA and the circular, LEAs were no clearer than they had been before as to the legal definition of adequacy with regard to the range, nature and volume of adult learning in any given area, and this became a focus of much campaigning in the 1990s, as LEAs moved to cut expenditure on adult learning.

Employment Department White Paper *Employment for the 1990s* (1988)

The conclusions of the Russell Report, the Venables Report (Venables, 1976), which considered the contribution of the OU to continuing education outside the undergraduate programme, and the various reports and publications of ACACE and the work of UDACE had all pointed to the importance of creating a comprehensive and flexible pattern of adult learning provision, giving the opportunity for individuals to move in and out of education and training. Despite this, *Employment for the 1990s* (Employment Department, 1988) concentrated on a narrow view of work-related skills. There was a continued refusal to accept the lessons from the past, to the effect that individual adults have moved in and out of different forms of education and training in their search for personal satisfactions, confidence-building, academic achievement and employment advancement. Attention was primarily focused on one aspect of adult learning: 'Above all, we must invest in the skills and knowledge of our people and build up industry's skill base, through a strategy of training through life, to enable Britain to continue to grow and to generate jobs.'

In 1988, the government wound up the MSC and replaced it with the Training Commission (TC), with the task of increasing the amount of adult training. Within a few months, following the decision of the TUC not to be a partner with employers' organisations, education providers and the government in a new programme for unemployed adults, the government replaced the TC with the Training Agency (TA). Very soon, the TA was itself replaced by the Training, Education and Employment Directorate (TEED). The 1988 White Paper also led to the creation of the Training and Enterprise Councils (TECs) in England and Wales and Local Enterprise Companies (LECs) in Scotland. TECs and LECs operated independent of government and were employer controlled. In terms of local policies and priorities, they responded to learning needs as defined by the minority of those local employers who were prepared to engage with the government's training agenda. There was little vision of the future, either with regard to the aspirations and requirements of local adults or the likely development of industry and commerce. As Hillage *et al.* (2000) comment: 'Their role is to assess local requirements and, within the limits of the resources available to them, ensure that the training and enterprise needs of local employers and workforces are met'. Employers and business and industry representatives gained considerable influence on priorities in adult learning through their membership of TECs. Following the 1992 Further and Higher Education Act, all establishments funded by the Further and Higher Education Funding Councils were obliged to have a nominee of their local TECs on their Corporation Boards. Colleges were required to consult with their local TECs on producing the College Strategic Plans.

Following the change of government in 1997 and completion of the reviews of post-school education and training, implementation of the Learning and Skills Act in April 2001 led to the incorporation of the education and training functions of TECs into the work of the newly created Learning and Skills Councils, but with additional responsibility for the work of Further Education. The work of the FEFC was absorbed into the national LSC.

Office for Standards in Education (OFSTED) (1990)

OFSTED was established by the government in 1990. Among OFSTED's many responsibilities was reporting to and advising ministers on the state of adult learning. In Appendix 1 of *An Education for the People?* Elsdon (2001) explains how HMI had operated from the early years of the twentieth century to fulfil their function 'to have a deep and thorough knowledge of the state of education in all its institutions and services throughout the country, and to advise the Minister of its state, of its needs and of the practical and policy implications'. He describes how files were built up over many years on every adult learning institution, organisation and service in the country, ensuring that each and every file contained up-to-date information available to HMI when visiting, inspecting or training. He then explains that this huge body of systematically accumulated knowledge and research resource was thought to have been destroyed at the time of the reorganisation and downgrading of the Inspectorate on the arrival of OFSTED. It was this alleged incident, together with the antagonism towards general and personal learning expressed by the government and OFSTED, which gave rise to the period being described as 'the age of the Philistines' in many adult learning circles. This invaluable historical archive, along with much other relevant material, disappeared. Even if it was thought reasonable for OFSTED to have decided that nothing could be learned from the comprehensive past records, the very act gave a strong indication of the marginality of adult learning in the spread of public education. The files of the National Archives are light on such documentation, from which much could have been learned. In the field of education, perhaps more than in any other fields of public and social activity, learning from past experience should be axiomatic. The absence of records, coupled with the loss of much knowledge gained by the specialist adult learning HMI whose role and influence had been marginalised, was a partial explanation for the perceived lack of interest of OFSTED in adult learning.

DES/ED White Paper *Education and Training for the 21st Century* (1991); Further and Higher Education Act (1992)

Before adult learning providers had had sufficient time or opportunity to come to terms with the consequences of the fundamental changes introduced as a result of the passing of the Education Reform Act of 1988, further radical change was outlined in the 1991 White Paper for England and Wales (DES, 1991) and its parallel White Paper for Scotland, 'Access and Opportunity: A Strategy for Education and Training'. The Act drew on the accumulated experience of the MSC and its various initiatives since 1974. National policy had increasingly concentrated on vocational education and skills training. Primarily, the White Paper and the Further and Higher Education Act which followed in 1992 were concerned with the 16–19 age group despite the presentation of the White Paper as covering post-16 education and training. The government foresaw the FEFC as being dedicated to the improvement and expansion of vocational and work-related education and training. The White Paper raised the issue of public and employer funding of education and training which could not be easily related to employment in general or the workplace in particular. Indeed, rather provocatively, the White Paper proposed that public funding should only be made available for 'useful' learning. Although this point was not incorporated in the Act in such crude terms, the clear intent of the government to differentiate in type and priority between different forms of adult learning was reflected in the Schedule 2/Non-Schedule 2 split (see below) and in the approach adopted towards the various forms of provision.

The aim of the 1992 Act was to privilege instrumental learning above all other and, thus, in this regard, to oppose and reject the conclusions and recommendations of the 1919 Final Report, the advice of ACACE and view of the Russell Committee expressed in the head quote to this chapter. The brief given to the Russell Committee had concerned non-vocational education for adults. In addition to non-vocational education for adults, the committee had paid regard to wider fields of adult learning, including education and work and adult students in higher education. Consistent with the evidence they had received and the experience of their members, the Russell Committee and ACACE had both urged governments to respect all forms of adult learning as being of equal importance. The value of adult learning was to be judged according to the motivation and expectation of the students and the degree to which their learning needs were met. In spite of this, the White Paper sought to reinforce the division between education and training and between different forms of learning provision, and the Act gave legislative power to this view.

According to the dominant political view, publicly funded education and training for adults was to be seen to be part of the developing market-driven society. The White Paper argued that public funds should be applied to adult learning with explicit academic, qualification and vocational purpose, together with courses offering access to higher levels of study, literacy, numeracy and English for speakers of other languages and programmes for adults with other special educational needs. These were the 'Schedule 2' subjects. These aspects of government-favoured adult learning were most likely to be provided by colleges in conjunction with the FEFC. Little regard was given, in the White Paper, to the millions of other adults whose learning was dismissed with the comment that it could have a valuable social function. These included not only the general public, but also the retired and elderly, parents at home with young children, people with disabilities, those requiring special learning opportunities in a non-educational social setting, prisoners and long-stay hospital patients. Rhetoric about value for money and the economic imperative replaced the views expressed in the Russell Report, the 1919 Report and ACACE publications, that adult learning should be seen to have personal, community and social value for individuals and society, in addition to general economic benefit.

This Act removed Further Education Colleges from the control of LEAs, making them free-standing corporations in receipt of central government funds via the newly formed FEFC. Colleges became subject to inspection by the FEFC inspectorate and, thereby, accountable to the FEFC. The government's intentions to detach further education from local government were confirmed by the decision that local authorities would not have places on the college corporation boards as of right. Some 430 colleges were accountable to the FEFC in this way. The designation colleges included the WEA and a small number of specialist adult education establishments, in addition to further, tertiary, art, agriculture and sixth form colleges which were substantial providers of adult learning.

For the first time, a legislative distinction was drawn between different forms of adult learning. The Act specified that: 'It shall be the duty of every local education authority to secure the provision for their area of adequate facilities for further education to which this subsection applies . . . where the education is provided by means of a course of a description mentioned in Schedule 2 of this Act.' Schedule 2 identified the areas of further education particularly designated as falling within the remit of the FEFC to offer funding, but did not specify what other learning activities should be secured by the LEA. LEAs retained a power to provide Schedule 2 learning if they so decided, but their main task would be as providers or commissioners of 'non-Schedule 2' work. Once again, a wide range of adult learning was being described in negative terms. Legislation still contained those undefined and unsatisfactory words 'secure' and 'adequate'. How was an LEA meant to 'secure provision' if it had no sanction to impose on a college should the college not accept the judgement of the LEA that certain 'facilities' were needed? By what criteria was 'adequate' to be measured? The outcome was that in the years that followed many LEAs significantly reduced the funding and, therefore, the amount of provision within their areas and were not subject to any penalty from central government (Fieldhouse *et al.*, 1996, pp. 75–6, 104–5).

The Further and Higher Education Act gave the legislative backing to the creation of the HEFC, responsible for distributing and monitoring the use of public monies to higher education establishments and to further education colleges in respect of higher education level programmes they provided. After implementation of the 1992 Act, the balance of contributions to adult learning from different providers varied considerably from place to place. Where the LEAs had a long history of direct provision of adult learning programmes, direct provision often continued, ensuring that the LEAs maintained sufficient strength and credibility so as to be important partners with further education colleges, universities and the WEA in coordinated local programmes. On the other hand, in situations where the LEAs had made little direct provision, or where the LEAs employed few full-time adult educators or, third, where the LEAs showed little interest in playing a leading role in the provision of adult learning programmes, LEAs frequently contracted out their provision to stronger further education and higher education establishments. The impact of the Act was to encourage competition between providers seeking to maximise student numbers rather than to respond to the needs of those who had bene-fited least from the public education service and whose learning needs were the greatest. It was an accountant's, rather than an adult educator's, view of adult learning.

While striving to enrol more students above achieving any other objective, providers devoted fewer resources to essential community development and community support work. Community-based outreach work, so effective and emancipatory during the period from the 1960s, became increasingly associated with marketing and publicising adult learning programmes, as defined by the providers. Previously, such work was concerned with listening to and learning from people in the community as they articulated their learning needs and participated in designing and implementing programmes to meet the needs. Cooperation between LEAs and voluntary and community organisations was reduced. Imaginative and creative initiatives involving traditional education providers and non-education interests became less evident. One year after the implementation of the Act, the National Association of Teachers in Further and Higher Education (NATFHE) published a report on the impact of the Further and Higher Education Act 1992 on adult education (NATFHE, 1993). The conclusions of the report were not controversial. They reflected experience throughout the country. In direct conflict with the aspirations of the Russell Committee for stronger, better staffed and resourced and relevant adult learning for all, the NATFHE survey found that there had been a reduction in the number of buildings and sites designated as centres for adult learning. An increase in daytime provision, coinciding with a reduction in evening and weekend provision, indicated a move away from education for personal development and fulfilment towards work-related or job-specific training. There had been a measurable reduction in the number of organising and teaching staff in LEAs employed to deliver programmes related to Russell work. Student fees had risen. The range of concessionary fees had reduced and some LEAs and further education colleges had introduced full-cost recovery courses or income generation activities, thus distorting the balance of provision, and pricing out sections of the local communities.

European Commission White Paper *Growth, Competitiveness, Employment: The Challenge and Ways Forward into the 21st Century* (1994)

This White Paper sent strong messages to governments of the member countries of the EU to the effect that public funding of the broad range of lifelong learning for all people would be beneficial to economic productivity, social inclusiveness and to the well-being of individuals. The inclusive approach to lifelong learning adopted in the European White Paper differed from the pattern then existing in most EU member countries, where a separation of general adult learning programmes from job- or work-related training was evident. A feature of this separation concerned funding. Generally, governments were more supportive of adult learning programmes with an explicitly vocational or academic purpose. The commitment of the Russell Committee to the maintenance of parity of esteem between all forms of learning and all subject areas had guided much thinking among providers in the years after the publication of the report. This view was reinforced by the conclusions and recommendations of ACACE (1982a) in *Continuing Education: From Policies to Practice*. Nonetheless, the UK government argued, in its 1991 White Paper, *Education and Training for the 21ˢᵗ Century*, that such public funding as might be available should be applied to vocational and academic courses and courses with an overt relationship to national economic priorities. After much pressure, the government modified its view to enable LEAs to fund adult learning not leading to qualifications or certification. The government's initial proposal, coupled with the threat to reduce or withdraw social security benefits from people who were referred to learning programmes but did not attend, would have been bound to fail to satisfy individuals and the wider world of employment. The purposes and motives of learners cannot be derived from the name given to courses. Experience also showed that people could not be bullied or forced into effective learning.

The Disability Discrimination Act (1995); The Kennedy Report
Learning Works: Widening Participation in Further Education (1997)

Despite the recommendations of the Russell Report and of ACACE, access to learning for adults with disabilities became more difficult. Closure of many centres for adult learning in town centres and residential areas, increasing cost and unreliability of public transport, difficulty of access to teaching rooms and lack of specialist equipment, were all elements of a major problem. There has been little evidence of the Disability Discrimination Act affecting the provision of adult learning or the numbers of disabled adult students or trainees, although the people who met the definition of disabled person under the Act constituted approximately 12 per cent of the population. The regulations associated with the Act provided that 'disability is any physical or mental impairment which has a substantial and long-term adverse effect on . . . normal day-to-day activities . . . disability may for example relate to mobility, manual dexterity, physical coordination, incontinence, speech, hearing or sight, memory, and ability to concentrate, learn or understand.'

The Kennedy Committee was established by the FEFC in 1994 and reported in 1997. Thus, it was deliberating when the Disability Discrimination Act was passed in 1995. There is no indication, however, that the Kennedy Report (Kennedy, 1997) was influenced by the debates and consultation preceding the passing of the Act. Whereas the Act necessarily paid regard to general issues acting against achieving equal opportunities for disabled people, the Kennedy Committee specifically considered widening participation in further education. Although the committee argued that learning for work and learning for other purposes were inseparable, the funding mechanisms and priorities of the FEFC militated against widening participation across all aspects of adult learning. The incoming Labour Government was pleased to pick up the Kennedy Report, and rapidly published its response. Very soon, matters relating to widening participation became one element of social exclusion to be handled centrally by the Social Exclusion Unit in the Cabinet Office. Lack of imagination and determination by providers, unwillingness of governments and quangos, especially the FEFC and TECs, to establish ways of applying regulations and guidelines flexibly, and maintenance of long-standing barriers to access, including organisational, financial and physical barriers, have limited the rate and extent of progress towards equity of treatment and consideration for all. Thirty years after Russell, both widening participation and equal opportunities in learning for disabled people remain as aspirations.

8
The changing world of adult learning 1972–97

We believe that the time has come for this country to give the same serious attention to the education of adults as it has given to the education of children.
(ACACE, 1982a, p. 1)

At a time of rapid economic, social and technological change there is increasing pressure on individuals to shape their lives to new circumstances, needs and opportunities, whether at home or at work. The expansion of continuing education, therefore, is not merely desirable but essential.
(NIACE, 1990)

The difficult tasks lie ahead, since strategies for the recruitment and motivation of traditional non-participants are likely to be complex and require a willingness to change traditional practices which has significant resource and staffing implications for education and training providers. The task will not be achieved by a 'quick fix'.
(NIACE, 1993, p.13)

Developments and changes in adult learning after Russell

For many years after the appointment of the Russell Committee in 1969, government policies and programmes were primarily designed to increase the range and improve the skills of workers to the general benefit of the national economy. At the same time, providers of adult learning programmes continued to express a broader commitment to the public by offering opportunities to satisfy the learning wishes of individual adults, whether for employment, financial gain or personal interest. This created a tension that characterised most debates about adult learning in the following two decades and still resonates in current debates. Whereas the Russell Committee, according to its terms of reference, was called upon 'to assess the need for and review the provision of non-vocational adult education in England and Wales', ACACE was established 'to advise generally on matters relevant to the provision of education for adults in England and Wales'. At the time of the establishment of ACACE, in 1977, the DES stressed that the phrase 'education for adults' was to be interpreted as being wider than 'adult education', however adult education might be defined. With diffidence, the Russell Committee had also sought to establish a wide interpretation of its terms of reference. In paragraph 4 of the Introduction to their report, the committee stated:

> Our terms of reference direct us to 'the provision of non-vocational adult education' but define our field of study no further. In practice, and in the terms of the Education Act 1944, there is a spectrum called further education which at one end is clearly vocational (though still not unconnected with personal and social development) and at the other is personal, social, cultural and non-vocational. It has often been represented to us in evidence that what makes a course of study vocational or not is the student's motive for taking it: if he [sic] takes it to qualify for a job it is vocational; if he takes it for the pure love of learning it is not, whatever the subject; and there will be relatively few courses that are composed wholly of one type or the other. We therefore see no virtue in attempting a sharp line of division anywhere across this spectrum, but have taken our terms of reference as being simply a convenient way of indicating that we should exclude the major areas of higher, technical and art education.

Regrettably, the committee did not explain why it had both broadened its interpretation of the terms of reference while, at the same time, excluding certain areas of learning which attracted many mature adult students. For most practitioners at the time, these excluded areas were essential elements of adult learning, undifferentiated in principle from others and thus thought to have been unjustifiably set aside.

In 1979, the incoming Conservative Government made clear its intentions to reduce public expenditure generally and, as far as adult learning was concerned, to reduce or eliminate national funding for adult learning not directly related to employment and skills. It encouraged LEAs to do the same at the local level. In political terms, it seized the space that had been created by Prime Minister James Callaghan's 1976 Ruskin College speech, in which he had called for a 'great debate' about the relationship between education and work. This political space was then exploited for ends which had little or nothing to do with the learning aspirations of adults. Thus, only six years after the publication of the Russell Report, and while ACACE was working with a brief to think of adult education as wider than whatever definitions of the term might have been considered valid at the time, liberal education for personal interest, satisfaction and growth came under threat. By the end of 1979, a national Save Adult Education Campaign had become established. It grew from modest but indicative beginnings in the Nottingham area, where the WEA and Nottingham University Department of Adult Education joined together to challenge the expressed intentions of the county LEA to greatly reduce expenditure on adult education by a combination of three measures:

- an increase in student fees
- the removal of concessionary fee arrangements designed to assist those on low incomes or with special educational needs, and
- the closure of many of the County's school-based evening centres.

Two leading international thinkers in adult learning at the time of the publication of the report, and for many years thereafter, were Ivan Illich and Paulo Freire. Their work featured in training courses for adult learning practitioners and activists, community workers and community development activists. In the late 1960s and early 1970s, their thinking greatly influenced the ideas and practice of those involved in EPA- and CDP-related work in Liverpool, community and social development workers in major cities, overspill estates and new towns, and community education workers in inner London. Illich's *Deschooling Society* and Freire's *Pedagogy of the Oppressed* became standard reference works for people committed to the belief that improvement in the present systems was not sufficient to ensure a better future. Systems had to change. Illich advanced a more radical argument and encouraged all involved in community learning to accept that institutions per se were blocks to learning. On the other hand, Freire adopted, adapted and advocated the two fundamental principles of community developers. First, that the cultures and values of groups or sections of populations with which adult learning activists work, should be respected at all times. Second, that learning starts from the point determined by the individual learner not by the person in the teaching role. This complex and challenging assertion became greatly simplified in the statement 'start from where people are'.

Learning at work

Further acknowledgement of the personal and employment-related benefits of adult learning came in the late 1980s and early 1990s through the creation and expansion of Employee Development Schemes (EDS). The first and best known in the UK was the Employee Development and Assistance Programme (EDAP) established in 1987 by the Ford Motor Company (Tuckett, 1991). By the year 1989/90, 45 per cent of eligible staff had participated, of whom 70 per cent had not previously participated in any organised form of adult learning. The company's business objectives were:

- to change the workplace culture by funding learning activities for hourly paid and salaried staff, during non-working time
- to improve levels of literacy, numeracy and basic skills

- to raise employee morale and motivation
- to establish a shared understanding and commitment to quality at work and improving industrial relations.

The trade unions' objective was to increase the range of non-wage benefits open to their members. Courses funded through EDAP, because they were to take place in employees' own time, were not to be job-related. Company training was a quite separate department, with a budget much greater than that of EDAP. A tripartite partnership of the company and unions representing the two categories of employees agreed the purpose of EDAP during the annual contract and pay negotiations. EDAP was designed 'to offer employees a wide range of personal and career development education and training, retraining and development activities and to make available a variety of employee assistance services to encourage healthier lifestyles'.

Many courses took place at the workplace, with a purpose-built learning centre in place at Dagenham by the mid-1990s. This enabled flexibility in programming to accommodate shift-work patterns. For many employees, it also reduced or removed the burden of travel time between the place of work and the place of study. The success of the EDAP was significantly underpinned by the working partnership between the promoters of the EDAP and local providers of adult learning programmes. Another factor was the evident valuing, by employer and unions, of general adult learning organised through, and sometimes taking place in, the workplace. The partnership between education and industry has been valuable beyond simply the provision of courses. From basic skills, including literacy, numeracy and English for speakers of other languages to honours degree courses, employees enjoyed an extensive choice. By the time Ford EDAP received the Department of Employment's Individual Commitment Award in May 1995, the evidence was overwhelmingly clear that the EDAP had acted as an inspirational example of imaginative good practice in what had become a higher performing workplace. This award publicly confirmed the positive outcomes from providing workplace and work-related learning wider than job-related training. The EDAP initiative had proved to be good for business and good for employees, individually and collectively. More modest outcomes, but similar in principle, have been documented in respect of EDS elsewhere, including the EDS at Peugeot and Rover, Lucas Industries, a number of local authorities and at NIACE itself (Forrester et al., 1995).

Paragraphs 270–3 of the Russell Report discussed different forms of 'educational leave'. Compulsory day or block release for young workers under the age of 18, for 'such further education . . . as will enable them to develop their various aptitudes and capacities and will prepare them for the responsibilities of citizenship' had been explicit in the Education Act 1944 but never implemented. The committee regretted the fact that such release from work for study as became available was given only for vocational study or apprenticeship training. Even that type of release was limited: in 1969, 40 per cent of young men employees took day-release courses but day-release study was only available to 10 per cent of young women. In 1964, the UNESCO general conference had invited member countries 'to grant workers leave, paid if possible, necessary for training in the framework of permanent education'. The view, at the time, was that such arrangements, under detailed consideration by the International Labour Organisation (ILO) since 1965, 'would embrace general, social and civic education, training at all levels, and trade union education' (paragraph 271). The Russell Report commented that some countries had introduced legislation to allow for paid educational leave. It argued that the CBI, the TUC and appropriate government departments should act 'to ensure that we do not lag behind other European countries in affording adequate opportunities for educational leave' (recommendation 48).

It is a matter of regret that there has been very little progress in developing Paid Educational Leave (PEL) since the Russell Report. Some release has been provided by employers, especially for basic education (Forrester *et al.*, 1995, pp. 98–111), in both the private and public sectors. David Miliband's work at the Institute for Public Policy Research (IPPR) helped to keep discussion of paid educational release alive (Miliband, 1990). From the Kennedy Report (1997) onwards, there was a clear desire to re-evaluate the overall learning needs of employed adults. A secondary, but important pressure for action was the evidence from existing workforce training and skills development programmes that productivity and profitability would be enhanced, the workforce would display greater motivation and loyalty, and customer care would improve. The question of a statutory minimum entitlement to PEL has been raised since the 1960s, when the debates took place within UNESCO and the ILO about how PEL might relate to a broader adult entitlement to learning. If PEL were an entitlement of all employees, should there not be a similar entitlement for people who do not happen to be in employment? If PEL is considered to be of benefit to individuals as well as companies and the economy, more broadly, should there not be arrangements to include people unemployed but seeking work, people of working age otherwise committed as parents, unpaid carers and volunteers, men and women unable to work due to illness and disability and people who have retired from paid work? Such a general entitlement was called for in the NIACE (1990) Policy Discussion Paper on Continuing Education, *Learning Throughout Adult Life*, which included the recommendation that the government should 'consider means for the provision of a free-of-charge entitlement for every adult to learning opportunities equivalent to at least 60 hours of study per year on an accumulating basis, to be used for either education or training'. NIACE believed two advantages would accrue if all adults were to be offered a minimum entitlement to learning, at a time, in a place and of a type chosen by the prospective learners: there would be an increase in the number of adult learners, and they would come from a wider cross-section of the total population.

Within the context of adult learning and industry, the Russell Committee identified the education of trade unionists as one of the fastest growing points of 'role education' in the early 1970s. The report recommended that 'the education of trade unionists should be expanded and more tutors should be trained for work in this area of adult education' (recommendation 45). A major influence on policy and practice in this aspect of adult learning provision from its formation in 1969 to the early 1990s, when it ceased to function, was the Society of Industrial Tutors (SIT). In an article in *Adult Education* in 1974, Geoffrey Stuttard outlined the growth of the SIT and its position with regard to the recommendations of the Russell Report. One of the SIT's first actions was to submit evidence to the Russell Committee. The SIT aimed to 'advance the general education of men and women in industry and commerce' and 'to help and support tutors to maintain in their work the spirit and independence of the adult education liberal tradition' (Stuttard, 1974). In its evidence to the Russell Committee, the Society made three specific assertions:

1. Liberal adult education of people in industry and commerce should be seen as a growth area.
2. The students to be drawn from industry and commerce were from that section of the total population often not touched by adult learning providers, often with limited school education and, therefore, a priority target group.
3. The industrial background of the students was seen to be 'increasingly important in social, economic and political terms, at a time when key concepts in industry are those of participation and interdependence'.

Immediately following publication of the Russell Report, the SIT was actively involved in pushing forward a number of the report's recommendations. A policy statement approved at the SIT annual conference in 1973 made particular reference to seven topics, most of which featured strongly in the recommendations of the Russell Report: statutory day release; a new long-term residential college; regional consortia to coordinate work; influence on and through the media; strong Industrial Relations study centres; tutor training courses and facilities; and, finally, student participation. Special mention should be made of the role and contribution of the SIT in discussions leading to the establishment of the Northern College of Residential Adult Education. In 1973, membership of the SIT was approximately 250. However, it 'punched above its weight' in influencing policy. Much of the influence was by way of well-considered publications and responses to governmental and other official reports and papers. In 1974–5, the Society worked with Michael Foot, Secretary of State for Employment, and his civil servants on aspects of the Employment Protection Act 1975, notably Clause 57 which gave 'lay trade union officials a statutory right to day release for industrial relations training'. Despite the obvious progress achieved by the SIT's various interventions and contributions to policy thinking and programming, an article by Bruce Spencer (1991) commented pessimistically: 'When the Russell Committee reported in 1973, many felt that it was heralding a new era, but with hindsight we can say it was essentially recording adult education convention and its recommendations were largely displaced by funding problems and by the perceived needs of the "economy" for qualifications and training.' Such pessimism was understandable in 1991, given the plight of learning providers in face of the cuts and constraints to which they were being subjected. However, during this bleak period it was still possible to reflect on what had been achieved since Russell and what would have been even more at risk had the Russell Committee not been established.

The Ashby, Russell and Alexander reports, recommended that universities should increase provision of vocational and professional courses as they diversified provision and widened participation. In the early 1980s, the DES began to exert pressure on universities to programme more of this work, just as LEAs and other bodies were being urged to give greater priority to education and training related to jobs, employment and work skills. This led to the DES initiative in 1982 known as PICKUP (Professional, Industrial and Commercial Updating). PICKUP was established to be a means whereby higher education would respond to training needs as defined by business and industry. Employers were expected to pay for short, part-time, flexible and cost-effective training. Training was to be post-experience rather than initial and would be specifically vocational for people already in employment. While there was no reluctance on the part of the universities to increase post-experience vocational education, there was much concern that, at a time of scarce resources, the DES diverted funds to PICKUP from the Responsible Body budget allocation for England and Wales. Scottish university extra-mural departments experienced a reduction in their governmental grants to fund PICKUP work in Scotland. Some new targeted funds were made available by the government to cover a proportion of the cost of PICKUP. Consequently, the ability of the universities to maintain their traditional liberal programmes was severely reduced. Throughout the 1980s, a constantly rising proportion of university continuing education, within specialist adult learning departments and the universities as a whole, was related to PICKUP and similar activities.

Some of the companies, public authorities and voluntary organisations, large and small, which had established EDS, were quick to seek the award of Investors in People (IiP) status. Having been seen by their employees and the wider community as committed to adult learning through work, the next step was for companies to achieve recognition for their commitment to employee training.

Funding for IiP became available from TECs. Employers, unions and educational establishments largely welcomed the IiP initiative and the kitemark it brought. Despite its success, IiP continued to beg a crucial question: firms that wanted the award had to show that training was related to their actual business requirements, yet who was to say what the balance should be of general educational development and job-specific training? Generally, employers and TECs preferred to fund the job-specific training rather than the general educational development.

English as a second or additional language

As will be noted towards the end of this chapter, Russell did not differentiate in any way between the different educational needs of disadvantaged adults. On the other hand, *The Disadvantaged Adult* (Clyne, 1972) has a whole chapter on the educational needs of adult immigrants. For the Russell Committee, immigrants with poor skills in English were one example among many of the way disadvantage was threaded through society. In 1977, having consulted widely with practitioners and community organisations, the BBC launched a significant series of English language programmes (*Parosi*) for South Asian women. The programmes were designed to be used in a variety of settings – in the homes of individuals, in conjunction with one-to-one teaching and learning arrangements, in groups arranged by Asian community and religious organisations and, finally, in adult education centres and institutes. This pattern confirmed the appropriateness of the Russell Committee's view that learning programmes should be promoted in places and organisational arrangements appropriate to the needs and situations of the prospective learners. In the Freirean phraseology of the time, providers of learning should 'start where people are', intellectually, educationally and in other ways.

It was assumed that, whereas most South Asian women would be likely to require separate and special programmes to assist in the learning of English, men would be more likely to pick up English at work, while their children would acquire the language at school. These assumptions were misplaced. It soon became accepted that language learning could not be left to chance. Structured programmes were required in the workplace and at schools. In a number of areas of high immigration, Industrial Language Training Units were established to teach English within the workplace. In 1978, the National Association for Teaching English as a Second Language (NATESLA) was founded. Its initial aims were:

- disseminating and supporting the development of English as a Second Language (ESL) materials and methodology

- placing the narrow focus of language teaching constantly within the wider economic and social reality of the UK
- representing bilingual students and their needs to national bodies.

By the 1990s, the emphasis of English language teaching came to focus more on refugees and asylum-seekers, many of whom had been traumatised by war, famine and displacement. They brought with them a further range of challenges to policy-makers and to adult educators.

Working with older people

The University of the Third Age (U3A) was established in the UK in 1982, ten years after the first U3A was created in Toulouse, France. The French initiative followed an evident expression of frustration on the part of a number of older people that learning opportunities were few and far between. This expression coincided fortuitously with a central government requirement in France that universities should make provision for older people. While the French initiative acted as a spur to action in the UK, the organisation and structure of the U3A differed in the two countries. In France, groups of third-agers, through their committees, negotiated with local universities for use of accommodation, facilities and staff expertise. In the UK, the shape of the U3A owed much to the writings of Peter Laslett, whose report, *The Education of the Elderly in Britain* (Laslett, 1980), called for due recognition of the cultural and intellectual importance of older people.

Supported by a £9,000 grant from the Nuffield Foundation in 1982, the U3A grew rapidly as a network of independent local U3As. In 1983, the Third Age Trust was registered as an education charity. Further national development funding was received that year from The Gulbenkian Foundation and the NEC. Later, in 1986, the national U3A received a grant of £14,900 for a period of three and a half years from the DES. By 1994, there were nearly 250 local U3As in membership of the Third Age Trust, plus a few local U3As that had taken the decision not to join the national body. From its earliest days, given that the Third Age Trust was a registered educational charity, all local groups have sought to ensure the primacy of the educational purpose. Inevitably, differences have existed between individuals and groups over where the balance should be struck between academic and social activities. In keeping with the Russell Committee's acknowledgement of the importance of community-based voluntary organisations and their role in the broad provision of adult learning, the U3A has been an excellent example of self-help. The 1919 Adult Education Committee would have recognised the operation of a learning cooperative, run along mutual lines. Local U3As are largely self-funded and self-managed, using and valuing the accumulated skills, knowledge and experience of members. By the later 1980s, and continuing into the early 1990s, the national U3A was sufficiently strong and confident to play an important part in the Save Adult Education Campaign and in the VAEF. At the same time as promoting their own learning programmes, many local U3As campaigned and lobbied in defence of public funding for liberal and non-vocational adult learning.

Family education

As a major educational charity, with 40 years' experience in pre-school and adult learning, the Pre-school Learning Alliance (PLA) [previously the Pre-school Playgroups Association (PPA)] reaches more than 500,000 families each day through its member pre-schools. Despite its designation as an organisation concerned with early years learning and care, the PLA is a major provider of adult learning programmes. Through the more than 250,000 actively involved parents working regularly as volunteer helpers in pre-schools, and the participation of most of these adults in courses promoted at pre-school, regional and national levels, the PLA was the largest single contributor to parent and family learning during the period 1972–97. Although the PPA was established before the Russell Committee started its work, the recommendations of the report with regard to parent and family learning, coupled with some of the documented outcomes of the EPA initiatives following the Plowden Report (1967), gave an impetus to the conjoined early years and parent education work. Participation in courses and group work on topics as varied as child development, family learning, parents as teachers, intergenerational learning, understanding education and committee work laid the learning foundations for many people. It is a matter of record that the involvement of large numbers of parents, primarily women, in pre-schools and associated courses has resulted in examples of individual progress and success previously unimaginable by the individuals concerned. The routes from pre-school activity, as volunteer helpers, to trained and qualified teacher or social worker, or to university lecturer, school governor, elected councillor or MP may have been long but they are routes which have been taken.

In the 1990s, interest in the field of family education was revived. This was mainly due to concern that adults with negative experiences of education found it difficult to support their children at school, and in some cases were passing on their own negative perceptions of school to their children. It soon came to be recognised that family education promoted through schools (usually primary schools) had advantages for both parents and children. Adults were able to raise their own self-esteem and educational level and better support their children in activities such as reading and homework and in their general attitudes towards education. It was the ongoing support of NIACE which kept debates about family education alive through the 1990s, in particular through the NIACE publication *Riches Beyond Price* (Alexander and Clyne, 1995) and associated conferences and lobbying activities.

Following the election of the Labour Government in 1997, family learning came to be seen increasingly as a central part of the social inclusion agenda. Viewed in this light, what family education tends to play down are the real material constraints which make family life stressful for poor parents. Peter Robinson, an economist, came to the conclusion that longitudinal studies demonstrate the 'dominant impact of social and economic disadvantage in impeding basic skills development' (Robinson, 1997, p. 3) He concluded that 'over the long run the most powerful "educational" policy is arguably one which tackles child poverty, rather than any modest interventions in schooling'. The most successful adult learning initiatives with 'parents' (usually mothers) are those that have begun to open up the possibility of a second chance at education, and ultimately access to well-paid jobs rather than the low-paid irregular work which is so often the lot of women with young children.

ILEA

The ILEA was in the vanguard of many developments in adult learning during the 1970s (Tuckett, 1988). Some initiatives followed the publication of the Russell Report. Others preceded and influenced the report. Evidence to the Russell Committee was published as an appendix to the agenda of the ILEA Education Committee meeting of 18 February 1970. In view of the size and nature of the adult education service in inner London, it was inevitable that the evidence should have assumed national importance. According to William Devereux (1982) the evidence made two specially important contributions to the national scene:

1. The survey of students undertaken by ILEA's Research and Statistics Division put the spotlight on those who were not being served by ILEA – which had done more than most to make facilities widely available.
2. Its detailed consideration of the effect on student enrolment of the level of fees charged.

In consideration of the first of the two points made by Devereux, namely the identification of those sectors of the population not served by ILEA's adult education service, the evidence to the Russell Committee, in its conclusion, asserted that 'the service exists to educate and not just to continue the education of the educated'. ILEA judged that a 'community fieldworker' approach was required, with appropriate staff appointed to adult education institutes or to suitable voluntary organisations funded substantially by the authority. For this approach to be effective, it was considered essential to have crèches, playgroup and nursery provision, and classes and group work at reduced fees 'for mothers'. This outreach approach stressed not just the needs of individuals in poor communities, but also their collective interests as expressed through organisations such as tenants associations, black and ethnic minority groups and older people's organisations. Such group work was characteristic of ILEA outreach work. The history of outreach or community education work in adult learning in inner London is well documented in Devereux's (1982) book and in reflective accounts published well after the demise of ILEA in 1990 (Payne, 1995; NIACE, 2000). The first ILEA outreach worker was in post in the autumn of 1971 and was followed by a number of others by the middle of 1972. Outreach work fell victim to the economies of the 1980s and 1990s. It was labour intensive, therefore expensive, while outcomes were hard to quantify. The title of Veronica McGivney's (2000) book *Recovering Outreach* was significant of the rediscovery of a way of working familiar to an older generation of practitioners.

With regard to fee levels, the evidence from ILEA to the Russell Committee stressed the importance of keeping fees low in order to ensure that because 'the object of the adult education provision by the authority remains as it has always been to provide an opportunity for any man or woman to develop his/her individual talents or interests, then it is difficult to consider fees which represent more than a modest percentage of the actual cost'. The phrase 'as it has always been' was to emphasise the consistent attitude of the Authority and its predecessor, the LCC since the period of World War I to the effect that providing institutes were enabled to vary or waive fees in circumstances judged by the staff to be appropriate. At the time of submitting written evidence to the Russell Committee, ILEA was controlled by a Conservative administration which decided that the 'modest percentage' should be about 20 per cent of the actual cost. By the time ILEA was invited to offer oral evidence, the recently elected Labour administration had decided that the guideline should be 10 per cent. This disagreement between the parties served to underline the point that, given that the total income from student fees for adult learning has been a comparatively small sum within the context of the total available education budget of an individual LEA, decisions to raise or lower fees have generally been taken for political rather than financial reasons. Often, raising individual course fees resulted in reducing the gross fee income to the LEA as a consequence of the reduction in student numbers. The low fees policy remained a characteristic of ILEA provision until abolition in 1990, together with generous concessions for groups such as older people, the unemployed and those on benefit. This represented a view that socially worthwhile services should be subsidised from public funds. It was a view that only a large authority such as ILEA was in a position to take, given the clear view from national government that public services should wherever possible be paid for by the users of those services, and that many public services might be more efficiently provided through private enterprises.

As the century drew to a close, after the impetus given by the split between Schedule 2 and non-Schedule 2 courses, as set out in the Further and Higher Education Act 1992, the percentage of actual course costs in adult and community learning (ACL) collected by LEAs rose significantly. At a NIACE conference on 10 December 2002, Ivan Lewis MP, Parliamentary Under-Secretary of State for Adult Learning spoke of 'The Strategic Role of Local Authority Adult Learning'. In the context of the funding review being launched by the government, he said: 'In ACL there are almost as many policies on fees as there are Local Authorities. In some instances, LEAs provide all courses free; in others they target particular types of course or client group. At present, fees from learners account for about 40 per cent of costs in ACL; about 25 per cent in FE. Without pre-empting the funding review, I believe we need a more standard set of principles for fees in ACL.' Lewis touched on an issue that has bedevilled publicly funded adult learning for many years. The Russell Report and governments since the 1970s have stressed the importance of providers working with local communities and meeting the needs of individuals and groups in ways suitable to their circumstances, including ability to pay. At the same time, governments have looked for uniformity and tidiness in common across-the-board arrangements. It would have been more sensible and effective for governments to simply set general principles or guidelines for LEAs and other providers to follow in establishing different arrangements in accordance with the very different local situations. Providing adult education for affluent, suburban areas of the south-east was a very different matter from providing it in large cities and declining industrial areas.

Partnership working

Following the Russell Report's recommendations regarding the need for providers of adult learning programmes to work in close association with other social services and agencies, a group of HMI gave attention to the use and meaning of 'community' when applied to issues of adult learning. Retired HMI, influential in advice and guidance to adult learning providers in the late 1970s and the 1980s, have suggested to the present author that the Community HMI Working Party discussions and internal papers greatly influenced the approaches adopted by HMI towards many community-based and community-related adult learning initiatives. HMI had difficulty placing much of this work within the acceptable, ever-broadening and changing mainstream of adult learning. Instead, it was often perceived as marginal to the traditional and highly structured main-stream, which was held to have been tried and tested over many years. Being thought to be marginal, adult learning through the processes of community work or community development was not given the respect and acceptance it merited. Practitioners in the post-Plowden EPAs, Home Office CDPs, ILEA adult education institutes and elsewhere gave heavy emphasis to enabling people, individually and collectively, to start their adult learning from where they were, physically and intellectually, and to progress at a speed and in directions of their choosing. Many HMI, in common with significant numbers of policy and decision makers in the DES, LEAs and universities, were concerned that such learner-led and *animateur*-supported activity was undisciplined, casual and possibly politically risky. Even as late as 1977, when outreach and community education workers had been active in some areas for a number of years, much of the work was considered, by the more inflexible and traditional of inspectors, to be untested and experimental.

A memorandum submitted by the Home Office Community Development Project as evidence to the Russell Committee in1970 argued that adult education in CDP neighbourhoods might well increase social and civic confidence among residents to participate in local planning, make representations to central and local government and fulfil leadership and representational roles, in addition to gaining personal enjoyment from learning. The terms used in the memorandum were similar to those used by the committee producing the 1919 Report, with recognition given to the social benefits of adult learning. The Russell Report paid regard to the special nature of the WEA as an organisation concerned to deliver learning in non-traditional ways and with sections of the population not generally served by other providers: 'Unique among the voluntary bodies is the Workers' Educational Association which has for many years been a pioneer not only in bringing university quality adult education to a wide public but also in the teaching methods it has fostered and the degree and kind of student participation it has encouraged' (paragraph 226).

Another unique feature of the WEA, among providing bodies, since its launch at the beginning of the twentieth century has been its continued concern and involvement with all phases of education. The WEA advertised in the souvenir publication for persons attending the conference of the NUT, held in Portsmouth in 1937. The advertisement, targeted at individual teachers, mentions that the NUT was affiliated to the WEA at the time. In keeping with its original 1903 commitment to campaign and press for fair and reasonable learning opportunities, the advertisement mentioned the aims of the WEA to be: 'To aid working people in furthering their education in relation to the interests of a full and varied life. To bring about a national system of education from Nursery to University.' With regard to public education, the advertisement continued: 'The WEA has campaigned ceaselessly for educational advance and against economies. Its statement of policy includes a demand "that teachers work under conditions of adequate leisure and professional freedom". It creates an informed educational opinion among organisations not primarily concerned with Education.' It is noteworthy that this WEA advertisement makes no mention of adult learning or adult education, thus underlining the concern of the WEA across all phases of education and the belief that education for a social purpose cannot easily be pigeon-holed. The language of the advertisement will now appear dated. However, the sense and purpose conveyed by the words will have been recognised and accepted by individuals and organisations associated with the development of outreach and community education work, as an essential element of adult learning provision, during the past 40 years.

In a paper written for a SCUTREA Conference, Alistair Thomson of the University of Sussex described partnerships in the provision of adult learning, involving universities with other organisations (Thomson, 1992). During the 1990s, such work became a significant part of the work of the Centre for Continuing Education at Sussex University (Stuart and Thomson, 1995). Thomson referred back to the fruitful partnerships between universities and voluntary and community organisations in the early part of the twentieth century which encouraged the writers of the 1919 Report to outline the importance of encouraging such work of the voluntary sector: 'The authors of the report were concerned that voluntary effort should not be stifled by local or central government control. They proposed that county-based joint university and voluntary association committees should co-ordinate liberal adult education provision, and that public funding should go to any voluntary providers of quality adult education, regardless of political or religious affiliation.' Consequently, despite the constrained national finances and the opposition of both the LEAs and the Board of Education, the Further Education Regulations of 1924, which designated 'Responsible Bodies', enabled central government funds to be channelled directly to the WEA, YMCA and the Educational Settlements Association. Although the authors of the 1919 Report may have had a wider range of voluntary providers in mind, this action emphasised the essential continuing contribution of the voluntary sector to liberal and non-vocational adult learning. Throughout the period to the 1960s, the contribution of the voluntary sector through bodies as different as the Councils of Social Service, trade unions, Drama League and the Arts Council was increasingly recognised.

Picking up the language and priorities from the evidence submitted by ILEA, Home Office CDPs, Liverpool EPA and other projects and organisations, the Russell Committee described the significance of 'outreach' and 'community' education initiatives and urged that they be accorded proper status as important elements of the overall structure of area and neighbourhood provision. In many places, the difficult financial situation following the international oil crisis of 1973 meant that many planned developments to serve the learning needs of unreached sections of the population were reduced or eliminated completely. Nonetheless, acknowledgement by the Russell Committee of the centrality of the voluntary sector in the provision of adult learning and, in particular, the role of voluntary organisations in community-based activities, gave encouragement and a measure of legitimacy to a number of initiatives. In some situations, this recognition was essential in the face of suspicion, opposition and, at times, hostility from traditionalist and conservative practitioners, especially in universities.

Hywel Francis, Director of the Adult Continuing Education Department in the University of Wales at Swansea, in an article in *Adults Learning* (Francis, 1991), discussed the Valleys Initiative for Adult Education (VIAE). Established in 1988 as a network of voluntary and statutory providers of learning opportunities for adults serviced and supported by the Department at Swansea, VIAE was designed to work for the salvation of the valleys communities, socially and economically seriously damaged by the consequences of coal and steel closures and the 1984–5 miners' strike. Francis reported that: 'As is often the case, the most innovative and exciting work takes place in the community, invariably through voluntary organisations. This should not be surprising, as they have the greatest experience and have the most knowledge of the needs of individuals and communities.' Reflecting on the Valleys Initiative some years later, it is clear that, whereas a number of LEA officers considered that it was difficult to identify any outcome causing a change to the nature of adult learning provision, many others believed that outcomes positively affected provision in a manner consistent with the recommendations of Russell. By focusing attention on ways of responding to the learning needs of people living in deprived communities, the initiative set a pattern of cooperation between statutory and voluntary agencies in working 'with' communities rather than 'for' them. Importantly, adult learning providers were able to revise their systems to take account of the proven success of partnership with communities and potential learners.

The special position of Wales
The Russell Committee was appointed in 1969 with a brief to consider the position of adult learning in England and Wales. Similarly, in 1977, ACACE was required to pay regard to the situation in both England and Wales. Even in those pre-devolution days, the easy linking of the two countries did not meet with universal approval. The Russell Report contained an extensive supplement 'on matters peculiar to Wales' produced by a member of the committee, Tom Ellis MP. Having set out his view of certain special factors, which he argued should have led the committee to include recommendations designed to protect and strengthen the Welsh language and cultural heritage, he then added a further note, also published as part of the supplement of the report. In his note, Ellis makes the case for differing from the views of other members of the committee in respect of three matters:

- First, he argued that the student intake of the long-term residential college, Coleg Harlech, should include at least a set minimum number or percentage of students from Wales. He based his case on his wish to ensure that the high proportion of students from England should not be allowed to squeeze out potential students from Wales and the need to ensure that there were sufficient opportunities for the study and development of Welsh culture on the back of the recruitment of sufficient Welsh-speaking students. The committee's view was that these were matters for the college authorities who, they felt sure, would pay regard to Tom Ellis's concerns.

- Second, Ellis argued against the view of the committee that future grant aid from the government to the WEA should be paid to the national association and not to the individual Districts. Ellis was concerned that the 'traditional democratic voluntarism' of the WEA in Wales would be put at risk. The committee disagreed and argued that the special characteristics and histories of the different Districts in both England and Wales could and should be respected and protected as factors influencing the manner in which the national WEA dispersed its funds.

- Third, he made the case for having separate Development Councils for Adult Education in England and Wales as a reflection of the increased recognition given by governmental and other official bodies to 'Welsh nationhood'. His other and, in his view, stronger point, was 'the significant differences, educationally, socially and politically which exist between England and Wales'. This point was not accepted by other members of the committee, who argued that the structures and delivery mechanisms for adult learning in England and Wales were basically similar. A Development Council, spanning England and Wales, was thought, by the other members of the Committee, to be able to allow for local and regional perspectives within its national thinking. LEAs, WEA, universities and other providers in the regions and localities were best placed to pay regard to community needs.

While these points of issue were relevant and important at the time, before the end of the century, the arrival of devolution and the creation of the Welsh Assembly dramatically changed the scene. Throughout the 1970s and 1980s, the attitude of most civil servants and politicians in the Welsh Office was not sympathetic to pleas for adequate funds for adult learning. Welsh LEAs were much the same. Generally, the regular programmes of the WEA and universities, plus the contributions of residential colleges and trade unions, were held to be sufficient. Direct provision by LEAs was not strong. Local government reorganisation in

1974 had a significant impact on adult learning in Wales, much greater than in most parts of England. Reorganisation came less than one year after the publication of the Russell Report and coincided with the first major cuts in LEA budgets for adult learning: 'Adult learning had a low priority in local education authority budgets, even in Labour strongholds like Glamorgan and its Mid Glamorgan successor' (letter from Ken Hopkins, then Director of Education in Mid Glamorgan and future Chair of NIACE Cymru to the present author, dated 6 June 2002). This view was a sad retrospective comment by a person who was known to believe, along with the Russell Report, that education 'must be a total system and that the effectiveness of the schools is jeopardised by the neglect of adult needs' (paragraph 51).

As was the case in many English LEAs, during straightened financial years, adult learning in Wales was an easy target for cuts. Had the Russell Report been published two years before local government reorganisation, it might have served as a guide to policy and programme development in preparation for the handover to the new LEAs. It would have been of more value as an aid to future planning had it come two years later. In the circumstances, according to Doug Jones, County Further Education Officer in Mid Glamorgan at the time (letter of June 2002 to the present author), its value in 1973/74 was as

> . . . a very useful weapon in protecting the good practice and provision already in place against determined attempts to trivialise and curtail adult education. We were able to quote Russell's eloquent justification of adult learning, its advocacy of the broadest possible curriculum, its insistence on accessibility, especially in terms of fees and location, and its concern for adequate provision for people with disadvantages and disabilities of all kinds.

Yet in Wales, adult education had retained the image of being 'night school' and was judged by most LEA senior officers and politicians as not sufficiently important to protect. Russell had called for an increase in the number of full-time adult learning staff. In Mid Glamorgan, the largest of the new Welsh LEAs, with much social and economic distress caused by the run-down of the coal and steel industries, one of the casualties of the budget cuts was the appointment of full-time adult principals, as recommended by Russell and already approved by the County Council. The Welsh Joint Education Committee (WJEC), as the body charged with coordinating and developing policy and practice, proved to be unable to give the necessary leadership and exert pressure on individual LEAs to give greater prominence to adult learning. In recommending regional cooperation, the Russell Committee had looked to the WJEC to act in Wales in the same ways that Regional Advisory Councils were expected to operate in England.

None of these financial and policy setbacks was unique to Wales. Precisely the same problems were evident in many LEAs in England. Although the recommendations of the report were modest in terms of their financial impact, the economic situation was such that few LEAs were able and willing to commit the necessary resources to enable the services to grow. With regard to certain special elements of adult learning, national and local resources were found to enable growth in volume and improvement in quality. The Russell Report had placed great emphasis on the learning needs of adults requiring basic education opportunities and language learning (English for speakers of other languages in England and Wales, and Welsh in Wales). Mention has been made of Tom Ellis's plea for adult learning programmes designed to preserve and foster the language and culture of Wales. Following the report, the demand for Welsh language classes in Wales grew rapidly. This was particularly true in the major urban areas of south Wales. This growth was not entirely attributable to the response to the Russell Report, as Doug Jones made clear in correspondence with the present author:

> In the years following Russell we saw a very significant increase in the demand for and the provision of courses to enable adults to learn Welsh, particularly in urban areas. So many factors combined to account for this, not least the corresponding expansion in primary and secondary education through the medium of Welsh, that it is impossible to attribute it solely or even mainly to the report. It is a phenomenon that must be noted, however, not least because once again it brought us new learners and introduced refreshingly new techniques of teaching languages to adults.

Other factors, including the lively debates about the roles and contributions of radio and television in adult learning and cultural affairs, had a major influence, as did growing pressure for devolved government in Wales.

Some 12 years after the publication of the Russell Report, NIACE Cymru (now NIACE Dysgu Cymru) was formed. Instead of accepting the committee's recommendation to create a National Development Council for England and Wales, or Tom Ellis's minority recommendation that separate Development Councils should be created for England and Wales, the Labour Secretary of State had established the Advisory Council (ACACE) for England and Wales in 1977. ACACE was brought to an end in 1983. Pressure in Wales for a representative body to be the voice of adult learning in Wales was recognised by NIACE. Doug Jones, one of the leading protagonists for adult learning in Wales at the time and a member of the management committee of NIACE Cymru, commenting on NIACE Cymru (letter to the present author of June 2002) states that

. . . despite its limited brief and meagre financial support from the Welsh Office, I think it achieved a great deal. It raised the profile of adult education in Wales. It built bridges between providers that had previously worked in isolation and sometimes in opposition to one another. It helped them to understand, value and respect each other's contributions. It demonstrated the full scope of adult education and endeavour. It created fruitful partnerships and it promoted and directly assisted staff development. It was able to show the distinctiveness of provision and need in Wales and it created a platform from which it drew attention to good practice and unmet needs. It was a powerful advocate with the Welsh Office and won influence and respect there.

A slightly different perspective on the general adult learning scene and the contribution of NIACE Cymru to adult learning in Wales since the middle 1980s is offered by Dewi Jones, currently Group Director, Education and Children's Services, Rhonda Cynon Taff County Borough, and previously a leading community educator in Wales and also a member of the management committee of NIACE Cymru. Having described the extent to which providers, especially the universities, WEA, Women's Institutes, trade unions and LEAs were making their different and distinctive contributions while, at the same time, cooperating with each other and sharing experience, he argues, in a letter of 14 August 2002 to the present author, that the strengths of NIACE Cymru have been 'its ability to bring together expert practitioners who were open and generous in sharing their practice' and 'identifying best practice and discussion and thinking around pertinent issues'. In keeping with the conclusions and recommendations of Russell and set out in the ACACE (1982a) publication, *Continuing Education: From Policies to Practice*, Dewi Jones asserts that 'some of the most effective forms of adult education haven't necessarily been labelled as adult education. There has been a growth in community development (voluntary trusts, outreach work, tenants' groups, community agencies, family literacy) and a great deal of it has had a significant effect on people's lives.' Reflecting on the changes during the period covered by this book, Doug Jones argues that

. . . adult education has become a predominantly selfish pursuit. We participate in learning for self-gratification, for self-actualisation, for self-advancement, and governments encourage our pursuit of these essentially selfish goals in the belief that our individual advances will aggregate to national prosperity and world economic leadership. It seems to me that individualism and community development are incompatible. Communities will develop and regenerate themselves only when a sense of community is rekindled and when mutual aid and the pursuit of common goals takes the place of self-interest.

The Work of the National Institute of Adult Continuing Education (NIACE)

NIACE has been a crucial coordinating organisation in England and Wales. Since it changed its name from the National Institute of Adult Education (NIAE) to NIACE in 1983 and, subsequently, adopted the designation 'The National Organisation for Adult Learning', it has grown in strength and significance as a recognised and respected national NGO. The Russell Report recommended that 'the National Institute of Adult Education and the Department should agree a five-year programme of expansion and the Department should undertake to provide sufficient grant to enable the institute to embark on the agreed programme' (recommendation 115). The Russell Committee could not have known, however, that the international oil crisis of 1973/74 and the public expenditure cuts of the 1970s would make implementation of the recommendation impossible. The Russell Report suggested five areas of development to ensure the continued centrality of the institute to adult learning in the country. These were library and information work, seminars and conferences, survey work, publications and international contacts.

In the years since the report was published, many attempts have been made, by the Institute alone and by the Institute in conjunction with other bodies, to strengthen the library and archive collections as resources for adult learning in the country. The library has expanded considerably and has become more accessible. Although the amount of archive material has grown, it has not been possible to find funding to fully catalogue and store the accumulated material appropriately in a place and in a manner to enable the documentation to be easily accessible to researchers and writers. Nonetheless, it continues to be a priority issue for the Institute. The amount of adult learning material held at the National Archives is limited. Important files and boxes of collected papers are currently held in basements, cellars and cupboards in buildings belonging to universities and professional organisations, and in private houses.

Since 1973 and, particularly since 1983, the Institute's programme of conferences and seminars has grown considerably. The Institute has an established reputation for good quality events dealing with topics of both historical and contemporary significance. Within the spirit of cooperation between organisations, as encouraged by Russell, the institute has regularly promoted events jointly with other bodies, both statutory and voluntary. Year by year, larger elements of the conference and seminar programme have been concerned with policy development and planning. In the past, the institute tended to be more reactive than proactive.

The third area of work, identified by Russell, was survey work. The report (paragraphs 425 and 428.3) referred to the research undertaken by NIAE (1970), published as *Adequacy of Provision*, and suggested that regular surveys of students and teachers in adult learning could be undertaken 'using the format of its 1970 survey as a model'. In the years that followed, the Institute conducted and published regular surveys of adult participation in learning and of the fees paid by learners. From time to time, survey work has been undertaken for other organisations or in partnership with other organisations. Much of the explanation for the high reputation of the organisation relates to the quality and immediate usefulness of the research and survey work.

Surveys and research are valued to the extent that they are accessible to those who wish to learn from the findings and conclusions. With foresight, as the fourth area of development, the Russell Committee urged the institute to produce a wider range of publications. During the last three decades of the century, NIACE increased the number of periodicals and other publications produced each year. NIACE has become a major publisher. In keeping with the Russell recommendation, it has not sought to compete with commercial publishers but has seen this aspect of its work as a major service to progressing the theory and practice of adult learning. In addition to its monthly magazine, *Adults Learning*, it now publishes a number of academic journals and an impressive range of both scholarly books and more practical guides and handbooks. Its annual yearbook is an indispensable directory for those working in the field.

The fifth area of expansion, suggested by Russell, was connected with increasing understanding in this country of changes in policy and systems throughout the world. It was evident to the committee that, although UK ministers, civil servants, HMI and adult learning practitioners had participated in international conferences and meetings, there was little sign of lessons from abroad having been learned and applied. For this reason among others, and recognising the growing importance of UNESCO, OECD, Council of Europe and the recently formed ICAE and European Association for the Education of Adults (EAEA), the committee urged NIACE to create 'an abstracting service covering the literature of adult education on a world basis'. The committee could not have foreseen the extent to which its suggestion would be met, in part, by broadening the range and increasing the number of the Institute's publications and, partly, by the dramatically effective use of the Internet as a means of communication, information and publication.

One development not foreseen by the Russell Report was the development of Adult Learners' Week from 1992, first at a national then at an international level. As Stephen McNair records in a profile of NIACE's long-serving director Alan Tuckett:

> Adult Learners' Week became not just a tool for celebrating adult learning in all its diversity but, by linking individual learners directly to politicians, it lifted NIACE out of the box in which it had been contained for many years, relating to government either through polite, friendly but marginal conversation with civil servants, or formally arguing in print with

Ministers. Adult Learners' Week gave NIACE direct access to, and credibility with, Ministers and the wider policymaking community which proved invaluable as Government's interest in adult learning grew through the 1990s. (Gilbert and Prew, 2001, p. 58)

It also provided a great deal of pleasure and encouragement to hard-pressed adult educators at a difficult period in the history of adult learning. As Judith Summers, Chair of NIACE from 1992–9 commented, 'the Week brings out the inventiveness and fun in adult learning which might otherwise be obscured by institutional rigour' (Gilbert and Prew, 2001, p. 127). Adult Learning Weeks have rapidly become a recognised part of adult learning in many countries.

Adult basic education

The Russell Committee's attention to adult literacy, and what was described at the time as work with and for 'disadvantaged adults', was not value laden other than to express concern that people's personal, social, economic and political horizons and potential are to a great degree limited by poor literacy skills. In the section of its report headed 'Adult Education and the Disadvantaged', the committee emphasised the importance of responding to the learning needs of individuals, stating (paragraph 278):

Blanket terms like 'the disadvantaged' or 'the handicapped' carry an implication that these are undifferentiated masses whose needs, once they are identified, will be alike ... the task of the education service will be to collaborate with social services and other relevant departments in ensuring that disadvantaged individuals are not debarred by lack of education from active participation in the life of their local communities.

The Disadvantaged Adult (Clyne, 1972), a study undertaken for the committee, influenced the conclusions and recommendations of the committee in relation to the links between educational disadvantage and other forms of disadvantage. The Russell Report suggested (paragraph 279) that

... the test of disadvantage is taken to be the extent to which such integration into active society is prevented [by] factors ... in three areas: personal capacity (which includes both physical and mental conditions), social disadvantage (which includes geographical isolation as well as poverty or social deprivation) and educational disadvantage (which might mean, not only a lack of basic education or literacy, but also such things as imperfect language in the born-deaf and isolation from the messages of the standard educational agencies through ignorance or rejection of the imagery and vocabulary they use).

Paragraph 279 was a clear expression of the belief of the committee that the required learning provision, in the jargon of a later period, called for 'joined-up government' and acceptance of the implications of low literacy skills for the 'socially excluded'. It was also testimony to the clarity of language and the caring commitment of Henry Arthur Jones, the person who drafted it.

The establishment of ALRA in 1975 brought not only a new professionalism but also a new vocabulary to the teaching of basic skills. Terminology employed to describe work with and for adults with literacy learning needs has changed greatly in the past 30 years. It is necessary to appreciate the meanings of words, as used in their contexts and times. Retrospective comparison can be unhelpful. It serves no useful purpose to suggest that definitions and meanings, appropriate and acceptable in 2006, can usefully be applied to the often different words used in 1973. Language lives and changes as a vehicle of communication. Unfortunately, much unreasonable and misguided criticism of those involved in teaching and organising adult literacy programmes in the 1960s has been based on a narrow concern with the terminology employed in describing the work of the 1960s, and indeed before.

During the years immediately preceding the establishment of the Russell Committee, there was little national effort made to coordinate adult literacy work, other than that taking place in prisons. During World War II and the period of National Service, literacy work in the army (for men only) was co-ordinated and led by the Royal Army Education Corps. Survey and investigative work undertaken for Russell indicated that approximately 50 per cent of LEAs were making provision. In addition, a number of LEAs supported voluntary organisations in providing teaching and learning. Some LEA activity was channelled through the work of Community Development Projects and EPAs.

Post-Russell literature has largely failed to register sufficient appreciation of the original and imaginative teaching and learning processes and of the materials generated by teachers and students in the 1960s and earlier. There is an implicit assumption and, sometimes, an explicit assertion that literacy work, as a national feature, started after Russell. This is, demonstrably, not the case. An abstract from a contemporary dissertation (Haviland, 1973) concluded that 'there exists in England a substantial number of people, perhaps as many as two million, who can be classified as either "illiterate", that is, having a reading age of seven years or less, or "semi-literate", that is, having a reading age of between seven and nine years of age'. This is the same general conclusion reached in the study undertaken for the Russell Committee. Haviland documented the great increase in the number of 'instruction programmes' during the period 1950 to 1973 and mentions the particularly rapid growth between 1967 and 1973. By contrast, in her chapter, 'Literacy and Adult Basic Education' (in Fieldhouse *et al.*, 1996), Mary Hamilton argues that ABE 'as part of adult continuing education in the UK emerged when central government support for adult literacy began in the 1970s'. Here, as elsewhere in the literature, there is an easy slide from the narrow term 'literacy' to the broader phrase 'adult basic education'. The Russell Report and *The Disadvantaged Adult* (Clyne, 1972) make the same linguistic move without defining the intended differences. While the Russell Report does not go into detail on either the 'literacy' or 'basic education' needs of adults, *The Disadvantaged Adult* has a whole chapter on the 'Education of adult immigrants' and refers to early English as a second (or additional) language practice. Little of this was included in the report. Surprisingly, the field of numeracy is not mentioned in either publication. Less surprisingly, information technology, now recognised by government as an additional basic skill, is not even hinted at.

As a direct response to the conclusions and recommendations of the Russell Committee, and in acknowledgement of the strength of the case made by the national campaign, variously entitled The Adult Literacy Campaign or The Right to Read Campaign, the government (through the DES and the Scottish Office) allocated one million pounds for one year (April 1975 to March 1976), in the first instance, to stimulate additional adult literacy activity, particularly teacher training, development of the curriculum and production of teaching and learning material. This programme was to be administered by an agency, ALRA, as a unit within NIAE. Very soon, the government confirmed the existence of ALRA for a further two years. With changes in emphasis and constitutional arrangements, ALRA became the Adult Literacy Unit (ALU) and then, in 1979, the Adult Literacy and Basic Skills Unit (ALBSU). In 1995, the new terminology was confirmed, and it became the Basic Skills Agency (BSA). The language has changed but the problem has not gone away.

The campaign took as its shared lead document the British Association of Settlements (1974) publication *A Right to Read: Action for a Literate Britain*. In addition to providing a comprehensive description of the size and nature of the national problem of adult illiteracy, the publication included a policy statement and recommendations designed to galvanise opinion and action. The campaign was given strong support by the BBC which, in the following year, broadcast a series of short programmes coupled with a national telephone helpline. 'On the Move' was a mould-breaking series with considerable impact. Countless local activists, both volunteers and paid, were encouraged by the quality of 'On the Move' and its strong message to the effect that adults with literacy problems were ordinary people with a particular learning need. Government action was prompted by a Private Members' Bill, introduced by Chris Price MP with all-party support. The Bill received government backing. Chris Price had been one of a number of MPs who responded positively to representations made by the national campaign. In his capacity as chairman of the Parliamentary Education

Select Committee, he was extremely influential in making the case for meeting the learning needs of disadvantaged adults, including adults with language and literacy needs, prisoners and their families. Specifically, the ALRA funds were not to be used to pay for what was already programmed, provided or projected by LEAs, voluntary organisations and other bodies, but to be used to pay for new activity. While the history of basic skills in England and Wales remains unfinished business, the progress made does serve to demonstrate the power of government action linked to a public campaign with broad support, even in times of economic retrenchment.

Towards lifelong learning

The narrow skills agenda being pursued by the Employment Department at the end of the 1980s may be contrasted with the continuing advocacy of a wider view of adult learning in the publication *Learning Throughout Adult Life* (NIACE, 1990). Members of the Russell Committee would have applauded and welcomed this publication, given that it touched on so many of the issues raised in the 1973 Report and commended to government, providers and others as meriting careful attention. The importance of this discussion paper lay, first, in its clear presentation of the essential need to guarantee effective coordination and cooperation between the many streams of adult learning as the foundation for future continuing education and training provision for adults. Second, it concisely addressed matters of funding for both general provision and individual students or trainees. Third, the body of recommendations, targeted at providers of education and training, employers and TECs, LEAs, central government and NIACE itself, pulled together outstanding issues, left unmet or unresolved since the end of ACACE in 1983, and arising from the work of UDACE, REPLAN, MSC and other bodies in the 1980s.

The discussion paper informed consideration of many of the government publications and proposals of the time. It clearly acknowledged that a basic problem with British education was that large sections of the adult population had benefited less than others from learning opportunities, a theme pursued assiduously by NIACE staff and publications through the 1990s. Among those most disadvantaged by previous learning experience were many women, black and other ethnic minority people, disabled and older people. *Learning Throughout Adult Life* argued that many of the imaginative strategies adopted in the 1970s and 1980s, including a number of outreach and community education practices, following Russell and the work of ACACE, should be properly funded and accepted as mainstream practices. The discussion paper also included the major recommendation, adopted for its election manifesto by the Labour Party in opposition in 1992 but dropped when in government in 1997, that 'all adults should have a minimum, regular and quantified entitlement to learning opportunities throughout their lives. Individual learners should be able to exercise their active choice over the learning on which to spend their entitlement'.

Learning Throughout Adult Life took, as its starting point, the ACACE (1982a) report *Continuing Education: From Policies to Practice*, which had offered a wide-ranging view of the current state and the future possibilities for adult learning. It noted that the changes of the 1980s had 'improved opportunities and provision for some people but reduced them for others'. In the post-Russell years, the Employment Department had exercised an overarching responsibility for vocational education and training. Thus, the leadership and direction of the totality of continuing education was shared between the Departments of Employment and of Education and Science. Margaret Thatcher, as Secretary of State for Education, had lost the argument in 1974 when the MSC was created and allocated to Employment as opposed to Education and Science which she favoured. After 1979, as Prime Minister, she took no action to end the divided leadership. The unhelpful split responsibility between the two departments continued. Yet through the successive changes outlined in Chapter 7, the amount of work-related education and training and special programmes for unemployed adults increased. Advice and guidance to actual and potential learners became more widely available, although in the 1990s there was a shift away from independent guidance agencies and towards internal guidance services run by providers. The number of access courses for adults also grew.

The work of PICKUP, targeted to meet employers' skills shortages, and of REPLAN, programmed to enable colleges to satisfy more of the learning needs of unemployed adults, was important. Open Colleges, Open College Networks and Federations and the development of NVQs, all made a positive impact on the learning providers to the ultimate benefit of students and trainees. Most claimed improvements in programme provision in the 1980s were directly led by labour market needs and, therefore, they tended to be oriented towards vocational education and training. Yet by the end of the decade, it was apparent that participation rates in adult learning among working class men and women, ethnic minorities and older people had not risen greatly. Overall, the participation of women in learning activities had increased but, in comparison with men, they received fewer opportunities. Inequities persisted regardless of changes in policies and funding arrangements.

Whereas the debates and policy proposals emanating from international organisations, particularly the OECD and UNESCO, had stressed the personal, social, economic and educational value of adopting a broad view of adult learning, the Education Reform Act 1988 and other government pronouncements and policy decisions by both the relevant departments (DES and ED) tended to concentrate on narrow vocational considerations. This indicated no advance in understanding or vision since the Education Act 1944. On the other hand, NIACE had changed its name in 1983, from the National Institute of Adult Education to the National Institute of Adult Continuing Education. This change was a clear statement of the importance of working to a wider agenda of learning than understood by the term 'adult education'. Emphasis was increasingly being given to 'recurrent', 'continuing' and 'permanent' as alternative descriptive terms. The concept of 'lifelong learning' had arrived in all but words.

Arguing for an expansion in the provision and funding of continuing education, the NIACE discussion paper asserted that: 'At a time of rapid economic, social and technological change there is increasing pressure on individuals to shape their lives to new circumstances, needs and opportunities, whether at home or at work. The expansion of continuing education, therefore, is not merely desirable but essential.' For people involved in the provision of adult learning at the time, this confident, well-founded and forward-looking assertion was neither controversial nor dramatic. However, appearing in a policy discussion paper in 1990, it coincided with the cold blast of a narrowing of public policy coupled with financial constraints and threats sufficient to prompt the launch of a renewed national Save Adult Education Campaign. Once again, excellent and enlightened proposals would fall victim to deteriorating economic circumstances. It was only in 1997 with the publication of the Kennedy Report (Kennedy, 1997) and the work of NAGCELL that a call for a wider view of the potential for adult learning was to coincide with improving economic prospects.

When considering the likely developing and changing needs in the 1990s, the NIACE policy discussion paper paid proper regard to the government's expressed determination to improve the country's economic performance while, at the same time, limiting public expenditure, encouraging business competition and urging individuals to invest in their own education and health care. This explicit move away from comprehensive publicly-funded services, accessible to all and free, or heavily subsidised, at the point of use had the in-built danger of unfairly, and increasingly, disadvantaging those adults with the greatest learning needs. NIACE argued for policies and action to redress disadvantage. The Employment Department White Paper, *Employment for the 1990s* (Employment Department, 1988), had described the frameworks for vocational education and training established in a number of other countries with the aim of improving national economic performance. In each of the quoted examples, there was a clear national commitment to education and training throughout life. This was at variance from the approach and funding priorities outlined by the UK government in the Education Reform Act 1988 and accompanying regulations. In each case, however, the opportunities were created for the proponents of a wider view of adult learning to bring their criticisms into the open.

The study by UDACE, *Financial Barriers to Access* (UDACE and Ames, 1986), had made clear that the lack of a national funding framework for adult learning had led to a postcode lottery: the opportunity to study or train often depended on where a person lived. In *Learning Throughout Adult Life*, NIACE argued 'for a comprehensive review of the means of funding and resourcing education and training, and defining an entitlement for the learner. For adults especially, lack of adequate financial support remains a barrier to achieving access, and this should be resolved as a matter of urgency and equity.' In the early 1990s, the discussion paper became an essential reference document for those individuals or organisations making representations to the government about the impact of reduced funding and the narrowed definition of adult learning thought worthy of public funding. Many of the points raised in the NIACE paper could be traced back to ACACE and Russell. They were also seen to inform some of the debates that took place in NAGCELL, established by the Labour Government in June 1997.

9
The vocation of adult education

If you want flowers, you must have flowers, roots and all, unless you are satisfied, as many people are satisfied, with flowers made of paper and tinsel. And if you want education, you must not cut it off from the social interests in which it has its living and perennial source.

(R.H. Tawney, 'Adult Education in the History of the Nation',
paper presented to the Fifth Annual Conference of the
British Institute of Adult Education, 1926)

The strength of Russell was that it recognised the complex ways in which adult education, attended by millions for different reasons, contributed in different ways to the quality of life.

(Keith Jackson, 1994, p. 24)

The world we have lived in

For those adult educators whose careers have spanned the period 1969–97, looking back at the Russell Report is an invigorating experience but also a depressing one. Invigorating because so many of the ideas that have illuminated and inspired our professional lives can be found in its pages. Depressing because, as suggested, the Russell Committee appeared to have abandoned well before publication of the report any attempt at drawing out a set of radical proposals which would make adult education central to educational, social and economic policy in England and Wales. Indeed, members of the committee would be fully justified in complaining that such was not their brief. In Chapter 5, the Russell Report was characterised as a 'significant and forward-looking document'. Yet it is not possible to read Russell now without a profound sense of how the world has changed. It is a 'world we have lived in' but certainly not the professional world we inhabit today. Despite the stress on local and regional initiatives and partnerships with the voluntary sector, the document is permeated by a sense that government is the chief actor in the development of adult learning. It is government that will offer the leadership and provide the resources. While in Chapter 5, Elsdon *et al.*'s (2001) view that Russell marked 'the end of a period of hope and expansion for adult education, and not the dawn of a new and happier era' was criticised as unduly pessimistic, it is true in this one limited sense: the hope that government policy and action alone would somehow 'produce' the learning that adults required to function in times of rapid social and economic change has been shown to be false.

With this important caveat, that for the twenty-first century reader the Russell Report overstates the scope for government action, nevertheless Russell was a forward-looking document in tackling the theme which in one way or another has dominated public policy ever since – modernisation. For readers of the report in the 1970s, the urgency of such modernisation was marked by the extent of low productivity and unproductive social conflict, particularly that between trade unions and employers in both private and public sectors. During the 1980s, modernisation was interpreted from an ideological perspective that approved the running-down and closure of traditional heavy industry, the growth of the service sector, the ending of subsidies to declining industrial sectors and the privatisation of public services (or at least the introduction of elements of competition into public monopolies). Both Richard Hoggart and Raymond Williams, who have been noted in this book as important social commentators committed to adult education, had grown up in a more 'traditional' world of working class culture, politics and self-help that was now placed firmly on the back foot.

Apart from his success as a writer on social issues, Hoggart had worked for UNESCO and at Goldsmith's College, University of London. He was also Chair of ACACE. Williams had enjoyed a successful career as a university extra-mural department tutor and continued to take a lively interest in adult learning even after taking up a more conventional academic career. As noted in Chapter 1, Williams believed that adult learning was both part of the engine driving social change and also itself promoted social change. Both Hoggart and Williams, in their separate ways, reflected on the growing importance of the mass media, and the different sources of information and ideas available to adults. In his essay 'Resources for a journey of hope' in *Towards 2000*, Williams (1983b) plotted a course that linked older values of participatory democracy and citizenship with newer concerns such as 'identity politics' (the new social movements, including the women's and environmental movements) and the need to find a new settlement between collectivism and individualism. These challenges remain as current today as they were in 1983. Williams' essential thesis in this essay was that public life had become dominated by what he referred to as 'Plan X politics' in which technical efficiency is all, and change is seen as an inevitable process that is beyond the grasp of people (Margaret Thatcher's well-known TINA – 'there is no alternative'). For Williams, new technologies meant new choices, both for society and for individuals. Adult education is seen as one of the ways in which society decides its own future, but also the vehicle through which individual people respond to change. As early as 1959, Williams had written that 'the man who thinks his education is complete at 15, or 18, or 21, is not educated' (Williams, 1959).

For adult educators, one key issue of how the 'modernisation agenda' was applied in the 1980s and 1990s was the recreation of inequality after a long period in which gaps between rich and poor appeared to be closing. There was a continuing tension in professional publications and practice between on the one hand the desire to provide general opportunities for people to come to terms with technological and economic change, to retrain for new jobs in the new economy, to make good deficits in their previous education, and on the other hand the desire to be a force for progressive social change. This desire pointed to a levelling-up within society. For many adult educators, this conflict was resolved in their commitment to specific groups who were seen to be 'disadvantaged' by particular facets of their educational experience, by issues of gender and 'race', and by specific disabilities. Thus while adult education did something to soften the contours of the new inequality, it cannot be claimed that it contributed in more than a marginal way to reducing social and economic inequalities. As stated at other points in this book, adult education has never been, and cannot ever be, a panacea for society's ills. Those seeking to tackle the problems of society head on were few in number: Ian Martin, in Fieldhouse (1996, pp. 123–30) refers specifically to the work of Tom Lovett, Jane Thompson and Keith Jackson. But he also reminds us that much Second Chance work (much of which evolved into access to further and higher education courses) was relatively conventional in form and content. That is not to say, of course, that it was not of great benefit to individual women, working-class activists or members of community groups. Simply that its parameters fitted more easily within those of conventional adult educational initiatives concerned with individual rather than collective advancement.

While society was evolving in ways that members of the Russell Committee could not have accurately predicted, other geopolitical changes were beginning to have an impact on the work of adult educators. At the time of the Russell Committee, the remit of the committee to consider adult education in 'England and Wales' was seen as unproblematic. In England there was little sensitivity to the cultural traditions of Wales; in Wales, demands for a recognition of the special identity were muted, and that identity was often conceived of in a regional rather than a national way. It was left to one member of the committee to write a dissenting note within the report in response to the section dealing with 'Matters Peculiar to Wales'. In few places does the report seem as archaic as in this title. As was emphasised in Chapter 8, the most significant demand made by Ellis was for a separate Development Council for Adult Education in Wales in recognition of the reality of 'Welsh nationhood' and the 'the significant differences, educationally, socially and politically which exist between England and Wales'. Since Russell, not only has demand for greater autonomy in Wales increased, but a substantial measure of devolution is now in place with a separate Welsh Assembly and ministers. Half of the Assembly members speak Welsh as a first or second language, and the First Minister, Rhodri Morgan, is bilingual. Even in South Wales, which remains substantially English-speaking, the Welsh language is a significant curriculum area for adult education providers.

Northern Ireland had not been mentioned in the Russell Report. Unlike Scotland it did not have its own report. Yet in 1974 the Northern Ireland Council for Continuing Education was established. Paul Nolan, now of Queen's University of Belfast, began work as a WEA tutor-organiser in Northern Ireland in 1979. In conversation with the present editor, he stated that the Russell Report had had a galvanising effect on a generation of adult educators who viewed adult education as having a social purpose, and wanted to work alongside voluntary community organisations, whether through the WEA, through the universities, or through local authorities (the five Education and Library Boards). Tom Lovett had moved back to Northern Ireland in 1972 and joined the Community Studies Division of the Institute of Continuing Education at the University of Ulster, Magee College in Derry. He later established the Ulster People's College in 1982, with a group of 'community activists, trade unionists, community educators, peace workers and feminists' (Lovett, 1995, p. 279). In the meantime, attempts to work with the unemployed and community development workers had fallen foul of the sectarian divide in Northern Ireland. The revival of socially committed adult education in Northern Ireland in the 1990s owed much to the availability of EU funds for such purposes as community capacity-building, women's education and work with the socially excluded. This work found its theoretical underpinning reflected in the European White Paper (European Commission, 1995) and the Delors Report (UNESCO, 1996), rather than in Russell.

The changing perception of Wales and the peculiar difficulties of Northern Ireland are just two examples of the changing geometry of international relations. Yet such changes point in a number of sometimes contradictory directions: outwards towards Europe, outwards towards the world and inwards towards internal devolution.

Outwards towards Europe. The EU is a significant player in international affairs. Some issues, such as education, are considered to be covered by subsidiarity principles, which state that decisions should generally be taken as close to the citizens as possible. The EU has its own policies on (*inter alia*) training and social policy, even if it has few powers to influence directly national policies in this field. In particular, European Social Fund monies have provided for support for adult learning initiatives in almost every part of the UK and Ireland. The emphasis has generally been on those broad educational skills that underpin the more specific skills called for in employment. The use of such funds covered fields as varied as family education, language and literacy, and work with the unemployed. TECs used ESF funds to support learning at work, including EDS. EU support for 'lifelong learning' was an important influence during the 1990s. The designation of 1995 as European Year of Lifelong Learning led to the eventual adoption of the term lifelong learning by, first of all, the professional community, and later by the UK government. By the beginnings of the twenty-first century, the EU's commitment to a 'social Europe' remained an important counterweight to the concerns of multinationals and the WTO to cut the 'social costs' of employment.

Outwards towards the world. Again, this book has demonstrated the ways in which UNESCO approaches to and policies on adult education influenced debates in the UK. In the same way, OECD was one of the major forces for economic and social 'modernisation' and its policies were influential, without having any kind of binding force. Beyond OECD lay a developing stratum of international economic bodies which gathered importance towards the end of the century, in particular the World Trade Organization (WTO). Their concern with stimulating the world economy by eliminating barriers to world trade led to charges that such policies were a major reason why some developing countries were becoming poorer rather than richer. While on the one hand poorer countries found it difficult to develop their own industries and services in the face of competition from foreign-owned multinationals, on the other hand they found it difficult to compete in agricultural goods where both the USA and the EU maintained subsidies to agriculture. By the end of the century, WTO meetings were besieged by protesters and negotiations on new trade agreements had stalled, a state of affairs which was in the interest of neither the advanced industrialised countries nor the developing countries. The developing countries demand the right to protect fledgling industries, while the industrialised countries refuse to remove subsidies on their agriculture. In general, the WTO approach has been considerably less subtle than the coaxing of the OECD, with its stress on developing human resources, the importance of the skills base for the economy, and the promotion of social inclusion as a key feature in sustaining the conditions for economic growth.

Internal devolution. At least partly in response to these globalising influences, the end of the twentieth century saw a substantial increase in nationalist sentiment, negatively expressed in ethnic violence, positively expressed in devolution in countries such as Spain and the UK, and the creation of new nation-states in Central and Eastern Europe. Boundaries that once appeared fixed now appeared as provisional and changeable. Control over education, including adult education, has usually been ceded to devolved governments. While some of these policies are concerned with building the skills base in order to attract multinational investment, other policies have pursued more cultural objectives (include learning local languages and histories) or have sought to meet particular social objectives of the devolved governments. This final point is important because it means there is greatly increased scope for developing more integrated policies between government departments at a devolved level than in a system dominated by large, independent-minded nation-state departments. Thus while aspects of adult learning policy may now look very similar as between England and Wales, there has also been divergence. Wales has its own lifelong learning strategy *Wales – The Learning Country* (National Assembly for Wales, 2001). Although legislation from the Westminster parliament may cover both countries, the ways in which laws are interpreted in Wales is able to respond to Welsh circumstances and priorities. In Scotland, community education and popular education (the preferred terms) have developed their own characteristic approaches to creating a bridge between education and community development.

Adult learning post-Russell

The issue of development

The issue of development was a key dispute in the years following the publication of the Russell Report. As was emphasised in Chapter 2, the remit of the committee was unlikely to raise undue hopes in adult education circles. The emphasis on the most efficient use of available resources suggested stringency rather than expansion. Yet the Russell Report *assumed* development, in a way that was characteristic of the times. There had been a substantial growth in adult education provision, especially by LEAs, during the preceding years, and the assumption was that this would continue. Recommendation 4.4 referred to the creation of a 'Development Council for Adult Education for England and Wales'. Recommendation 9 referred to a 'Local Development Council for Adult Education' in each LEA area, on which providers, users and students would be represented.

The reality of the matter was rather different. Successive Conservative and Labour governments resisted the implications of the word 'development' – that an increasing amount of public resource would be placed at the disposal of adult educators. This resistance was not necessarily ideological. For example, Chapter 5 has emphasised the work of Gerry Fowler as Minster of State at the DES in both the setting up of the Russell Committee in the late 1960s, and the arguments about its implementation in the mid-1970s. The resistance was much more a pragmatic response to the economic circumstances at the time. At the back of this resistance it is also possible to see the powerful influence of multinational bodies such as the International Monetary Fund (IMF). Thus the imposition of tough structural terms to the 1976 IMF loan, especially cuts in public expenditure, coincided with Prime Minister Callaghan's 'Ruskin College' speech in which he called for a much closer alignment of education and economic policy. This became a mantra of government policy for the next 20 years, cutting right across many of the recommendations of the Russell Report which continued to see adult education as a general social good that might be justified in a variety of ways.

Once development was seen to be off the agenda, what then could adult education 'do'? The great expansion of adult education in the 1960s had been most marked in the field of LEA provision. Here the main emphasis was on creative, recreational and physical exercise activities, and to a lesser extent on formal academic courses and on basic skills (mainly literacy). What followed in most LEAs was an attempt to sustain such a service while reducing the cost by substantial fee increases – no talk of 'contributions' here! Fees for academic and vocational courses were generally lower than for the kind of activities variously described as 'leisure', 'recreational' or 'non-vocational', while basic education remained a free or very cheap service. Only a small number of LEAs, most noticeably ILEA, continued to promote a view of adult education as a service responding to a wide variety of social needs, and a wide variety of learner motives ad purposes. The ILEA report *An Education Service for the Whole Community* (ILEA, 1973) noted a significant under-representation of manual workers in the adult education student body. It proposed much closer links between different parts of the education service, and a better use of educational buildings to meet community needs. It also laid out an important strategy of development through the dissemination of local innovatory 'research and development projects':

> It has to be recognized that the detailed implications of broadly agreed policy cannot be laid down from the centre and uniformly imposed. On the contrary, the philosophy of innovation strategy outlined above, calls for pragmatic tactics. In the simplest terms, we have to identify success, shout about it, encourage others to examine their own circumstances in the light of it and support growth as soon as it springs from the ground. (ILEA, 1973, p. 39)

This particular approach was to acquire greater significance in the coming years, as adult education, shorn of a central role in transforming and modernising the country, became instead an outstanding example of how social and economic change might have been dealt with in a more rational, planned way, if there had been the political will for that to happen. 'Development' happened, but usually at the margins of both policy and practice.

In this difficult context, it was unsurprising that much of the Russell Report fell on deaf ears. There were isolated successes. The OU was so close to the heart of the Labour Party, and quickly gained such an international reputation as a model for distance learning, that it was possible during the years 1974–9 to build a solid edifice that could only be tampered with but not destroyed. Yet its ability to compensate for unsatisfactory initial education was limited by its requirement to charge relatively high fees, and the gradual erosion of student support facilities. Given the link between educational qualifications and earning levels, it was precisely those who had most to gain from the OU (unqualified, working-class adults) who were least likely to become its students. Those who gained most from this particular 'second chance' were those who already had some qualifications, but at sub-degree level. Another lasting success, the creation of which had been stoutly supported by the Russell Report, was Northern College. With the support of many local authorities in the North of England, and of the trade union movement, Northern College became an important centre for genuinely 'second chance' education for unqualified adults, and developed strong links not only with the trade union movement but with many voluntary community organisations in the northern counties.

Economic change and learning for work

The central point in understanding the impact of Russell and post-Russell developments is the recognition that although the world that developed in the later 1970s and 1980s was not one that the Russell Committee could have anticipated easily, the Russell report did recognise the importance of the impact of social and economic change on people in three areas:

1. The increase in knowledge and the need for new ways of keeping abreast of it.
2. 'The need for education in social and political understanding'.
3. Education to make the best use of increasing leisure time.

In the event, the first of these (increasing knowledge) was not developed in any detail and the issue of learning at work to deal with new technologies or the challenge of computers was not addressed. The second continues to be a nettle that adult education has consistently failed to grasp. The third rapidly acquired a rather empty ring to it, as unemployment climbed past the million mark in the late 1970s and to over three million in the early 1980s. It was the return of mass unemployment, rather than the arrival of mass leisure, that presented the greatest challenge and the least satisfactory response. The increasing use of the Employment Department and the MSC to take responsibility for work with unemployed adults meant, as suggested above, that many of the pressing educational needs of the unemployed were not dealt with. As outlined in Chapter 7, where there was an apparent attempt to tackle the impact of social and economic change on people's lives through adult learning, it was usually in the form of rather narrowly conceived training or retraining courses organised through the Employment Department. Such courses were designed to get people off the unemployment register as soon as possible. Many people simply went from one training scheme to another, or from training scheme to temporary job, back to the unemployment register and then onto another retraining scheme. In many cases, narrow training courses trained people for non-existent jobs. MSC finance encouraged a privatised training sector that, despite the commitment of individual trainers, had neither the skills nor the remit to tackle deep-seated educational deficits. The majority of these interventions, in retrospect and despite the best will of many of the trainers and other staff involved, seemed to be set up to fail: that is to say that there was no congruence between the scale of the problem of mass unemployment and the official response. The fact that the MSC was subsequently to go through a number of reincarnations as TA, TD and TEED does suggest a high level of uncertainty and improvisation in government thinking.

At the same time, the one feature of learning at work policy which had been successful – the Industrial Training Boards (ITBs) – was allowed to wither on the vine. Some employers (usually those with little commitment to training) had always resented the levy-grant system by which money was collected from all employers and redistributed to those who provided training for employees. Abolition of the ITBs meant that the interests of the bad employers were allowed to override the overall interests of industrial sectors and of the economy as a whole. It is interesting and significant that two large industrial sectors (construction and engineering) continued to have ITBs and use variations on the levy-grant system throughout this period. Within the employed workforce, the 1999 Labour Force Survey showed that monthly training participation rates had grown from 10.5 per cent in 1986 to 15.9 per cent in 1999, while failing to highlight that all but 1.1 per cent of this growth had taken place between 1986 and 1990. As Ewart Keep, a member of the Skills Task Force Research Group of the UK National Skills Task Force (1997–2001), has consistently argued, a truly 'modern' economy would create jobs demanding high levels of skills, while too many actual jobs require only routine skill levels:

> A different type of skills strategy is required at national level, without which the chances of employers delivering in any substantial way on life-long learning for all in the workplace are slim to non-existent. Such a strategy would turn existing policy on its head, and, instead of assuming that the key to the desired 'skills revolution' is the supply of more skills, concentrate on stimulating demand for higher levels of skill, through seeking to upgrade product market strategies, enhance product and service quality and specification, and re-design jobs and work organisation so as to minimise dead end, low skill jobs and maximise the opportunities for the entire workforce to both acquire and utilise higher levels of learning and skill. (Keep, 2000, p. 25)

Despite the heroic efforts of a relatively small number of employers, 'learning at work' during the period 1969–97 was characterised by the failure of employers.

On the one hand they blamed schools for the poor quality of recruits, on the other hand they tried to both contract out of existing training arrangements and to shift the burden wherever possible onto the state. The case of EDS is especially instructive. Despite the proven success of such schemes in improving skill levels and motivation to learn, and in generating better industrial relations, EDS failed to become a great movement of employers. Rather, it was left to the government to attempt to persuade employers, through various promotional grants, to opt into such schemes. The benefits that might have accrued from a mass development of EDS did not materialise. The importance of the links between education and the economy, emphasised in Callaghan's Ruskin College speech in 1976 had been generally accepted. At the same time it appeared a curiously lopsided argument with employers repeatedly demonstrating their reluctance to take their share of the responsibility for the nation's skill shortages.

ACACE and after

As outlined in Chapter 6, it was within ACACE and its successor organisations that many of the dramas of attempting to put together a coherent educational response to social and economic change and personal misery were played out. The 1981 report *Protecting the Future for Adult Education* gives some indication of how difficult the task ahead was. While the report follows in general terms the lines of the Russell Report itself, there is a greater urgency in dealing with the challenge of economic change:

> It scarcely needs repeating that the nature of our society and the environment in which we live is undergoing constant and accelerating change. Technology changes the physical environment . . . and indirectly it changes the roles of the individual and the state, of employer and employee, of teacher and student, of man and woman, of parent and child, as well as the significance of family life, and the inter-dependence of people. Change calls for adaptation, adaptation requires understanding, and understanding depends on education. The provision of education must keep pace with the implications of change so as to help all of us cope as effectively as possible with the decisions which as adults we are continually having to make. (ACACE, 1981, p. 8)

The gap between such statements and the kind of tokenistic training and retraining courses being offered by the MSC in the late 1970s/early 1980s is obvious. The report was addressed in particular to the financially straightened LEAs, and there is a note of some desperation in the plea for clearer central government guidance and financial support: 'It is fruitless for the Council to enquire into and advise on a whole variety of aspects in the provision of adult education, unless the local education authorities are at least encouraged to main-

tain a firm financial and organisational base on which the future can grow'
(ACACE, 1981, p. 51).

Yet 'enquire into and advise' was exactly what ACACE did, as recorded in
Chapter 6. Not only did it enquire into subjects which had become pressing
issues since Russell (education for the unemployed; educational guidance for
adults; adult basic education) but it also ventured into the potentially
dangerous waters of the political education of adults. Under the steady leadership of Richard Hoggart, ACACE held its nerve and continued to keep the
'Russell agenda' alive into the decade following its publication. Of especial
importance was *Continuing Education: From Policies to Practice* (ACACE,
1982a). The very title was a reminder of the 'development' aspects of Russell,
and at the depth of the economic crisis caused by incautious and accelerated
industrial restructuring, it represented a remarkably forward-looking document.
The use of the term 'continuing education' was of particular note, with its
broader remit than the by now rather dated term 'adult education'. This
allowed the enquiry to range across further and higher education, MSC-
sponsored courses and distance education, as well as LEA work. For the first
time in a publication of this sort there was a more positive approach to the
MSC Training Opportunities Scheme (TOPS), pointing out the increasing
proportion of such courses held in further and higher education, and the
increasing proportion of women on these courses (one tragedy of the early
1980s was that there was little that could be offered to men in, for example,
traditional, isolated coal and steel communities with few other employment
possibilities). A whole chapter was devoted to 'Barriers to Access', a theme that
remained ever-present in policy documents for the remainder of the period in
question, while 'Information, Advisory and Counselling Services' was also
deemed to merit a chapter to itself.

The need for ongoing learning in adult life was attached once again to social
and economic change, but this time in a way which linked it explicitly with the
Russell theme of 'disadvantage':

New technologies reduce the demands of work and enhance opportunities
for leisure, but they also put a premium on the adaptability of knowledge
and skills not possessed by those with only limited educational attain-
ments. Particularly at risk are: those women whose level of educational
experience and aspiration often put them at a disadvantage; members of
ethnic minority groups who are often locked into multiple deprivations of
poor education, poor housing and poor employment prospects; those
manual workers who left school at the minimum age and have had no
further education or training; young people entering the labour market for
the first time, often with few skills to offer; and the retired, particularly the
growing number of those retiring early, still physically and mentally active

but with far fewer opportunities to contribute to society in any satisfying and constructive way. (ACACE, 1982a, p. 182)

At the time, this was a clear statement of those groups who were suffering most because of social and economic change. But as other parts of the economy began to pick up, from the late 1980s onwards, it also became a statement about those groups who were not sharing in the new wealth of the country. Indeed, one of the great ironies that appeared from 1990 onwards was the coexistence of rising general standards of living with growing inequalities of wealth and opportunity, usually correlated with educational experience and attainment.

The work of ACACE, then, was an old vision played out in new circumstances. Many of its themes (adequacy of provision; a service for the whole community) went against the grain of current thinking in political circles. 'Social policy', like social services, had come to be seen as residual provision for those who were unable or unwilling to hep themselves. Yet other parts of the work of ACACE could be said to reflect that same sense that were 'special groups' in society who would only be able to play a full part in society and the labour market with additional support, a position that could be focused equally well from socially radical and conservative positions. In no small part the success of ACACE could be put down to its ability to hold together antagonistic forces: the tensions between a service for the whole community and a service for special, disadvantaged groups, and then the tension between differing motivations (charity and social justice) for wanting to support those people disadvantaged by the pace and direction of social and economic change.

The work of UDACE and REPLAN (itself stemming from a recommendation in the ACACE (1982a) report *Policies to Practice*) maintained these creative tensions through into the more receptive political atmosphere of the 1990s. To some extent there was a drawing together of the government's instrumental view of adult education and an older liberal conception of its role that stressed the links with citizenship and culture. Certainly it had been necessary to think deeply about the nature of the adult education response to mass unemployment, to diversity and ethnic tensions, to people's need for guidance and help in rene-gotiating their lives. Both the drawing together and the differences are vividly illustrated by the example of REPLAN. This was established, as outlined in Chapter 6, to look at the educational response to unemployment. While the MSC, through the TOPS programme, continued to stress a relatively narrow training agenda, REPLAN stressed the broader educational needs of adults inde-pendent of employment status. It should also be noted that this corresponded to the reality of unemployment. Many more people experienced unemployment in the 1980s than the actual peak number of unemployed in any given month. While in some areas unemployment became a way of life, giving rise to the pessimistic and negative theory of an 'underclass' in society, for many other unemployed people it was an experience sandwiched between more or less satisfactory periods of employment, but which emphasised unresolved issues about the adequacy of their initial education and training to equip them with the skills required in a rapidly changing world.

Organisations, particularly those known by acronyms, come and go. It might be thought that organisations such as ACACE, REPLAN and UDACE, together with political casualties such as ILEA, left only empty holes behind them. This was far from the case. All of these bodies, together with NIACE itself, were important through their lobbying work, conferences and publications in offering both inspiring visions and concrete examples of how adult learning might benefit individual adults and the country at large. The concept of adult education as a profession or vocation suggests both individual talent and collective resources. While major figures were indeed lost to the field when organisations were abolished, many others reappeared in new guises. The case of the abolition of ILEA is particularly instructive. Over the decade following abolition in 1990, ILEA adult education staff turned up in many settings, including colleges, universities, local authorities and voluntary organisations. In these ways the Russell vision was kept alive, deepened and refined in response to new challenges in the years from 1969–97. By 1997 there was a body of professional knowledge vastly superior to what had existed in 1969. There was pressure for change, for adult learning to at last emerge as a major feature of government social policy. It is for others to decide whether in the years since 1997, the promise has been fulfilled or dissipated.

Adult learners and the prospects for adult learning

The world of 2006 is self-evidently not the world of 1969 when the Russell Committee was established. In particular, there has been a diminution of reliance on and expectations of the state as far as social policy is concerned. The period since 1969 has seen great changes in civil society, in particular the growth of identity politics, reflected in large-scale social movements such as the women's movement and the environmental movement. Many NGOs have budgets and staff as large as those of medium-sized corporations or government departments. In political terms, the characteristic political organisation is no longer the political party but the pressure group. This is not the place to go into any detail about such developments, but to suggest the implications for adult learning. First and most obviously, adult education is only one among many sources of information and ideas about what is going on in the world. The large NGOs, through their mass membership, are able to influence large numbers of people, often at a global level. Individuals, whether members of such organisations or not, will use the Internet to obtain information and ideas they feel they require, often sharing them with other interested family members or friends at a local level. Local voluntary community organisations continue to thrive and meet locally defined learning needs. Since individuals and communities have more choices about how to meet their learning needs, what might be termed the 'learning economy' is much more varied and decentralised than it ever was in the past. It was suggested above that during the 1980s public policy on adult learning (and social welfare issues such as health and social services) became increasingly a 'residual' matter. Public policy referred to those who were unable to make arrangements for themselves. Whereas private school education, with its severe financial implications for family budgets, remained beyond the reach of most people and school education therefore still a central theme of public policy, the same cannot be said of adult education. As 'student contributions' reached an ever higher percentage of actual costs, the adult education student was increasingly seen as a consumer of a service that might be provided by any one of a number of private or public agencies, or organised by the learners themselves, or voluntary bodies to which they belonged.

Thus one of the cornerstones of the Russell Report, the provision of an adult education service for the whole community, seemed increasingly less likely to be the subject of public policy. In arguing for the importance of adult learning, the allocation of public resources to it, and the potential of adult learning as an arm of public policy, adult educators have had to become much more subtle in the arguments they deploy. At the beginning of this book, there was some reference to the debate about different types of adult learning: vocational or non-vocational, education or training. At the beginning of the period in question, there was considerable support for the notion of a 'seamless robe' of learning, different in kind, but all of equal value. By the end of the period, following two decades in which the education–training debate was used to justify the involvement of two separate government departments in adult learning, and during which expenditure on education itself (school and post-school) was more and more seen to be justified by its economic contribution, the argument over terminology seemed increasingly sterile.

What generally seemed absent from the debate was the rather hard-headed notion that the viability and profitability of economic enterprises was based on a number of factors – their intrinsic economic value, their exploitation of the available skill base, and the existence or not of social stability and cohesion favouring investment and enterprise. Some slight reference has been made in this book to the social conflicts of the 1970s; rather less has been said about ongoing conflicts during the 1980s and 1990s which suggested that all was not well in the society. While some residual social policy was undoubtedly supported by humanitarian concerns, a lot more support was generated by a sense that unless these social conflicts were dealt with, then an important precondition of a successful economy would not be met. This has had a profound influence on adult education policy from the emphasis on disadvantage in Russell to the concept of 'social inclusion' that emerged towards the end of the 1990s. It is also important to recognise that it is not an argument for equality: social inclusion proposes that all will be well provided that those left behind are not left too far behind, that ladders of opportunity exist and are seen to exist, that social optimism can be encouraged and supported in practical ways. In a sense family education is emblematic of this approach, providing educational support to families that can only ever partially make up for the educational failings and misfortunes of the parent generation, while at the same time encouraging parents to think of the education of their own children in more positive ways.

At this point in the consideration of social policy, it is necessary to return to the issue of skills. Few would now deny that the rate of technological change means that the front-loading argument (that initial education and training provides people with the skills and knowledge they will need through their working lives) is redundant. Rather fewer commentators have recognised a further aspect to this argument. Not only do people have to learn new skills, acquire new knowledge, as they move through lives increasingly affected by technological change, but they live longer. The extension of the average lifespan well beyond the age of retirement has important consequences for social policy, for example in the fields of pensions, health and social care. But it also has implications for adult learning, in such areas as learning related to the volunteering activities of older people, to financial management, to the strong relationship identified between an active, learning old age and a healthy old age. In general, the first part of the argument – relating to learning needs during working life – has been much higher profile than the argument about learning post-work. Yet it seems inevitable that in the coming years social policy will be directed towards this new challenge.

Participation studies have added considerably to our knowledge of what kinds of adults participate in adult learning and how frequently. We know rather less about *why* they participate, the pleasures and benefits they derive from learning, the difficulties and problems they encounter while learning. This complicates adult education as a form of social policy. We now know a lot about participation, but still not enough about learning and biography. People learn for a variety of reasons, and generally governments have tried to reflect this by supporting (for example) learning related to paid work rather than leisure. Yet if we take the single example of information and communication technologies (ICT), people learn computer skills for a variety of reasons, related to work, family and leisure, and their involvement in voluntary community organisations. The same person may indeed learn for all three sets of reasons at the same time. The person following an ICT training course at work is likely to use these skills outside of work; the person learning in a community centre class may well use the skills at work. There is a sense in which the argument in favour of adult education 'for the whole community' contains an element of obvious truth: that people learn for their own purposes and apply learning in their own ways, so that a more general support for adult learning across society may end up producing more social benefits than a targeted policy that privileges certain types of learning. Throughout the period in question and on into the twenty-first century, there have been reported research findings about the value of a broad approach to the adult education curriculum and the wider benefits of adult learning. In a recent research review, Veronica McGivney (2005, p. 30) writes: 'The literature on adult learning constantly reaffirms that the education programmes that are most effective in attracting adults and sustaining their motivation are those that respond to their interests and aspirations.' It is a self-evident point that we must not ignore.

One important part of adult learning that is more fully recognised now than it was at the time of the Russell Report is 'informal learning'. Initially it was Alan Tough (1971, 1979) who reminded adult educators that learners learned characteristically without the help of educators, planning and executing a vast number of learning projects. This perspective has had only a marginal influence on adult education theory and practice. Forrester and Payne (2000) described this as a 'missed opportunity', taking the view that 'in so far as there is a problem about participation in adult learning, it is located in the apparent limited ability of formal providers of adult education and training to engage with the interests and enthusiasms of the adult population'. There is now a wealth of evidence about the extent of adult learning through membership of voluntary organisations (Elsdon *et al.*, 1995). Yet there has been a reluctance to recognise that what passes for 'adult learning' in this country is only a small part of the total learning going on in society. Some attempts have been made to make provision through voluntary community organisations, but there has been a reluctance to give serious consideration to this perspective as a way of putting the learner central stage rather than 'delivering' more of the same packaged in a slightly different way.

One particular difficulty of placing too great an emphasis on informal learning, however, is that it assumes that all learning is good, or at least neutral. This is far from the case, and even brief acquaintance with the Internet will reveal this clearly. For every group devoted to animal welfare, there will be another devoted to hunting and killing wild animals, for every group committed to ethnic harmony and diversity, there will be another committed to ethnic superiority and conflict. Michael Welton's most recent book confronts this dilemma directly:

> The word 'learning' often represents itself to Western consciousness as something inherently good. But clearly, humankind learns to imagine great and horrible things. We can learn to hate other peoples, races, religions, wealth. We can acquire techniques, carefully mentored or taught, to torture, maim, murder, bomb and harass. From the historian's vantage

point, when we lower the discourse of the learning society into the world in which it actually exists, we discover that the language of the learning society co-exists with many horrible practices in the world. (Welton, 2005, p. 3)

Public policy, then, must at some point dwell on the issue of curriculum, of what it is desirable to learn or not learn, whether that learning takes place in institutions such as colleges or universities, in local authority outreach project, in voluntary organisations or through distance learning, the Internet and the media.

Learning and social policy

It was the misfortune of the Russell Report to appear at a difficult time in the country's social and economic history. Yet in a sense, there were some advantages to this. The deepening economic crisis of the later 1970s and early 1980s meant that there were men and women with time on their hands. Committed adult educators, working generally on the fringes of public policy, were able to motivate learners who had suffered profoundly distressing and negative experiences to reconstruct their lives through education. That they were able to do so was due in great part to the stress on the disadvantaged in the Russell Report. The development of Second Chance and Access courses, and of educational guidance services, did not emerge of course direct from the Russell Report. The work of ACACE, UDACE and REPLAN, outlined in this book, served to interpret themes from Russell, to adapt them to changing circumstances and to promote and disseminate projects in these areas. Despite heated debate as to the appropriateness of the term disadvantage, the Russell Report (1973) and *The Disadvantaged Adult* (Clyne, 1972) had drawn attention to a number of groups in society who were not enjoying the full benefits of post-World War II prosperity. Ten years later those groups had grown markedly. The Russell Report had referred to three areas of disadvantage: personal capacity; social disadvantage; educational disadvantage. It had also become apparent that disadvantage was not just a state of being but a condition actively induced by processes of social and economic change driven by factors right outside the personal experience of those then described as 'the disadvantaged'.

Disadvantage as an active process may be briefly exemplified in the case of steel towns such as Sheffield. The steel industry in the UK, which as recently as 1980 employed over 150,000 workers, saw that figure drop to just over 50,000 by 1990. The run-down of the steel industry threw thousands onto the economic scrapheap of mass unemployment. Many were men with no qualifications and limited literacy skills who had grown up certain that their success in life depended on physical strength rather than intellectual ability. In the case of immigrant workers, they often knew very little English. Meanwhile the women in steel communities had to assume new social and economic roles, and often adult education was a way of acquiring not just useful skills for the labour market, but also new attitudes towards the value of education and the role that women might play in society. Similar changes took place in traditional coalmining and textile communities, while few communities, even in the south-east of England were entirely exempt from the social and economic turmoil of the period.

The importance of guidance at this period was a direct reflection of the depths of the upheaval. During the late 1970s and 1980s, educational guidance services grew up around the country (there was one, for example, in each inner London borough prior to the abolition of ILEA in 1990). These provided a service which:

- was directed specifically towards adults
- offered a range of service, including information, advice, counselling, advocacy and feedback (proposing changes in provision to make it more 'adult-friendly'), according to need
- provided support for adults across time as they moved through various stages of study and employment
- was free to users
- was independent of providers.

It is particularly unfortunate that the general availability of such services has not been considered a priority since 1990, and that where it does exist, educational guidance for adults is generally considered to be a residual service for those who appear resistant to other aspects of social policy rather than a generally available service for adults wanting to chart a path through social and economic change with the support of adult learning.

Yet even the most committed of adult educators must occasionally have asked themselves just what education could achieve, divorced from other interventions in society. As has been made clear in this book, the present author and editor do not accept that educational intervention *by itself* can reduce poverty or reverse community decline. To this list might be added environmental degradation and ethnic and religious conflict. (It is especially curious that there is no mention of the environment in the Russell Report, despite the fact that its publication coincided with the first wave of interest in environmental issues in Western Europe.) But accepting that adult education cannot *by itself* change society is very different from the claim that it has no role outside of those fields traditionally ascribed for it over the past half-century: leisure and cultural activities on the one hand and preparation for the job market on the other. Adult education has the potential to be not just one aspect of social policy but to provide an underpinning for a range of other activities. For example, adult educational work in ILEA during the

1980s benefited from the Greater London Council (GLC) 'cheap fares' policy which made it easier for adults to reach adult education centres, while outreach and community education workers were involved with community development projects run by both the GLC (until 1986) and the various boroughs. The same staff worked alongside health and social workers to identify the contribution of adult learning to other areas of social policy. The anti-racist policies of ILEA were intended to stand alongside those of the GLC and the London boroughs to ensure that the learning and other social needs of migrant communities were met.

These arguments for a higher level of coherence in policy-making did not in general mesh with the tone of the 1980s. The advocates of 'small government' preferred to give 'market forces' free rein. Government initiatives were deliberately intended to work on a limited departmental basis. In the 1990s, of course, came the rediscovery that in order to 'make a difference' in particular places damaged by social and economic change (for example, those hit by industrial restructuring in the 1980s, or by civil unrest in the early 1990s), concerted action was required: across government departments; between local and national government; between statutory agencies and civil society. The era of the Single Regeneration Budgets had arrived. Concealed as it were within this recognition that concerted social policy could make a difference in particular geographical settings was the broader truth that social policy itself might better be achieved through interdepartmental working. The phrase 'joined-up government' had been invented, even if it seemed to operate more in theory than in practice. Governments had begun to recognise that in a mixed economy of public and private provision and choices, government remained responsible for ensuring that the sum total of such choices contributed to a healthy, harmonious society.

Yet the difficult of implementing learning as part of cross-departmental social policy can be illustrated through issues of food and health. At one level, it would be perfectly straightforward to mount public information campaigns, or to put on a large-scale programme of adult learning about the relationship between health and food. Yet in practice, it is not straightforward at all. The availability of good quality food itself depends on:

- how the agricultural industry is regulated (itself a responsibility shared between the UK government and the EU)
- the work of the Food Standards Authority, and the planning system over issues such as the building of out-of-town supermarkets which can reduce availability for those who do not drive cars
- rural policy and how to keep village shops open.

This is before delving into debates about organic versus non-organic food production, or the use of genetically modified (GM) food-stuffs, or the relationship between departments responsible for health, community development and education.

The practical difficulties of applying learning as an overall vision across public policy are further complicated by the contrasting tendencies in policy formulation to emphasise either the overarching vision or the practical suggestions for improvement. Russell was already a compromise between these two, suggesting a vision but preferring to make recommendations that could make a difference within existing resource constraints. Such compromises run through public policy from Russell to NAGCELL. Reports that emphasise the big vision include Russell itself, the ACACE report *Continuing Education: From Policies to Practice* (1982a), the first report from NAGCELL (Fryer, 1997). Yet as is made clear in Chapter 7, government action during the period 1969–97 did nothing to resolve major issues about the legal status of adult education, and how a structure might be found that was responsive to the wide variety of factors that motivate adult learners. It is not surprising that other policy initiatives preferred to stick to more closely defined and, arguably, achievable tasks. Yet the end result is always that the adult education vision is a deferred vision.

The other obvious point that must be kept in mind about social policy is that public policy relates to social change: there is a difficult-to-define space in which a public mood is determined at any particular moment. Public policy is most effective when it 'fits' the social mood of a country, least effective when it cuts across the public mood. Thus during the period under discussion in this book, access courses for groups such as women or ethnic minorities did correspond to important sea-changes in civil society. Furthermore they did so in a way that cut across unhelpful blockages in public policy such as the distinction between vocational and non-vocational. Some access students have gone on to develop substantial new careers; for other the experience has been justified in terms of personal growth, and contributions made to family life or within a local community. In similar fashion, there is a general mood of support for ICT and a desire to learn the necessary skills to use these new technologies, that goes beyond questions of the use to which these skills will be put. The example mentioned above, of the relationship between food and health, is another case in point: the general public mood is that people are no longer prepared to put up with low quality food that is damaging their health. Despite the obvious difficulties of implementing social policy in this instance, there is widespread support for such initiatives within civil society. By contrast, the debate about promoting higher literacy standards in the adult population has faced constant public ambivalence over the issues. Adults who have spent many years honing their skills at avoiding situations demanding literacy are often reluctant to desert these tried and trusted techniques. Many employers acknowledge (in private of not in public) that the literacy demands on employees are very low. In one important area of social policy (disability) the social mood often seems to run ahead of public policy. The

Disability Discrimination Act, finally now coming into force, has been part of a major push within civil society by those with disabilities, their families and supporters. A large disadvantaged minority is no longer prepared to 'put up and shut up'. Yet many public agencies, including traditional providers of adult learning, are still struggling to comply with the act in the facilities they provide.

Observing the interface between public policy and public mood is not only a useful exercise in itself. It also suggests a possible resolution to one of the most long-standing debates in adult learning: that over 'need' and 'demand'. As has often been noted, those in greatest apparent need of adult education are often precisely the ones least likely to volunteer for it. Are there ways in which the social issue of what adults want for themselves and their families can be drawn more closely into the social policy definition of what should be publicly provided? In this sense the argument for adult education becomes precisely that for a participatory rather than a representative democracy. It is the Russell Report's education for citizenship redefined for a society that expects less of government in terms of direct provision, but which continues to demand that government should offer leadership and support in achieving generally agreed social goals. This is not to say that Russell was wrong as policy, rather that policy ripens as its essential vision responds and adapts to social change.

Conclusion: adult learning and the adult educator

The choice of language to describe the activities in which adult educators and learners engage is not just a matter of words. If adult learning is to develop a cross-departmental brief as a central feature of public policy, then the move from 'adult education' to 'adult learning' is essential. Adult learning can no longer be pigeon-holed as an issue of second order importance within a government department primarily concerned with schools. It is an advance that learning in relation to both work and other learner motivations is now coordinated through a unified Department for Education and Skills. Yet there is some way to go before the importance of adult learning is fully recognised in areas such as Social Services, the National Health Service, Arts, Libraries and Museums, Housing and Pensions. The contribution that adult learning might make to controversial issues such as GM food, the future of pensions, nuclear power or stem cell research, where wide public concern is often matched by wide public ignorance, is another area that merits exploration. It is ironical that some local authorities, excluded from direct responsibility for adult learning provision, are now looking at precisely the role of adult learning across the whole portfolio of local authority responsibilities.

If adult learning is to achieve a more central and comprehensive role in public policy, what are the implications for adult educators? Arguably, the professional identity of adult educators has always centred on the local authority sector with its bias towards leisure provision. Those who have taught adults in further and higher education have often identified themselves more as further or higher education teachers who happen to work with adults as part, or even all, of their brief. It is to the credit of NIACE, the national organisation for adult learning, that it has been able to conserve some sense of professional identity across all the organisational changes of the last 30 years. Yet this professional identity still seems to have weak foundations. The academic study of adult learning has stressed the psychological distinctiveness of learning in adults rather than children, but this is scarcely sufficient to justify the extended social role suggested for adult learning here. The contributions of radical thinkers such as Illich and Freire have been mentioned, but have often made adult learning appear even more marginal to public policy than it is. Some commentators have attempted to apply the perspectives of post-modernism to the field, but have seldom managed to provide illumination to either policy debates or practice.

Arguably, the most relevant theoretical work in support of a comprehensive role for adult learning in modern life has come from social thinkers, and in particular the work of Anthony Giddens and Jürgen Habermas. Giddens' often repeated observation that human beings are both structured and structuring is of particular help. While a key role of adult learning is adaptation to social and economic change, the learners will also acquire the skills and confidence to themselves influence the direction of change in the future. Habermas has drawn a broad contrast between a world of technical rationality that removes choice and agency from human activity, and a life-world in which people relate together free from the constraints and rules imposed by the state on the one hand and paid work on the other. Michael Welton has argued that a close study of Habermas's work is essential for adult educators:

> We turn to Habermas to learn more about one domain, civil society, in order to construct an adequate theoretical framework towards the achievement of a learning society that encourages active citizenship, nurtures people-centred work and fosters governance and public spaces that engage a significant minority of citizens in deliberative processes committed to the common weal. (Welton, 2001, p. 21)

Civil society (the life-world), in Habermas's view, constructs and mobilises its own knowledge vis-à-vis the power of the state. It places issues on public agendas which otherwise might not be there. Welton lists some of these – environmental risk issues, feminist issues, issues related to global economic inequalities and multicultural issues arising from movement of populations (p. 32). In Welton's view, education in support of civil society remains a realistic target for adult educators who want to see 'a just and honest learning society' (p. 33). Thus, to say that adult learning should inform all public policy is not to see the state as controlling all learning, but as helping to resource it within many social settings in local communities. It will always be important for adult educators to see themselves as rooted in civil society rather than in the state.

The renewal of that important sense of the work of adult educators as a vocation is of critical importance. This book has documented concerns that adult learning is always at threat from those who want to define it in public policy terms as of value only in so far as it relates to the labour market. Yet this particular threat is one part of broader concerns – Raymond Williams' 'Plan X' and Habermas' 'technical rationality'. It is Michael Collins (1991, p. 39) who articulates mostly clearly these links:

> The obsession with technique, or technical rationality, has induced modern adult education to evade serious engagement with critical, ethical, and political issues. It has effectively sidelined adult education as a social movement and supports initiatives that tend to de-skill the practitioner's pedagogic role. Thus, the distinctiveness of adult education as a field of practice has been seriously eroded. Therein lies the deepening crisis. A renewed sense of vocation in adult education is invoked as a prelude to the orchestration of technique on a more human scale and for the shaping of a genuinely reflective, emancipatory practice.

Adult educators in the future will need to know more about the social world in which they operate, and the contribution that adult learning can make to that world. They will need to be committed to a humanist perspective on human life which stresses diversity, autonomy and community. They will need, as well, to listen to the past, to the voices of other adult educators who have pursued similar ends in different circumstances: 'not . . . a luxury for a very few exceptional persons – but . . . a permanent national necessity, an inseparable aspect of citizenship . . . both universal and lifelong', as the Ministry of Reconstruction report stated in 1919.

Afterword

In the Introduction we posed four questions:

1. What, if anything, have we learned from the successes and failures of the past?
2. What can we learn from experience elsewhere for adoption or adaptation here in the UK?
3. Why do we still consider adult learning as a by-product of education or employment policies rather than as a core strand of social policy?
4. What are the values that underpin the concept of adult education as vocation and to what extent has this been replaced by a more straightforward approach to it as 'just a job'.

We hope that we have provided sufficient guidance for readers to understand our approach to answering these questions for the period 1969–97. We are conscious, however, that a more pressing issue for readers may be to seek out answers themselves for these questions for the period since 1997. Does what they know of the more recent period, through whatever combination of study and experience, suggest that we have learned from the past, that we have been able to learn from experience elsewhere in the world, that we have developed a view of adult learning as a core strand in social policy, or that we have a positive and committed view of our own professional field?

Can adult learning contribute to social justice? Can adult learning enhance the lives of individuals and communities? In our varied careers in adult learning, we have always worked as if the answer to these questions is 'Yes'. Despite all the changes that have taken place in adult learning, we believe there are still people out there prepared to take up this challenge. It is a challenge addressed to a younger generation than that of the present author and editor: how can we maintain and reinterpret the values that underpinned the 1919 Ministry of Reconstruction Report or the 1973 Russell Report in the changed world of the twenty-first century?

Acronyms

All organisations are within UK unless otherwise indicated

A Level	Advanced level examination (normally taken at 18 years and used for university entrance)
AAE	Association for Adult Education
ABE	Adult basic education
ACACE	Advisory Council for Adult and Continuing Education (1977–83)
ACL	Adult and community learning
ACSTT	Advisory Committee on the Supply and Training of Teachers (later Advisory Committee on the Supply and Education of Teachers, ACSET)
AEC	Adult Education Committee (of the Ministry of Reconstruction, established 1917)
AEC	Association of Education Committees
ALRA	Adult Literacy Resource Agency (then ALU, Adult Literacy Unit, then ALBSU, Adult Literacy and Basic Skills Unit, now BSA)
AONTAS	Irish non-governmental organisation for adult learning
APEL	Accreditation of Prior Experiential Learning
ARE	Association for Recurrent Education
ATTI	Association of Teachers in Technical Institutions (now NATFHE)
BAS	British Association of Settlements
BBC	British Broadcasting Corporation
BIAE	British Institute of Adult Education (forerunner of NIAE and NIACE)
BSA	Basic Skills Agency (previously ALBSU, ALU and ALRA)
CATS	Credit Accumulation and Transfer Scheme(s)
CBI	Confederation of British Industry
CCC	Council for Cultural Cooperation (of the Council for Europe)
CDP	Community Development Project (Home Office funded scheme from 1969)

CGLI	City and Guilds of London Institute
CPAG	Child Poverty Action Group
DES	Department of Education and Science (subsequently DfEE, now DfES)
DfEE	Department for Education and Employment (previously DES, later DfES)
DfES	Department for Education and Skills (previously DfEE and DES)
EAEA	European Association for the Education of Adults (previously EBAE)
EBAE	European Bureau of Adult Education (now EAEA)
EC	European Commission (executive arm of the European Union)
ECA	Educational Centres Association
ED	Employment Department
EDAP	Employee Development and Assistance Programme (Ford Motor Company)
EDS	Employee Development Scheme(s)
EPA	Educational Priority Area (late 1960s, early 1970s)
ERA	Education Reform Act (1988)
ESL	English as a Second Language (now usually ESOL, English for Speakers of Other Languages)
ESWC	Education Service for the Whole Community (within ILEA)
EU	European Union (previously EC European Community and EEC European Economic Community)
FEFC	Further Education Funding Council (now the LSC)
FEU	Further Education Unit (later FEDA, Further Education Development Agency, now LSDA, Learning and Skills Development Agency)
GCE	General Certificate of Education (examination taken at 16 years, now called the GCSE, General Certificate of Secondary Education)
GM	Genetically modified (food)
GNVQ	General National Vocational Qualifications
GLC	Greater London Council (abolished 1986)
HEFC	Higher Education Funding Council
HMI	Her Majesty's Inspectorate
HMSO	Her Majesty's Stationery Office
HSAC	Home and Social Affairs Committee (of the Cabinet)
ICAE	International Council for Adult Education
ICT	Information and Communication Technologies

IiP	Investors in People
ILEA	Inner London Education Authority (abolished 1990)
ILO	International Labour Office (also called International Labour Organization)
IMF	International Monetary Fund
IPPR	Institute for Public Policy Research
ITA	Independent Television Authority
ITB	Industrial Training Board
LCC	London County Council
LEA	Local Education Authority
LSC	Learning and Skills Council
MP	Member of Parliament
MSC	Manpower Services Commission (later TC, Training Commission, TA, Training Agency and TEED, Training, Education and Employment Directorate; subsequently replaced by TECs, and later LSC)
NAB	National Advisory Body (for Public Sector Higher Education)
NAEGA	National Association for Educational Guidance for Adults
NAGCELL	National Advisory Group for Continuing Education and Lifelong Learning
NATESLA	National Association for Teaching English as a Second Language
NATFHE	National Association of Teachers in Further and Higher Education (previously ATTI)
NCVQ	National Council for Vocational Qualifications
NEC	National Extension College
NGO	Non-governmental organisation
NIAE	National Institute of Adult Education (forerunner of NIACE)
NIACE	National Institute of Adult Continuing Education (England and Wales)
NIACE Cymru	NIACE in Wales (now NIACE Dysgu Cymru)
NOW	New Opportunities for Women
NUT	National Union of Teachers
NVQ	National Vocational Qualification
OECD	Organisation for Economic Cooperation and Development
OU	The Open University
OXFAM	Oxford Committee for Famine Relief (now an international aid agency)
PEL	Paid Educational Leave

PICKUP	Professional, Industrial and Commercial Updating
PPA	Pre-school Playgroups Association (now the PLA Pre-school Learning Alliance)
PRA	Pre-Retirement Association
RAC	Regional Advisory Council (for Further Education)
REPLAN	Development unit funded by DES, 1984–91(not an acronym)
RoSLA	Raising of the School-leaving Age (1972)
SCUTREA	Standing Conference on University Teaching and Research in the Education of Adults
SEO	Society of Education Officers
SHELTER	Charity for homeless people (not an acronym)
SIT	Society of Industrial Tutors
TA/TC/TEED	see MSC
TECs	Training and Enterprise Councils (replaced by LSC)
TG	Townswomen's Guild
THES	*Times Higher Education Supplement* (also known as *The Higher*)
TOPs	Training Opportunities Programme (of the MSC)
TUC	Trades Union Congress
TVEI	Technical and Vocational Education Initiative
U3A	University of the Third Age
UCAE	Universities Council for Adult Education (later UCACE, Universities Council for Adult Continuing Education, then from 1993 UACE, Universities Association for Continuing Education)
UDACE	Unit for the Development of Adult Continuing Education (1984–91)
UGC	University Grants Committee (now HEFC)
UNESCO	United Nations Educational, Scientific and Cultural Organisation
UK	United Kingdom of Great Britain and Northern Ireland
VAEF	Voluntary Adult Education Forum
VCC	Vice-Chancellors' Committee
VIAE	Valleys Initiative for Adult Education
WEA	Workers' Educational Association
WJEC	Welsh Joint Education Committee (pre-devolution)
WI	Women's Institute
WTO	World Trade Organization
YMCA	Young Men's Christian Association

Bibliography

ACACE (1979a) *Adult Students and Higher Education*. Leicester: ACACE.

ACACE (1979b) *Links to Learning*. Leicester: ACACE.

ACACE (1979c) *Towards Continuing Education*. Leicester: ACACE.

ACACE (1979d) *A Strategy for the Basic Education of Adults*. Leicester: ACACE.

ACACE (1980) *Present Imperfect*. Leicester: ACACE.

ACACE (1981) *Protecting the Future for Adult Education*. Leicester: ACACE.

ACACE (1982a) *Continuing Education: From Policies to Practice*. Leicester: ACACE.

ACACE (1982b) *Education for Unemployed Adults*. Leicester: ACACE.

ACACE (1983) *Political Education for Adults*. Leicester: ACACE.

ACSTT (1975) *The Training of Teachers for Further Education* (The First Haycocks Report). London: ACSTT.

ACSTT (1978a) *The Training of Adult Education and Part-time Further Education Teachers* (The Second Haycocks Report). London: ACSTT.

ACSTT (1978b) *Training Teachers for Education Management in Further and Adult Education*. London: ACSTT.

Adkins, G. (1980) *The Arts and Adult Education*. Leicester: NIAE.

ALBSU (1993) *The Cost to Industry: Basic Skills and the UK Workforce*. London: ALBSU.

Alexander, T. and Clyne, P. (1995) *Riches Beyond Price: Making the Most of Family Learning* (NIACE policy discussion paper). Leicester: NIACE.

Bains, M. A. (1972) *Report of the Study Group on Local Authority Management Structures*. London: HMSO.

Ball, S. J. (1994) *Education Reform: A Critical and Post-structural Account*. Buckingham: SRHE.

Board of Education (1926) *Report of the Consultative Committee of the Board of Education on The Education of the Adolescent* (The Hadow Report). London: HMSO.

British Association of Settlements (1974) *A Right to Read: Action for a Literate Britain*. London: BAS.

Brown, J. (ed.) (2003) *The Challenge of Change* (NAEGA occasional paper). Newcastle/Tyne: NAEGA.

Butler, L. (1984) *Case Studies in Educational Guidance for Adults*. Leicester: ACACE/NIACE.

Calouste Gulbenkian Foundation (1968) *Community Work and Social Change* (Gulbenkian Report). London: Longman.

Caute, D. (1988) *Sixty-eight: The Year of the Barricades.* London: Paladin.

CDP Information and Intelligence Unit (1974) *The National Community Development Project: Inter-project Report 1973.* London: CDP.

Central Advisory Council for Education (1967) *Children and Their Primary Schools* (The Plowden Report). London: HMSO.

Clyne, P. (1972) *The Disadvantaged Adult: Educational and Social Needs of Disadvantaged Groups.* London: Longman.

Collins, M. (1991) *Adult Education as Vocation: A Critical Role for the Adult Educator.* London: Routledge.

Commission on Adult Education (1983) *Lifelong Learning* (The Kenny Report). Dublin: Stationery Office.

Committee appointed by the Prime Minister (1973) *Adult Education in Ireland* (The Murphy Report). Dublin: Stationery Office.

Committee on Higher Education (1963) *Higher Education* (The Robbins Report). London: HMSO.

Corbett, A. (1978) *A Critical Survey of the Major Educational Reports.* London: Macmillan Education.

Council of Europe (1965) *Workers in Adult Education: Their Status, Recruitment and Training.* Strasbourg: Council of Europe.

Council of Europe Council for Cultural Cooperation (1970) *Permanent Education.* Strasbourg: Council of Europe.

Cushman, M. (1996) *The Great Jewel Robbery? Adult Education in Inner London since the Break-up of the Inner London Education Authority.* London: NATFHE.

Delors, J. (1996) 'Education for tomorrow', *The UNESCO Courier,* April 1996.

DES (1966a) *A Plan for Polytechnics and Other Colleges: Higher Education in the Further Education System.* London: HMSO.

DES (1966b) *A University of the Air.* London: HMSO.

DES (1969) *Report of the Planning Committee.* London: HMSO.

DES (1971) *Museums in Education.* London: HMSO.

DES (1972a) *Education: A Framework for Expansion.* London: HMSO.

DES (1972b) *Report of the Committee of Enquiry into Teacher Education and Training* (The James Report). London: HMSO.

DES (1973) *Adult Education: A Plan for Development* (The Russell Report). London: HMSO.

DES (1978) *Higher Education into the 1990s.* London: HMSO.

DES/ED (1981) *A New Training Initiative: A Programme for Action.* London: HMSO.

DES (1989) *Adult Continuing Education and the Education Reform Act 1988, Planning and Delegation Schemes* (Circular 19/1989). London: HMSO.

DES (1991) *Education and Training for the 21ˢᵗ Century*. London: HMSO.

Devereux, W. (1982) *Adult Education in Inner London 1870–1980*. London: Shepheard-Walwyn.

Eldwick Research Associates (2001) *Adult and Community Learning: What? Why? Who? Where? A Literature Review on Adult and Community Learning*. London: DfES.

Elsdon, K., Reynolds, J. and Stewart, S. (1995) *Voluntary Organisations: Citizenship, Learning and Change*. Leicester: NIACE.

Elsdon, K.T. *et al.* (2001) *An Education for the People? A History of HMI and Lifelong Learning*. Leicester: NIACE.

Employment Department (ED) (1988) *Employment for the 1990s*. London: HMSO.

European Commission (1994) *Growth, Competitiveness, Employment: The Challenge and Ways Forward into the 21st Century* (White Paper). Luxembourg: EC.

European Commission (1995) *Teaching and Learning: Towards the Learning Society* (White Paper). Luxembourg: EC.

Fieldhouse, R. *et al.* (1996) *A History of Modern British Adult Education*. Leicester: NIACE.

Flude, R. and Parrott, A. (1979) *Education and the Challenge of Change*. Milton Keynes: Open University Press.

Fordham, P., Poulton, G. and Randle, L. (1979) *Learning Networks in Adult Education*. London: Routledge & Kegan Paul.

Forrester, K. and Payne, J. (2000) 'Will adult learning ever be popular', in D. Jones and A. Jackson (eds) *Researching Inclusion: Proceedings of the SCUTREA Conference* (Nottingham, UK, July 2000). Nottingham: SCUTREA.

Forrester, K., Payne, J. and Ward, K. (1995) *Workplace Learning*. Aldershot: Avebury.

Fowler, G. (1988) 'On the nature of political progress', in F. Molyneux, G. Low and G. Fowler (eds) *Learning for Life: Politics and Progress in Recurrent Education*. London: Croom Helm.

Francis, H. (1991) 'A work culture and a learning culture. The right to be lazy', *Adults Learning*, May 1991.

Freire, P. (1972) *Pedagogy of the Oppressed*. Harmondsworth: Penguin Books.

Fryer, R. (1997) *Learning for the Twenty-first Century* (The Fryer Report). London: DfEE.

Gilbert, H. and Prew, H. (2001) *A Passion for Learning*. Leicester: NIACE.

Halsey, A.H. (1972) *Educational Priority: EPA Problems and Policies Vol 1*. London: HMSO.

Hargreaves, D. (1980) *Adult Literacy and Broadcasting: The BBC's Experience*. London: Frances Pinter Publishers.

Harrison, J.F.C. (1961) *Learning and Living 1790–1960: A Study in the History of the English Adult Education Movement*. London: Routledge & Kegan Paul.

Havilland, R.M. (1973) 'Survey of provision for adult illiteracy in England' (unpublished thesis). Reading: School of Education, University of Reading.

Hillage, J., Uden, T., Aldridge, F. and Eccles, J. (2000) *Adult Learning in England: A Review*. Brighton: Institute for Employment Studies/NIACE.

Hirsch, D. (1992) *City Strategies for Lifelong Learning* (The Hirsch Report). Paris: CERI/OECD.

HMSO (1969) *Report of the Royal Commission on Local Government in England, 1966–1969* (The Redcliffe-Maud Report). London: HMSO.

Hobsbawm, E. (1995) *Age of Extremes. The Short Twentieth Century 1914–1991*. London: Abacus.

Hughes, H. D. (1977) 'Adult education: Russell and after', *Oxford Review of Education*, Vol. 3, No. 3.

ILEA (1973) *An Education Service for the Whole Community*. London: ILEA.

Illich, I. (1971) *Deschooling Society*. London: Calder and Boyers.

Istance, D., Schuetze, H.G., and Schuller, T. (eds) (2002) *International Perspectives on Lifelong Learning*. Buckingham: SRHE and Open University Press.

Jackson, K. (1970) 'Adult education and community development', *Studies in Adult Education*, Vol. 2, pp. 165–72.

Jackson, K. (1994) 'From community to market in adult education', *NATFHE Journal*, Autumn 1994, pp. 24–26.

Jones, H.A. and Charnley, A. (1983) *The Adult Literacy Campaign: A Study of its Impact*. Leicester: NIACE.

Keep, E. (2000) *Employer Attitudes Towards Adult Training* (National Skills Task Force Research Paper 20). London: DfEE.

Kennedy, H. (1995) *Return to Learn: UNISON's Fresh Approach to Trade Union Education*. London: UNISON.

Kennedy, H. (1997) *Learning Works: Widening Participation in Further Education* (The Kennedy Report). London: HMSO.

Laslett, P. (1980) 'The education of the elderly in Britain', in E. Midwinter (ed.) *Age is Opportunity: Education and Older People*. London: Centre for Policy on Ageing.

Lee, J. (1965) *A Policy for the Arts*. London: HMSO.

Legge, D. (1982) *The Education of Adults in Britain*. Milton Keynes: Open University Press.

Lovett, T. (1975) *Adult Education, Community Development and the Working Class*. London: Ward Lock.

Lovett, T. (1995) 'Popular education in Northern Ireland: The Ulster People's College', in M. Mayo and J. Thompson (eds) *Adult Learning, Critical Intelligence and Social Change*. Leicester: NIACE, pp. 275–86.

Low, G. (1988) 'The MSC: A failure of democracy', in M. Morris and C. Griggs (eds) *Education – The Wasted Years? 1973–1986*. Lewes: Falmer Press.

Lowe, J. (1975) *The Education of Adults: A World Perspective.* Toronto: UNESCO Press and OISE.

Maclure, J.S. (1965) *Education Documents England & Wales.* London: Methuen.

Mayo, M. and Thompson, J, (eds) (1995) *Adult Learning, Critical Intelligence and Social Change.* Leicester: NIACE.

McIlroy, J. and Westwood, S. (eds) (1993) *Border Country: Raymond Williams in Adult Education.* Leicester: NIACE.

McConnell, C. (ed.) (2002) *The Making of an Empowering Profession.* Edinburgh: Community Learning Scotland.

McGivney, V. (2000) *Recovering Outreach: Concepts, Issues and Practices.* Leicester: NIACE.

McGivney, V. (2005) *Keeping the Options Open: The Importance of Maintaining a Broad and Flexible Curriculum Offer for Adults.* Leicester: NIACE.

Midwinter, E. (1972) *Priority Education.* Harmondsworth: Penguin Education.

Miliband, D. (1990) *Learning by Right: An Entitlement to Paid Education and Training* (Education and Training Paper No. 2). London: IPPR.

Ministry of Education (1947a) *Schemes of Further Education and Plans for County Colleges* (Circular 133). London: HMSO.

Ministry of Education (1947b) *Further Education: The Scope and Content of its Opportunities Under the Education Act 1944* (Pamphlet Number 8). London: HMSO.

Ministry of Education (1954) *The Organisation and Finance of Adult Education in England and Wales* (The Ashby Report). London: HMSO.

Ministry of Education (1960) *The Youth Service in England and Wales* (The Albemarle Report). London: HMSO.

Ministry of Reconstruction (1919/1980) *Final Report of the Adult Education Committee* (The 1919 Report). London: HMSO. (Reprinted with introductory essays by H. Wiltshire, J. Taylor and B. Jennings, Department of Adult Education, University of Nottingham, 1980.)

MSC (1981) *A New Training Initiative.* Sheffield: MSC.

MSC (1983) *Towards an Adult Training Strategy.* Sheffield: MSC.

NAB/UGC (1984) *Strategy for Higher Education in the Late 1980s and Beyond.* London: NAB.

NATFHE (1993) *Adult Education – A Survey Report: A Report on the Impact of the Further and Higher Education Act 1992 on Adult Education in Local Areas.* London: NATFHE.

National Assembly for Wales (2001) *The Learning Country.* Cardiff: Welsh Assembly.

NIACE (1990) *Learning Throughout Adult Life: A Policy Discussion Paper on Continuing Education.* Leicester: NIACE.

NIACE (1993) *The Learning Imperative: National Education and Training Targets and Adult Learners.* Leicester: NIACE.

NIACE (2000) *Aylesbury Revisited: Outreach in the 1980s.* Leicester: NIACE.

NIAE (1970) *Adult Education – Adequacy of Provision* (complete issue of *Adult Education*). Leicester: NIAE.

OECD (1977) *Learning Opportunities for Adults, Vol. IV, Participation in Adult Education.* Paris: OECD.

OECD/CERI (1973) *Recurrent Education: A Strategy for Lifelong Learning* (The Clarifying Report). Paris: OECD.

Open University (1969) *Report of the Planning Committee to the Secretary of State.* Milton Keynes: The Open University.

Parrott, A. (2002) 'Determining the value of lifelong learning', *Adults Learning*, Vol. 13, No. 8.

Payne, J. (1995) 'Adult learning in the context of global, neo-liberal economic policies', in M. Mayo and J. Thompson (eds), *Adult Learning, Critical Intelligence and Social Change.* Leicester: NIACE , pp. 262–74.

Percy, K., Butters, S., Powell, J. and Willett, I. (1979) *Post-initial Education in the Northwest of England: A Survey of Provision.* Leicester: ACACE.

Perry, W. (1976) *Open University.* Milton Keynes: Open University Press.

Pike, R.S., McIntosh, N.E.S. and Dahllof, U. (1978) *Innovation in Access to Higher Education.* New York: ICED.

Robinson, J. (1982) *Learning Over the Air, 60 Years of Partnership in Adult Learning.* London: BBC.

Robinson, P. (1997) *Literacy, Numeracy and Economic Performance.* London: Centre for Economic Performance.

Rogers, A. (ed.) (1976) *The Spirit and the Form, Essays in Adult Education in Honour of Professor Harold Wiltshire.* Nottingham: University of Nottingham Department of Adult Education.

Rogers, A. (1983) 'Research and development in adult education: some tentative thoughts', in J.V. Wallis (ed.), *Papers from the 13th SCUTREA Annual Conference*, University of Nottingham, 1983, pp. 1–15.

Rogers, J. (ed.) (1969) *Teaching on Equal Terms.* London: BBC.

Rose, J. (2002) *The Intellectual Life of the British Working Classes.* New Haven: Yale University Press.

Rubenson, K. (2002) 'Adult education policy in Sweden 1967–2001: From recurrent education to lifelong learning', in D. Istance, H.G. Schuetze and T. Schuller (eds) *International Perspectives on Lifelong Learning.* Buckingham: SRHE and Open University Press, pp. 203–16.

Scottish Education Department (1975) *Adult Education: The Challenge of Change* (The Alexander Report). Edinburgh: HMSO.

Simon, B. (ed.) (1990) *The Search for Enlightenment: The Working Class and Adult Education in the Twentieth Century.* Leicester: NIACE.

Simpson, J. (1973) *Feasibility Study in the Collection of Adult Education Statistics.* Brussels: Council of Europe.

Skills Insight (2002) *The Skills Review Update*. Guildford: South East England Development Agency (SEEDA).

Society of Industrial Tutors/TGWU (1988) *The Impossible Dream: The Future of Paid Educational Leave in Britain*. London: TGWU.

Spencer, B. (1991) 'Developments in British adult education', *The Industrial Tutor*, Vol. 5, No. 4.

Stephens, M. (1981) 'Trends in research in adult education in Britain since 1970'. Paper presented at the Annual SCUTREA Conference 1981 (available at: http://brs.leeds.ac.uk/cgi-bin/brs_engine).

Stuart, M. and Thomson, A. (eds) (1995) *Engaging with Difference: The 'Other' in Adult Education*. Leicester: NIACE.

Stuttard, G. (1974) 'Industrial tutors – a case study of a society', *Adult Education*, Vol. 46, No. 5.

Thompson. J. (ed.) (1980) *Adult Education for a Change*. London: Hutchinson.

Thomson, A. (1992) 'New cultural contexts for university adult education: the potential of partnerships with non-traditional agencies', in N. Miller and L. West (eds) *Changing Culture and Adult Education*. Papers from the 25th Annual Conference of SCUTREA, University of Kent, July 1992, pp. 71–4. Canterbury: SCUTREA.

Tight, M, (1982) *Part-time Degree Level Study in the United Kingdom*. Leicester: ACACE.

Tough, A. (1971) *The Adult's Learning Projects*. Toronto: OISE (1st edn).

Tough, A. (1979) *The Adult's Learning Projects*. Toronto: OISE (2nd edn).

Trenaman, J. M. (1967) *Communication and Comprehension*. London: Longman.

TUC (1968) *Training Shop Stewards*. London: TUC.

Tuckett, A. (1988) *The Jewel in the Crown*. London: ILEA.

Tuckett, A. (1991) *Towards a Learning Workforce: A Policy Discussion Paper on Adult Learners at Work*. Leicester: NIACE.

UDACE (1986) *The Challenge of Change: Developing Educational Guidance for Adults*. Leicester: NIACE.

UDACE and Ames, J.C. (1986) *Financial Barriers to Access: A Project Report*. Leicester: NIACE.

UNESCO (1972) *Learning to Be* (The Faure Report). Paris: UNESCO.

UNESCO (1984) *Campaigning for Literacy*. Paris: UNESCO.

UNESCO (1996) *Learning: The Treasure Within* (The Delors Report). Paris: UNESCO.

Venables, P. (1976) *Report of the Committee on Continuing Education* (The Venables Report). Milton Keynes: Open University Press.

Ward, K. and Taylor, R. (eds) (1986) *Adult Education for the Working Class: Education for the Missing Millions*. London: Croom Helm.

Wedell, E.G. (1970) *The Place of Education by Correspondence in Permanent Education: A Study of Correspondence in the Member States of the Council of Europe*. Strasbourg: Council of Europe.

Welton, M. (2001) 'Civil society and the public sphere: Habermas's recent learning theory', *Studies in the Education of Adults*, Vol. 33, No. 1, pp. 20–34.

Welton, M. (2005) *Designing the Just Learning Society: A Critical Enquiry.* Leicester: NIACE.

Westwood, S. (1993) 'Excavating the future: Towards 2000', in J. McIlroy and S. Westwood (eds) *Border Country: Raymond Williams in Adult Education.* Leicester: NIACE, pp. 224–36.

Westwood, S. and Thomas, J.E. (eds) (1991) *Radical Agendas?: The Politics of Adult Education.* Leicester: NIACE.

Williams, R. (1959) 'Going on learning', *The New Statesman*, 30 May 1959, in J. McIlroy and S. Westwood (eds) (1993) *Border Country: Raymond Williams in Adult Education.* Leicester: NIACE, pp. 218–21.

Williams, R. (1983a) 'Adult education and social change', in J. McIlroy and S. Westwood (eds) *Border Country: Raymond Williams in Adult Education.* Leicester: NIACE, pp. 255–64.

Williams, R. (1983b) *Towards 2000.* London: Chatto and Windus.

Wiltshire, H. (1976) 'The nature and uses of adult education', in A. Rogers (ed.) *The Spirit and the Form, Essays in Adult Education in Honour of Professor Harold Wiltshire.* Nottingham: University of Nottingham Department of Adult Education.

Woodhall, M. (1980) *The Scope and Costs of the Education and Training of Adults in Britain.* Leicester: ACACE.

Index